Royal St James's

A London Courtesan: Mrs Patience Russell, c. 1675

One of Mother Elizabeth Cresswell's mignons, *a beautiful and charming
girl, well-regarded at Court and mistress to Lord Rochester, who left her
£150 in his Will*

Royal St James's

Being a Story of Kings, Clubmen and Courtesans

by

E. J. BURFORD

ROBERT HALE · LONDON

Robert Hale Limited
Clerkenwell House
Clerkenwell Green
London EC1R 0HT

British Library Cataloguing in Publication Data
Burford, E. J.
  Royal St. James's: being a story of kings,
  clubmen and courtesans.
  1. Saint James's (London, England) – Social
  life and customs.   2. London (England) –
  Social life and customs
  I. Title
  942.1'32   DA685.S143

ISBN 0-7090-3274-9

Photoset in Linotron Palatino by
Rowland Phototypesetting Limited, Bury St Edmunds, Suffolk
Printed in Great Britain by St Edmundsbury Press Limited
Bury St Edmunds, Suffolk
Bound by WBC Limited

Contents

List of Illustrations

Picture Credits

Frontispiece, pp. 6, 22–3, 30, 32, 37, 43, 51, 66–7, 72, 80, 114–15, 119, 122, 125, 136–7, 158, 160, 164, 166, 169, 171, 174, 178, 184, 187, 192, 198, 202, 206, 208, 210–11, 214–15, 226, 231, 234, 237, 238, reproduced by courtesy of the Trustees of the British Museum; pp. *xiv*, 11, 33, 35, 45, 46–7, 77, 83, 85, 181, 197, reproduced by courtesy of the Westminster City Libraries, Archives and Local History Department; p. 5 based upon the original survey now in the Public Record Office; pp. 8, 62, 69, 79, 126, 128, 130, 132, 134, 142, 157, reproduced by courtesy of the Greater London Council, Records Office Department of Prints; p. 88 by courtesy of Yale University; p. 222 by courtesy of the Courtauld Institute of Art. All other items from material in the author's own collection.

Acknowledgements

I wish once again to express my sincere thanks and appreciation for the help given in my research for this work to Miss M. J. Swarbrick, Archivist at Westminster City Council Library, and her colleagues Mr R. Harrison and John Sargent, particularly regarding the choice of illustrations. My thanks are also due to the young ladies in their department, Alison Kellie and Elizabeth Cory. Also in respect of the illustrations I must pay tribute to my good friends John Phillips, Keeper of Prints at the Greater London Council, and Duncan Smith of the Print Room of the British Museum. Mr James R. Sewell, Deputy Keeper of Records at the Guildhall helped very greatly with information about various City worthies and unworthies. My thanks too to Mr Richard Bowden, Archivist at St Marylebone Library.

My friends at the Lewis Walpole Library in Farmington, USA have earned my thanks and gratitude for their invaluable help, in particular Mrs Catherine Jestin, the Librarian, now enjoying her well-deserved retirement, and Mrs Frank Sussler, Curator of Prints.

I am also mindful of the assistance of those long-dead but indefatigable compilers of the Rates Collectors' books for Westminster whose work forms the real basis for this book – sadly, they can only be thanked posthumously.

E. J. BURFORD

To my dear wife and helpmeet
on the occasion of our Diamond Wedding

Preface

The story of St James's is basically a tale of rags to riches – or more correctly from pest house to palace and how a remote, bleak field sheltering leprous maidens became one of the most aristocratic quarters of a great metropolis.

During the centuries of transition its activities ran the whole gamut of human experience – from extreme piety to pornography, from feudal serfdom to the dawn of parliamentary democracy, from abysmal ignorance and illiteracy to the age of science and the humanities.

'St James's' here means that area bounded by the Haymarket, along the south side of Piccadilly to St James's Street, down to the Palace and along Pall Mall, including the great park, thence to Charing Cross where it all started.

The reader must try to imagine an older scene of the plain-looking palace frowning on the kaleidoscope of noisy gilded coaches carrying bewigged and sworded courtiers and their ladies, and loose ladies in lacy finery with hoops and powdered wigs, their faces powder-patched, as well as ambassadors coming and going with their retinues, royal messengers riding furiously, their horses jostling with the sedan-chairmen, grooms, porters, artisans and hucksters, thieves and pickpockets and confidence tricksters, pimps and panders and procuresses and hosts of beggars. Nor should one forget proclamations stentoriously announced at the palace gate, and the pillory for malefactors and religious dissidents alike – in short, the joys and miseries of centuries.

Herein the reader will find details of the *real* lives of the inhabitants from royalty down to rascality, from the coffee-shops to the great gambling clubs, from the mob to the macaronis and, for the first time, that great sexual magnet, the King's Place 'nunneries' and their famous abbesses – the so-called *Bordels du Roi*, and their frequenters, in plain and unexpurgated language.

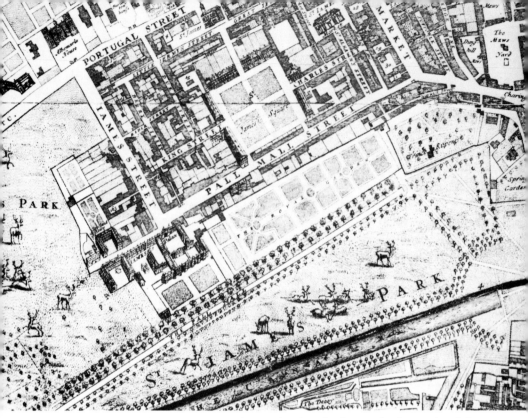

Ogilby and Morgan's map of 1681 showing the deer park, the canal and the Duchess of Cleveland's estate along St James's Street

Today the hurly-burly has gone but the Georgian royal quarter remains with five royal palaces and many palatial mansions lining the quiet, elegant, prestigious streets, disturbed only by the Changing of the Guard every morning at St James's Palace and its neighbour, Buckingham Palace, for the free entertainment of thousands of spectators.

The beautiful park is still open for the use of 'the idle publick', and although the deer and other fauna have gone, the great lake and its birds are a constant delight. Refreshments can be obtained but no longer 'milk straight from the cow' at a penny a cup.

The coffee-houses in St James's Street are also gone but three of the famous clubs, White's, Boodles' and Brooks' aloofly regard the passing scene, and King's Place has lost all its 'nunneries'. St James's Square retains its air of exclusivity but *paille maille* can no longer be played in Pall Mall.

With this book in hand the reader can recapture briefly the sights and scenes of St James's romantic period.

1 From Fields to Bailiwick

Strange and gruesome as it may seem, the origins of the present highly esteemed parish of St James the Less go back to the time just after the Norman Conquest in 1066 when the horrible disease of leprosy was introduced to England by the Normans returning from the Crusades. The first of the 'lazars' or 'spittles' was established outside Canterbury in 1096 and dedicated to St James the Less, Bishop of Jerusalem, for 'the care of mayden lepers'.

In the year 1100 the Conqueror's son, Henry I, in order to secure the dynasty married the pious Scotswoman Edith (niece to the unlucky heir to the English throne, Edgar the Atheling). She changed her name to Matilda to please Archbishop Anselm and the Normans – the awkward fact that the young lady was a nun was conveniently brushed aside by the wily political cleric.

In 1117 Queen Matilda founded a hospital in St Giles-in-the-Fields for 'fourteen leprous Persons'. Soon afterwards, 'Some prominent Citizens of the City of London established an hospital . . . west of Charing Cross . . . on two Hides of land . . . in the parish of St Margaret's Westminster . . . for fourteen Sisters, maidens that were leprous . . . living chastely and honestly in divine service. . . .'

These prominent citizens were goldsmiths: Leofstane, the immensely powerful and rich Master of the Goldsmiths' Company was Provost of the City of London, and the goldsmiths were prodigious philanthropists.

The ancient laws of the City forbade '. . . leprous Persons . . . to sojourn by Day or by Night about the City under pain of Imprisonment . . . [they were allowed] . . . an Attorney or Proctor to go every Sunday to the parish churches . . . to collect for their sustenance . . .'. This proctor then delivered money and victuals to the unfortunates.

St Giles and St James were far enough away to avoid contagion.

Sometime before 1189 Henry II gave a Charter '. . . to the leprous Maydens of St James without London by Westminster of all their lands and holdings, with soc and sac, tol and theam, infangthief and all liberties and customs [free] and quittances . . .'. This was renewed in April 1242 by Henry III, who also granted forty acres of land in Hampstead. These provisions gave the Bishop of London sovereignty over St James's, but in a bitter dispute in 1222 the Pope decided that this jurisdiction was to be the prerogative of the abbot of Westminster. During the riots which followed, the lazar house was burnt down but it was rebuilt a little later.

The foundation was well financed because 'divers Citizens gave fifty-five pounds rents thereunto', and after this 'sundry devout men of London gave . . . four Hides of land in the field of Westminster and in Hendone, Calcote and Hamsted eighty acres of land and wood, etc . . .'.

In 1242 the lazar housed in addition to the maydens eight brethren, of whom six were chaplains. As a further measure of assistance, in 1275 the 'Taxors of the Twentieths' were ordered to discharge the tax entirely '. . . on the goods owned by the infirm Women of the Hospital of St James without Westminster . . . by the King's special Grace . . .'.

Regrettably the brothers and sisters did not behave as their rules required. In 1277 the prior of Westminster had to remind them that brothers were not allowed to eat and drink with the sisters, 'nor enter their houses', and that 'vigils at the deaths of a brother or sister were to be held . . . without unseemly noise'.

In 1290 King Edward I confirmed the charters and in addition '. . . was pleased to grant a licence to . . . these leprous Maidens of the Hospital of St James . . . the right to hold an annual Fair . . . on the site of St James's Farm . . . on the Vigil [1 May], Feast and Morrow of St James and for four days following . . . the profits therefrom being for their upkeep . . .'. The King referred to sound citizens who were spreading the disease 'by the contagioun of Polluted breath and by sexual intercourse with women in the stewes and other secret places detestably frequenting the same'. He ordered their removal from the City within fifteen days.

The Master and his assistants had meanwhile acquired twenty-two acres of land and also two acres of meadows for rent 'in the town of West Minster and Fulehame and a further eight acres in Westminster' for which they received a Pardon from the King (Edward I) in 1306. In 1317, however, it was disclosed that the prior was often drunk, and had embezzled the funds; what was worse, the weekly chapters had not been held. The Black Death killed off all the inmates except the Master, who was deposed in 1351. By 1384 there were no inmates so that Master Thomas Orgrave sub-let most of the buildings to Elizabeth, widow of Edward, Earl Despenser, 'for life . . . paying forty shillings for the Hanaper . . .' (a hanap was a two-handled silver cup used to measure out ales and beers).

By 1401 it was once again a convent, the King's own physician, Louis Recouchez, having been appointed warden, and it now became clear that the grant of 'sac and soc' was of value in establishing that St James's Hospital and its appurtenances were actually sanctuaries.

The rights of the 'socman' – the lord of the soke – overrode the ordinary law as regards the grant of sanctuary. ('Nicholas Cusack, an Irish man stole a Bay Horse worth Thirty Shillings from a Man at Woxebrygge [Uxbridge] . . . he claimed Sanctuary. The Constables of the Liberty of the Abbey came to the Chaplain, William Cave . . . so assaulted them and made fast the Gates of the Hospital . . . [and] permitted the said Nicholas to go away. . . . The King pardons the said William. . . .')

The soke-man also had rights of 'infangthief' – he could pass judgement on any thief within his 'soke'; in ancient days he actually had the power of life and death over malefactors within his territory (only the City of London had the right of 'outfangthiefe' – the power to send its officers to apprehend malefactors for offences outside the City) so that he could rightfully send away or attack any beadles or bailiffs or constables from outside. (The Irishman had been saved from certain death.)

By about 1450 leprosy had practically disappeared from England, so the house was no longer a lazar but a convent, '. . . with the leprous Virgins nowe gone . . . the gentle Sisters had a sheltered Life in Prayers and Solitude'. There were unwanted interruptions, however, as in July 1455, when there was '. . . grete grudgynge insomuche as ye Erle of Shrowsburie . . . hadde lodged hymselfe at the hospital by Lorde Cromwell's wishe . . .' to safeguard him from his enemies.

In 1467 the King granted the hospital and perpetual custody of all rights and appurtenances to William Westbury, Provost of the College of 'St Mary of Eton by Windesor' and the chaste sisters could enjoy a quiet life for a while.

When in 1512 Henry VIII's palace at Whitehall burned down, the King took the opportunity and '. . . buylt ther a goodlie Manoir house annexing thereuntoe a parke closed aboute by a Wall of Bricke nowe called St James's Park . . .'. A *Surveigh* in 1549 reported, however: 'Ther was a ffeld calld Sent James ffeld by estimacioun xl Acres wich was comen and owght to bee Comen and in Clossed by kinge henry viij . . . wich was Arrable And nowe ys ye Meadowe. . . .' (The King had enclosed common land; it had been arable but now was a meadow.)

Henry VIII then created the bailiwick of the manor of St James, which encompassed parts of the parishes of St Margaret's West-minster, St Martin-in-the-Fields, Fulham and Chelsey, which had by then been surrendered by the Provost of Eton College. The Bailiwick was bisected from east to west by 'ye waie from Colbroke [Colnebrook] to London', the northern part of which was by 1585 to be known as Piggadillo or Pickadilla. The King then proceeded to parcel out his newly acquired lands to friends and relations.

'St James's ffelde' was used for mustering troops or manœuvres. On 8 May 1539 Henry VIII made use of the City's ancient annual parade, the so-called Marching Watch – to make 'a great Muster from Mile End, fifteen thousand men in all in bright Harness with Coats of white Silk and Chains of Gold which passed through London to Westminster . . . round about the Park of St James and returned through Old Borne . . .'. In 1551 his son, Edward VI mustered his troops, 'the Kinges Maistre [Majesty] sytting on Horse-backe on a Hill by St James with his maiestries Privie Counsell withe him'. (The top of the hill was where St James's Street meets Piccadilly.) Some years later his sister Queen Mary mustered her troops against Sir John Palmer and his friends who were supporting her sister, the future Elizabeth I. Sir John and his friends were executed after their attempted *putsch* failed; Elizabeth had a lucky escape.

The 1549 *Surveigh* of Pall Mall Close or Field is the earliest indication that the Italian game of *palla maglia* (ball and mallet) was already being played thereabouts. In 1567 Mary, Queen of Scots, and her lover Bothwell '. . . were playing richt oppinlie at the fieldis with the Pal Mal and Golf . . .' in Edinburgh.

(Opposite) *A plan from Queen Elizabeth's time (1585) of the northern part of the bailiwick showing the divisions of the lands formerly held by the Abbey of Abingdon; and the Hospice of Burton Lazars (St Giles'), where prisoners on their way to execution at Tyburn were presented 'with a grete bowle of Ale to be their last refreshinge in their lyfe!' The Conduit Fields belonged to the City of London: one of the pumping conduits is shown on the Piccadilly roadway (the site is now Burlington House) and there was another at the western corner of Beak Street. Much of the land was leased to Thomas Wilson, then involved in a lawsuit with John Bristowe. Several patches were leased also to the Poulteneys*

date 1585

Q1 The Queene; in the occupacion of Mr.Bristow and Abingdon

Q2 The Queene to Mr.Pewltney

H The House of Mr.Howicke

GH Gunpowder House

SC Scavengers Close

R Rounde Ringill

G The Gravell Pitt

P Pewltney

W In the the tenancy of Mr.Wilson; the land in question

The Waye from Charrynge called Seynt Martins

The Waye to Hoggesmewe

Burton Lazar

Marshland

Lane to St.Gilles

St.Martins Fielde

St.Martins Church

The Mewes Close

The Mewes

Charrynge Cross

Dung Hill

Wilson

Burton Lazar

St.Gills Fielde

Burton Lazar

The Waye from Charrynge

GH

SC

Wilson

Widdowe Golightly

Abingdon

Colman Hedge Lane

Burton Lazar

Burton Lazar

Wilson

Wilson

The Waye to Charrynge (Haymarket)

Denham

Windmill Fielde

Abingdon

Shug Lane

(Marybone Lane)

R P

Geldings Close

Wilson

Wilson

Warwick St.

Widdowe Golightly

St.James Fielde

(Oxford Street)

The Waye from Uxbridge to London

W

Wilson

Q1

Wilson

Abingdon

R.

Wilson

G

The Queene

Abingdon

Wilson

Q2

Wilson

Thomas

Wilson

Abingdon

Conduit Head

The Waye from Colebroke to London

Mr.Pewltney

(Piccadilly)

Wilson

Conduit Meadowe

City of London

(Great Swallow St.)

By 1599 there was an approach road down the slope from Piccadilly to the palace – now the line of St James's Street – but only a handful of houses lower down on the east side. In that year St James's Fair was moved to the open space in front of the palace; it stayed there till 1636, when it was moved to a spot adjacent to the Haymarket.

By now too the game of *paille-maille* had become popular. In September 1625 King James I made a grant to the Scotsman Archibald Lumsden '. . . for the sole furnishing of the malls, scoops, and other necessaries for the game of *Pell Mell* . . . within his grounds in St James's Fields . . . and such as resort thereunto shall pay him such sums of money as are according to the ancient order of the game . . .'. It was then explained that this was a long alley where a ball was driven through a suspended iron hoop. This alley was on the site of a pre-Saxon highway from Charing Cross westward to the then important settlements of Coln-brooke and Reading. It was certainly the track to the lazar house and from about 1347 to the Lock Hospital and Chapel (for venereal diseases) established in Edward III's reign at 'Cnihtesbricge'. (Knightsbridge is mentioned as early as 1042, its gravel pits being thought to have therapeutic properties.)

In 1629 Charles I turned over the whole bailiwick to his Queen, Henrietta Maria, in trust for his son, the future Charles II.

By 1638 there were a few more dwellings on the east side of St James's Street, one of which was occupied by Michael Poulteney, a

The Lock Hospital as it was in 1720. Edward III in 1347 ordered: 'All leprous people to leave the City . . . to certain lazar houses . . . at some good distance – to wit at Ye Locke, at Knightesbridge west from Charynge Crosse . . .'

descendant of that Poulteney to whom Henry VIII had granted some estates in St James's Fields.

There was still only a handful of dwellings when Oliver Cromwell's Proclamation of 11 August 1656 'stayed all building . . . in St James's Fields . . .', but with the restoration of Charles II in 1660 the great leap forward started. He succeeded to the bailiwick and appointed new trustees, one of whom was his close friend (and probable brother-under-the-blanket) Henry Jermyn, who was to become the principal developer, but quite early in 1660 St James's Street is mentioned in connection with the King's grant of Berkeley House to his favourite mistress, Barbara Castlemaine, soon to be Duchess of Cleveland. The Cleveland estate comprehended all the former Poulteney estate from the front of the palace up the western side of St James's Street to Park Place.

In front of the palace was that monument to contemporary civilization the pillory, upon which many a Jacobite and other malefactors were to suffer.

St James's Street was declared 'fitt to be pav'd' by a Statute of 1661. In July the next year John Evelyn, Commissioner for the Improvements of Streets, 'ordered the paving of the way from St James's North, which was a quagmire . . . also the Hay Market and about Pigadillo . . . for the better keeping of the streets cleane'. In a different cleansing, '. . . several Whores and Infamous Persons . . . including one *Tory Rory* . . . were removed to the House of Correction, for Indecent Conduct'. ('Tory' is Erse for a robber!)

In 1662 and 1663 Charles granted Henry Jermyn a great property which included *inter alia* '. . . a roadway leading to the Palace gates from the roade to Readynge running through St James's Fields . . . the Haymarket in the west . . . the Conduit in St James's Square made of Bricke next unto the Rounde House of Stone . . .'.

At the same time William and Ralph Wayne petitioned the King '. . . for Permission to convey Water to the Inhabitants of Piccadilly . . . and Neighbourhood from the manie Springs nearby at Reasonable Rates on account of the greate Expence in the Invention of a newe Type of Engine with perpetual Motion'. The Water Tower stood at the corner of what is now Regent Street and Beak Street. Formal consent was given on 25 June 1664.

The most important event in 1664 was the petition in April by the inhabitants of the bailiwick to the House of Commons for the separation of St James's parish from that of St Martin-in-the-Fields and the erection of their own parish church. Despite strenuous opposition from the clerics of St Martin's as well as from Henry Jermyn, the petition was granted. The foundation stone was laid in

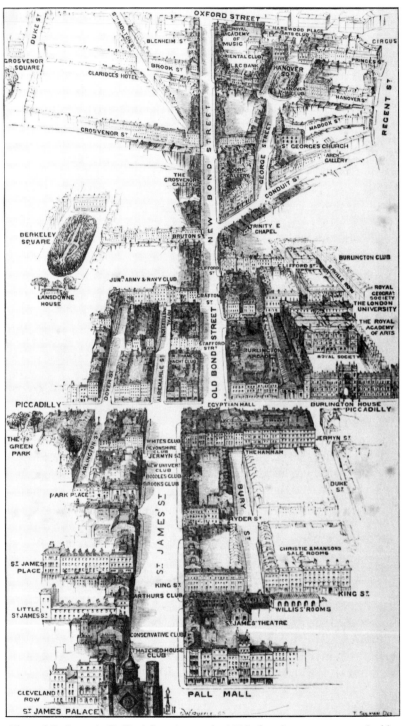

Plan of St James's Bailiwick as it was in 1880 showing some recognizable landmarks

April 1676, the consecration took place in 1684, and in June 1685 the new parish boundaries were demarcated.

In 1664 permission was given for 'a Market on Mondays, Wednesdays and Saturdays on the Square . . . originally intended for a Mercato Place and Mercato-house', but the market house was not opened before 1666. In 1665 the King gave the freehold of St James's Square to Henry Jermyn's nominees, the poet Abraham Cowley and Baptist May. In 1667 Jermyn Street was opened to link the Hay Market with St James's Street, and thenceforward the whole series of streets and alleys making up Ryder Street and King Street on the east side and Arlington Street on the west side.

It was the advent of the coffee-houses which gave St James's its especial character, as well as St James's Park, which was opened up to the public by that much maligned 'Bandy-legg'd Presbyterian' James I, who was no killjoy. It was a shrewd political move which cost him nothing and gained him great popularity.

The 1680s saw an increasing demand for building space, and one of the first casualties was St James's Fair which in 1688 had to be moved to 'the greate Brooke Feilde Market for Livestock' north of Piccadilly (now Shepherd Market) where '. . . the ffolke enjoy's Musicke Drinkinge Rafflinge Gameing Lotteries Stage Playes & Drolls as well as Prize-fightes Bull-fightes Beare-baitinges & other cruel Sportes . . . with all manner of Boothes & Gingerbreades in the shape of Tiddy Dol . . .'.

Then, on 10 April 1691, 'This Nighte a'sudden a terrible Fire burnt downe all the Buyldynges . . . at White Hall . . . consuminge other Lodginges of suche lewde Creatures who debauch'd both Kinge Charles II . . . and were his destruction. . . .' The seat of royalty had to be transferred quickly to the nearby palace at St James's, and the courtiers and their doxies found suitable accommodations nearby. A great new district was born to adorn the coming new century.

2 St James's and Buckingham Palaces

St James's palace goes back only to the time when Henry VIII acquired the former lazar in 1531. He had been married to Katherine of Aragon for more than twenty years, and she had given him only a daughter, Mary. He desperately needed a legitimate male heir – he already had a son by Elizabeth Blount, a lady in waiting, which occasioned a remark by *The London Chronicle*: 'Then dyd the Kyngges bastard Son, Douke of Rechemonde come atte Seynte James beyonde Charyngecrosse . . .', when the young Henry Fitzroy had been created Duke of Richmond.

By 1527 the King was seeking a divorce but Pope Clement VII was unable to do him this favour, and Henry was soon scheming to release himself from the shackles of the Church of Rome. The emergence of Lutheranism undoubtedly aided this objective, as did the venality of some clerics. For example, in 1528 '. . . the custody of lands in Sainte James Felde whiche belonged to Stephen Chese, deceased . . . had been . . . appropriated without Licence by the Abbot of Westminster and the Master of St James . . . and given to John Broke, Clothier of the City of London . . .'. Henry then utilized a Statute of Richard II of 1393 which banned the Pope from exercising any jurisdiction in England, and in 1539 he dissolved the monasteries and seized all their properties, which included St James's Hospital, described in 1530 as 'a large hospital or almshouse the outbuildings of which reach as far as the crest of the hill abutting the western road . . .' (Piccadilly).

By this time Anne Boleyn, a beauty with great charm and good French manners, was tempting the King. By the middle of 1531 he had decided to house his future bride in St James's. The Provost of Eton College, Roger Lupton, was forced to concede on 24 December '. . . the King shall have the site etc . . . of their House in St

ST JAMES'S PALACE and part of the CITY of WESTMINSTER.

A view from Pall Mall north in 1660, attributed to Wenceslas Hollar. The water-conduit tower is seen in the foreground

James in the Field with 185 acres . . . in exchange the College to have land and manors in Dartford . . . and other places . . .'.

Demolition started immediately and 'a goodlie Manoir . . . of red bricks and blue diapering . . . with four courts' was erected under Thomas Cromwell's supervision. The swamp was drained and fenced in and became St James's Park where 'tenys' and 'boulinge aleys' were available. A keeper-bailiff, Thomas Alvard, was appointed in 1533 to receive rents and profits.

There were only a handful of 'leprous sisters' in April 1536. It was reported: 'Joan Harvard . . . having held, along with other women an habitacion . . . was awarded an annuity of £6.13s.4d, as well as Agnes Starkey, Widdowe, Dame Katherine Vanpage, Widdowe and Anne Power, Widdowe', the King thereby discharging his liabilities.

Anne Boleyn moved in, was married, bore another daughter, Elizabeth, and having failed to produce a male heir was executed on 19 May 1536. With indecent haste Henry married Jane Seymour, but she never lived there. The next residents were his bastard son, the Duke of Richmond, and then Thomas Cromwell, whose tenancy ended with his beheading on 28 July 1540.

From 1543 Henry began to live in the palace, holding meetings of the Privy Council and in 1545 an investiture of the Knights of the Garter. His son, the boy-king Edward VI, resided there occasionally, but his uncle the Lord High Admiral, Sir Thomas Seymour, had his apartments there. Henry's last queen, the gentle Katherine Parr, lived there, as did his daughter Mary, who occupied a large suite of rooms 'wherein there was great concourse of friends and especial good cheer for them'. Her half-sister the Princess Elizabeth 'had a great liking' for the palace and frequently stayed there. Edward founded the Royal Library as well as the choir of the Royal Chapel, 'in which boys were impressed'.

11

Edward VI died there on 6 July 1553 and Mary became Queen, using Whitehall for official functions, but she preferred her manor of St James for her private residence. Because of her general unpopularity, there was a conspiracy to kill her while she walked in St James's Park which was discovered in time. During Sir Thomas Wyatt's rebellion bands of soldiers were posted 'on the hill opposite the palace Gateway', and a battery of cannon and a squadron of horse were posted along a line from Jermyn Street to Bennet Street. The eventual battle took place at Charing Cross, where 'the noise of women and children was heard so great and shrill in St James's'.

Mary went from the palace to her coronation and held splendid functions there but when she realized that her apparent pregnancy by Philip of Spain was only dropsy she 'crept to St James's a dying woman'. After her death, her body was eviscerated and embalmed and removed to the Chapel of St James's Palace on 10 December 1558.

Queen Elizabeth stayed there only occasionally after a heavy journey.

On 25 July 1560 it was reported: '. . . the St James Fayer by Westminster was so grete that a man could not have a Pigg for money and the Bear-wiffes hadd nother Meate nor Drinke before iij of the Cloke . . . and Chese went verie well awaie for one Penny of the pounde . . . besides the mightie armie of Beggares & Baudes that ther were. . . .'

In September 1561 Queen Elizabeth made 'a Great Progress from Enfield', all the hedges being cut down and the ditches filled in all the way 'to the door of St James's'. In July 1588 she rushed from Richmond to St James's to hear the good news about the defeat of the Spanish Armada. Crowds of noblemen and courtiers thronged the palace for days on end.

Her successor, King James I, before he arrived from Scotland, on 11 January 1603 ordered that the St James's Fair be postponed for a week or two 'because it would draw away the crowds from his coronation'. In the following year the palace was prepared as a residence for his son Henry, Prince of Wales. The Earl of Worcester's order to the Clerk of the Signet dated 14 July 1604 noted 'Whereas St Jameses howse is appoynted by his Majestie for the Prince to lye att, untoe the whiche there is neyther Barne nor Stable belongynge, the which want, of necessitie must be supplyed. . . .'

After Inigo Jones had altered and improved the interior, on 10 May 1610 the Prince held a brilliant Court. His household consisted of more than 400 persons 'of whom 295 were in receipt of regular salaries'. He forbade all blasphemy, swearing or bad language – offenders were fined on the spot, and the money was put in a box for distribution to the poor. Unfortunately this excellent young man died before he was nineteen, and the palace was then occupied by his brother Charles, then Duke of York, who established his Court there early in 1613.

Once more there is a reference to the palace as a sanctuary, for a debtor named Thomas Geare. The sheriffs 'and some hundreds of shouting Apprentices rushed pell-mell into the palace . . . demanding of Sir John Vaughan, the Comptroller to produce Geare. . . . When he refused to do so they assaulted him as he was getting into his Coach. . . .' For this all the offenders were punished for *lèse majesté*.

In 1624, when Charles was negotiating marriage with Henrietta Maria, sister of Louis XIII of France, he was compelled to agree publicly that '. . . she would have no further liberty but for her own family and no advantage for Recusants at home' in the use of a Catholic chapel to be erected in the palace grounds. After he had ascended the throne in March 1625, he married Henrietta Maria by proxy. The chapel, however, was not finished and she complained on arrival that it was 'just a Closet'. Charles riposted that she could use the Great Chamber for Mass, but if that was not large enough, St James's Park was 'the fittest place of all'! This was hardly a nice greeting for a bride but worse was to follow.

The numbers of the Queen's French attendants had swollen from sixty to more than 400. More to the point, they were costing £240 a day for their keep. When the King, out of patience at last, ordered them to depart 'at once', '. . . they behaved most indecorously . . . rushing to take possession of the Queen's Wardrobe and Jewels, not even leaving a change of bed-linen . . . moreover the palace servants complained that the French servants had so defiled the place that a week's work would not make it clean. . . .' It cost the King more than £5,000 to ship them all home.

In the violent quarrel which ensued, the King 'dragg'd the Queen to her apartments' and she retaliated by breaking many windows and smashing some of the furniture.

Despite all this conjugal bickering and a stillborn child in May 1629, there was great rejoicing when a year later a boy, Charles, was born. A daughter, Mary, followed the next year, and on 14 October James, Duke of York. Nevertheless, the monarchy was becoming more and more unpopular, especially when Charles seemed to show leanings towards Catholicism. This unpopularity was openly manifested during the visit in 1638 of the King's mother-in-law, Marie de' Medici. From Harwich to St James's '. . . so enthusiastick was her welcome from the Citizens of London that it was with the greatest difficulty that the souldiers could protect her from the crowds who wanted to lynch her . . . three people were killed in the scrimmage outside the palace gates. . . .' She stayed for more than three years in the greatest extravagance and luxury – costing more than £3,000 a month. Despite hints and nudges, she refused to move until at last Parliament voted £10,000 to get rid of her and she left just before the King's own misfortunes of 1641. This 'stately magnificent Woman, Mother to a King and of two Queens' died in the direst poverty in a garret.

Charles left the palace, to go to war, in 1642, with his two elder sons, Charles and James, leaving his son Henry, Duke of Glouces-ter, and his daughter Elizabeth. In July 1643 both children were placed in the care of Mary, Countess of Dorset. In 1644 the House of Commons sequestrated the estates of the King and all his adherents. The King's treasures were disposed of in June – on the 14th of that month Charles's forces met with disaster at Naseby. His son James was captured and sent to join the other children at St James's, conducted thither 'with a sumptuous retinue of Coaches and Nobles'. Charles's daughter Henrietta was in the care of the Countess of Dalkeith, who managed an escape by dressing the child as a boy.

The King's overriding need was to get James out of the hands of the Parliamentary army, and in 1648 he asked Colonel Joseph Bampfylde to rescue him. The Colonel, aided by his mistress Anne Murray – later Lady Halkett – entered the palace, and Anne changed clothes with the young Prince, who was 'good-looking and well-made and very pretty in women's clothes'. They made it to Gravesend in a barge and thence to the Netherlands.

The King, now himself a prisoner, was taken to Windsor and later to St James's. He complained: '. . . all Night he had a couple or more of louzy Souldiers stood Sentinel in his Bedchamber, talking and smoking-out his Eyes with their stinking Tobacco. One Sentinel used these very words. "You! with a Pox on you! must have Fifteen Pound the Daye allowed for your Table but wee poore Souldiers that stand in the cold will not have more than fifteen Shillings to releave us with. Well! Old Stroaker! wee shall be quit of you ere long."'

When Charles arrived at St James's, he was first treated as king but after a fortnight the officers of the New Army ordered '. . . that thenceforth all State ceremony or accustomed Respect be forborn . . . the number of his Menials to be lessened: Accordingly the

King's Meat was brought up by Souldiers, the Dishes uncovered . . . no Cup was served upon the knee . . .'.

The palace by now had become a barracks under Colonel Pride's command. Cromwell's troops, though disciplined, were no respecters of elegant mansions or their contents: the library was a shambles open to the sky with the books lying in heaps in the dust or mildewed with rain, while rats and mice ate the volumes. Many of the rooms had been gutted, the furniture damaged or destroyed.

The King was taken to Whitehall for his execution. Later the Royalist Duke of Hamilton, Earl of Holland and Lord Capell were decapitated in the palace yard.

The palace had now become a military prison overcrowded with officers and men indiscriminately. The conditions were appalling, and nothing was done to relieve the situation since all were considered traitors. Not until December 1651 were the majority of the prisoners set free, some on condition that they would serve in Ireland and the rest 'taken a day's march outside the City . . . so they might not beg nor lurk there to do further mischief . . .'. As late as January 1655 there were still a few officers incarcerated there.

One side-effect was that in July 1651 the St James's Fair was forbidden to be held; the presence of great hostile crowds outside the very gates would have led to dreadful violence.

On 29 May 1660 King Charles II restored St James's status as a royal palace and ordered immediate renovation and enlargement. The royal servants had not been paid for more than fifteen months.

Isabella Lumsden asked for one of the tenements which had been promised to her father '. . . who had spent £425.14s.0d keeping the sport of *Pall-mall* . . . for which he had a Patent. The Lease had been left to his wife who had been deprived of it during this distracted time . . .'. Mrs Elizabeth Elliott applied for a pension because she had been the King's foster-sister: '. . . it was the greatest Happiness to be suckled at the same Breast as so great a Monarch . . .'.

St James's Fair was revived, but '. . . many lewd and infamous Persons were committed to the House of Correccion . . . some very impudent had uncovered their nakedness when these Whores were drunk as they so often were . . .'.

There were also religious problems to be resolved. The King allowed his Queen, Catherine of Braganza, to build a chapel in St James's Palace, where '. . . she heard Mass on Sundays amid a throng of Friars in their Habits, Priests in gewgaw Costumes with Crosses and Images . . . surrounded by Protestant Maids of (dis)-

Honour . . .'. The resultant row forced Charles in July 1662 to order that, 'no English be allowed to attend these Services . . . on pain of punishment'. Pepys noted sadly that 'My Lady Castlemaine, tho' a Protestant did wait upon the Queen to Chapel . . . after the Mass a Fryar did preach a sermon in Portuguese. . . .' James, Duke of York, the King's brother was also in residence at St James's. The labyrinth of rooms enabled him to conduct his various amours, such as those with Lady Anne Carnegie (later Countess of South-esk) and Lady Elizabeth Butler, Countess of Chesterfield – until her husband 'plucked her away to their home in wildest Derbyshire'; the Duke also had a try with Lady Robarts, 'then in the Zenith of her Glory', but old Lord Robarts had no intention of being made a cuckold and whisked her away to Wales. Later Arabella Churchill and after her Catherine Sedley were to occupy suites temporarily.

Meanwhile the Duchess of York gave birth to a daughter, Mary, in April 1662, and she was baptized in the Queen's Chapel 'in accord with the rites of the English Church'. The Duchess now had her own Court, choosing the prettiest maids of honour, one of whom was the lovely Frances Jennings who dodged the Duke's advances and married Dick Talbot, Earl of Tyrconnel.

In 1664 Lady Castlemaine's lodgings in Whitehall caught fire and the King ensconced her in a suite over the Holbein Gate where he could visit her at leisure. His brother was having an affaire with Goditha Price, one of his wife's maids of honour as well as Lady (Margaret) Denham, wife of the poet Sir John Denham, after she had been rebuffed by the King!

James and his Duchess were recklessly extravagant, spending £20,000 a year more than their allowance – nevertheless, in 1668 they had the palace thoroughly overhauled. The Duchess died in the spring of 1670, and James at once negotiated for the hand of the fourteen-year-old Mary of Modena – who up to that time had never even heard of England! In early 1676 came the Roman beauty Hortense Mancini, Duchess of Mazarin – niece of the great Cardinal – to be welcomed effusively by Charles II. He lodged her in superb apartments, giving her an allowance of £4,000 a year, despite strident objections from his mistress Louise de Quérouaille, whom he had created Duchess of Portsmouth. Hortense died on 11 June 1699 'in mean circumstances in Chelsey'.

In 1677 James took Catherine Sedley as his mistress, ousting Arabella Churchill into the wilds of St James's Square.

In King Charles's 'Golden Reign' Lord Brouncker had kept a 'harem' in his apartments over the Eugene Court. Henry Purcell had a room under the Clock Tower where Dryden often stayed with him and went for walks in the park – it was also conveniently close to Anne Reeves' lodgings in Pall Mall.

On ascending the throne in 1685 James II granted the palace to Mary of Modena 'for the term of her natural life'. Their son James – later 'the Old Pretender' – was born there in May 1688.

James II, 'that Monastick Bigot', did not long enjoy his residence, for the country was not going to countenance another Catholic monarch. A call was sent to Prince William of Orange, who was married to James's Protestant daughter Mary. On 5 November 1688 his troops landed at Brixham in Devonshire. James marched his army to Salisbury, only to be deserted by his own adherents. William offered the compromise that James could still have St James's Palace as 'his personal habitation'. Rushing back to London the King had the mortification of finding all his Ministers gone to greet William and seeing his palace guarded by Dutch soldiers. On 11 December he fled from London and managed to get abroad on Christmas Day, never to return to England, dying in 1701 at St Germain, a forgotten man.

William and Mary entered the palace on 11 December 1688, Viscount Radcliffe reporting '. . . that Mary came laughing and jolly as to a wedding . . . unseemly levity in a Queen and at the plight of her Father!'. In fact, neither of James's legitimate daughters had any affection for their father.

On 26 December William summoned the Commons to meet him, requiring that 'the kingship be offered by the Will of the People and not as of Divine Right'; he and Mary were crowned in April 1689. The Dutchman proved to be one of the best rulers Britain had ever had – his great achievements being the Bill of Rights and the Act of Toleration which required *inter alia* that all future sovereigns should be members of the Anglican Church.

William had a dour manner, partly because he could not stand fools gladly and also because he suffered from asthma and did not care much for the atmosphere of the palace – indeed, one of his first actions was to buy the Earl of Nottingham's mansion in Kensington, '. . . being in free air and but a small distance from London, the Smoak of whose Coal-fires much incommoded him . . .'.

He had 'a royal way' built between Hyde Park and St James's Park, 'enough for two Carriages abreast' to enable easy and comfortable access to St James's.

William used St James's Palace only for official functions, which were described by a contemporary critic: '. . . that asthmatick Skeleton, *Phlegmatick William* . . . [had] such Dutch misanthropy that . . . his Courtiers resembled Mourners at a Funeral . . .

and Ladies, even of the First Coach were regarded less than before. . . .'

The only person allowed to dine with him was his old friend Marshal Schomberg – he never exchanged a word with any of the English noblemen present. His only known mistress was Lady Elizabeth Villiers, whom he had met in Holland. She accompanied him to England but in deference to his wife's feelings he broke off the liaison, resuming it only after Mary's death, when he created Elizabeth's husband, Lord George Hamilton, Earl of Orkney. The only untoward incident was in 1691 when Queen Mary's rooms in Whitehall caught fire and '. . . she was dragg'd half asleep in her Night Gown into St James's Park and thence into the Palace . . .'. Three years later she died of smallpox, to William's great distress.

In the following year he decided that Mary's sister Anne must be heir to the throne. He made over to her the palace and 'all its appurtenances'. She was to live there most of her life. In 1697 what remained of Whitehall was completely destroyed, and thereafter William decided that all State ceremonies should be held 'at his Court of St James' and to make access easier and safer 'had three hundred Lanterns . . . strait hanging from a line of trees from Kensington to St James . . . to thwart Thieves and Highwaymen'. A large ballroom was added, together with a number of extra rooms, which occasioned the remark that, 'It was a fine Palace within but a poor-looking one without!' Peter the Great, Tsar of Russia, after a visit to Greenwich Hospital recommended '. . . that You remove your Court thither and convert Your palace into an Hospital'.

Then suddenly William was killed by a fall from his horse, and James II's second daughter, Anne, who had been brought up in her uncle Charles's dissolute and bawdy Court, became Queen – a function for which she had never been trained. She was married to the handsome blonde 'but extremely stupid both when drunk or sober' Prince George of Denmark. She was a sickly woman, a condition aggravated by a long series of miscarriages (a consequence of her father's legacy of syphilis), only one child surviving to eleven. She also suffered intensely from gout, which was not improved by her heavy consumption of brandy. She was carried '. . . verie ill of the Goute and in extream agony to her Coronation' in Westminster Abbey in April 1702.

Given the state of medicine and hygiene, with the ever-present risk of puerperal fever and other complications, her gynaecologist Dr David Hamilton did well to pull her through. When in 1708 she dubbed him a Knight, the Commissioner for Excise, Sir Basil Cochrane, quipped:

> Rise, Sir David, said the Queen,
> The first Cunt Knight that e'er was seen!

However, her steadfast Protestantism and common sense gradually made her respected and eventually popular: she was a decent and religious woman with elements of compassion not usually associated with the Stuart family.

St James's Palace was far too uncomfortable for an obese and constantly sick woman – and moreover she was a great gourmandizer. She would come down from Windsor – which she preferred – for the infrequent assemblies and banquets, and from over-eating and over-drinking she was prone to an unfortunate gastric inconvenience, described at great length in Thomas D'Urfey's satire of 1711, entitled *The Fart*:

> When at Noon, as in State, the Queen was at Meat
> And the Princely Dane sat by her
> A Fart there was heard, that the Company scared
> As a Gun at their Ears had been fired.

The satire was really directed against the obsequiousness of the nobility and clergy, describing how each blamed the other in turn, finally blaming a Yeoman of the Guard who was outside.

> But the Truth of the Sound
> Not at all could be found
> Since none but the Doer could tell.
> So to hush up the Shame
> The Beef-eater bore the blame
> And the Queen, God be Praised, dined well!

Farting and belching were commonplace at home and in public and occasioned little comment; food was in general of poor quality and ill-cooked so that gastric upsets were an accepted part of life.

The Queen led a very moral life and during her reign tried often to prevent immorality in public, though gambling was excluded from her category of sins. Although her Courts were dull and uninteresting, fashionable life centred around St James's. The Queen's Theatre in the Haymarket was famous, at first for its routs and ridottos and when these became pornographic they were phased out and replaced by Italian operas under the direction of John Jacob Heidegger. The Queen issued several 'Proclamations Against Indecency' in 1704, and another in 1712 'Against Vice', as well as 'Regarding Riots' aimed at misbehaviour in all public places including brothels. In the theatres gentlemen were forbidden to climb on the stage to play with or fondle the actresses. None of these proclamations had any real effect.

In January 1703 Anne made new regulations for the park: no menials to walk on the grass, no disorderly people, beggars or rude boys to be admitted; hogs and dogs were forbidden, and everyone must walk on the gravelled paths. In May the orders were strengthened: 'Sentinels and Gatekeepers' to watch out for 'mean persons or anyone carrying a burthen'; no coaches to be allowed except that of the Duke of Buckingham and the Earl of Bradford – and they only from their houses through the mews into St James's Street. No carts were allowed in; nobody was to disturb the deer or the wildfowl, or sell anything or wash and dry linen. Finally all servants were forbidden to accept 'gratituities for opening doors or gate, the Park being at pleasure and *gratis*'.

Nonetheless one ancient amenity established by Henry VIII on the south side of the park was still allowed to function. This was The Royal Cockpit. Oliver Cromwell had prohibited this cruel sport by an Act of 1654, but it had been re-opened at the Restoration although by Queen Anne's time it was already known as 'the Resort of the Cheat and the Pick Pocket'. It was 'Repair'd and Beautified' in 1731 and cock-fights were to be carried on there until 1810 when the lease expired and the Governors of Christ's Hospital, to whom the ground now belonged, gave orders for the 'immediate erasement of the building'.

When the Stuart dynasty was nearing its end, the complexion of the aristocracy was also changing, which occasioned Daniel Defoe's bitter satire *The Peerage of the Nation*:

> This Off-spring, if one Age they multiply,
> May half the House with *English* Peers supply:
> There, with true *English* Pride they may contemn
> *SCHOMBERG* and *PORTLAND* – new-made Noblemen;
> *French* Cooks, *Scotch* Pedlars and *Italian* Whores
> Are all made LORDS – or Lords' Progenitors.
> BEGGARS and BASTARDS by the new Creation. . . .

Marshal Schomberg, Willem Bentinck and other Dutchmen had been raised to the peerage by William III because of their help in his wars to free the Dutch nation and because of their services when he came to be ruler of Britain; other peerages were granted automatically to the many royal bastards of the Stuart kings.

On 29 July 1714, following a violent quarrel between Lord Oxford and Lord Bolingbroke in the Queen's Council Chamber,

Anne was seized with an attack of apoplexy, and she died two days later. On that same day Georg Ludwig, Elector of Hanover, was proclaimed King of the United Kingdom, as George I.

Georg Ludwig of Hanover was born in 1660. His wife, the Princess Dorothea of Lüneberg-Celle, who had brought him a great fortune and vast estates had been shut away in the feudal castle at Ahlden because of her affaire with Count Philip von Königsmarck. Georg Ludwig was thus able to enjoy a carefree sexual life with his two mistresses in his comfortable palace at Herrenhausen. A brave soldier – he had been with John Sobieski of Poland in the great battle which drove the Turks out of Central Europe – he was a pugnacious little despot, bad-tempered and impatient, of narrow education and devoid of any royal 'presence' or wit. One saving grace was his financial rectitude.

Georg Ludwig was thus understandably upset to be awoken at two o'clock in the morning by the English Envoy, Edward, third Earl of Clarendon, with the news of his translation to a higher sphere. He '. . . heard him out, yawned, expressed vexation, turned over and went to sleep again . . .'. He was not keen on the job and it took some persuasion to get him to go to the land of the King-killers.

On 18 September 1714 he landed at Greenwich with an *entourage* of some 700 persons including his two mistresses, his two Turkish *valets-de-chambre*, Mustapha and Mehmet (the Turkish version of Mohammed) who had been captured at the battle of Vienna; and a host of minor attendants down to hairdressers, cooks and maids. Two days later he entered St James's Palace and recorded in his diary: 'The first morning after my arrival I looked out of the window and saw a Park with Walks and a Canal, which they told me were all mine . . . Next day Lord Chetwynd . . . sent me a fine brace of Carp out of my Canal and I was told I must give Lord Chetwynd's servant five Guineas for bringing my own Carp out of my own Canal in my own Park!'

King George spoke no English, nor did he ever try to acquire it. He never clearly understood the parliamentary system and laws. As a Lutheran he thought all the Tory peers were Jacobite Catholics, but was somewhat reassured by his coronation according to the Anglican rites. His accession caused the Funds to go up by seven per cent, but his reception by the mass of the people was far from enthusiastic.

It was the time of the great swindle known as the South Sea Bubble when fortunes were being made by bankers and merchants, the nobility and gentry, including the King's mistresses,

A Allard exc c Pr

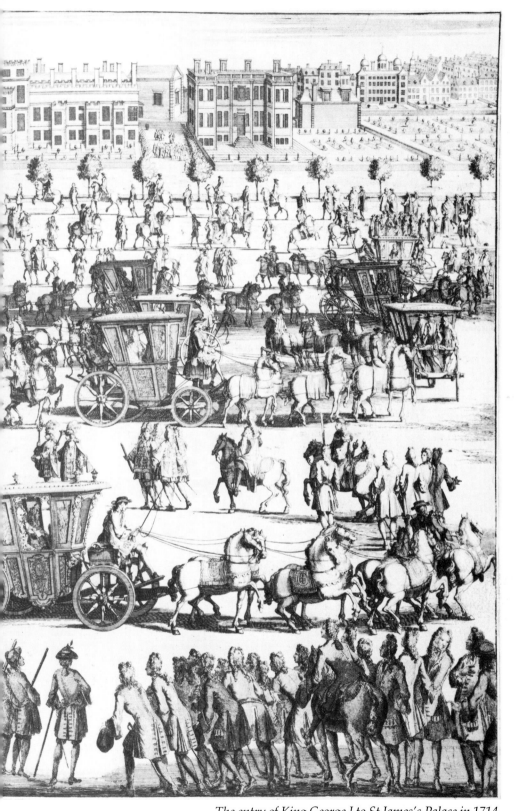

The entry of King George I to St James's Palace in 1714

the Countess von Platen and the Countess von der Schulenberg, and almost all his entourage. In consequence, 'There was a great demand for Jewellers, Engravers, Printers, Watchmakers and so on . . . and for Architects for the grand new Mansions being erected in St James. . . .' Contrariwise, for the poor, '. . . housing was bad, overcrowding was everywhere, a family in one room. Lack of money made any legal rights a mockery [for] many had no reserves nor any way of acquiring any because wages were too low and there was no place to save except in stockings . . . prices had risen . . . the ill lacked illusions and old age pounded the poor into paupers. . . .'

The public particularly resented the barefaced rapacity of the two royal mistresses, who were often mobbed and jeered at when they went abroad – as witness the famous anecdote when 'The Maypole', (the beautiful and very slender Countess Ehrengard Melusina von der Schulenberg) was booed at by an angry crowd and cried out, 'Goot peoples, ve haf come only for your goots!', the crowd jeering 'Aye! Damn ye! and for our chattels too!'

George himself, at first, was thrifty – he would pay for his 'Candles and Firing every Saturday Night' but in the end he joined the spending throng and by the end of his reign had to ask the House of Commons for half a million pounds to pay his debts – in 1723 the servants in the Royal Chapel in St James's Palace had to ask Sir Robert Walpole, First Lord of the Treasury, for their wages which had not been paid 'for a year since last Michaelmas'. The King's main vice was gambling – he would 'play at Hazard in the Groom-Porters' Lodge in the palace' almost every evening.

Domestic life in the palace was very dull – there was no queen to oversee balls and festivities. Moreover there was unpleasantness owing to the hatred which the King bore against his son, George Augustus. (The King maintained that he was a bastard by Dorothea and one of the Turks.) One cause for friction was George I's dislike of his son's wife, Princess Caroline of Anspach. The Prince and his wife were cooped up in mean suites with neither money nor influence – indeed, at one point Sir Robert Walpole told the King that, '. . . the heir to the Throne cannot be shut up in his room like a naughty schoolboy!'

Matters came to a head with the birth of their son in the palace in 1717. During the christening the Prince took offence at the behaviour of one of the guests, and there was an angry scene leading almost to a duel. The Prince now demanded his own establishment, but the King insisted that, if he went, the child be left with him. Only under great pressure from Sir Robert Walpole did he then grudgingly allow *'cette Diablesse, Madame la Princesse'* to enter the palace to see her child! He then had the baby sent to Kensington Palace, where it died shortly afterwards. The Prince was expelled to Leicester House in Leicester Field.

To save himself expense and trouble, the King often used the device of holding a Drawing-Room which was much less costly than a Reception. At one of these in 1716 Horace Walpole gossiped: 'Happening to meet the Duchess of Portsmouth [Louise de Quérouaille, mistress to Charles II] and the Duchess of Orkney [Elizabeth de Villiers, mistress to William III], My Lady Dorchester [Catherine Sedley, mistress to James II] exclaimed "Damn Me! Who would have thought that we three Whores would have met here?"'

Ten years later, the originally svelte Duchess of Orkney was described by Lady Mary Wortley Montague at a similar function: '. . . she exposed Behind a great mixture of Fat and Wrinckles, and Before a considerable Pair of Bubbies a good deal withered, and a great Belley that preceded her. Add to this the inimitable Roll of her Eyes and her grey Hair . . . embellished with a great deal of Magnificence and Jewels which made her as big again . . .'

The two Turks did well also. Mehmet apostatized in 1716 and was baptized Ludwig Maximilian Mehmet and was ennobled as Ludwig von Königstreu, marrying the daughter of a wealthy Hanoverian merchant. He was appointed a Groom of the Bedchamber and was also unofficially Keeper of the King's Privy Purse. He divided his time between Hanover and England and when he died in 1726 Mustapha took his place. Mehmet's mother and Mustapha's son lived near the palace and 'were well provided for'. Both Turks had been in the King's service from 1686, and were his most loyal retainers and honest servants.

At the end of 1726 'the despotic little king' took into his bed the twenty-four-old 'pretty, slim and wilful' Ann Margaret Brett, daughter of the profligate Countess of Macclesfield, but this David and Bathsheba romance lasted only a few months. On 3 June 1727 King George I died of an apoplexy, and his mistress quickly married Sir William Lemon and lived happily ever after.

His successor, George II had an 'official' *maîtresse en titre*, Lady Henrietta Howard *née* Hobart, newly created Countess of Suffolk, a gentle, cultivated, witty and not at all avaricious woman. In her own suite she held court to such as the playwright John Gay, the poet Alexander Pope and Jonathan Swift, the satirical Reverend. The King used to stroll over to her apartments once or twice a week and have a coffee and a chat and then walk back again.

The accession of the libertine George II made an immense difference to the manners and morals of St James's Palace. In addition to the 'Drawing Rooms' to which those who wished to fawn or to solicit could attend, grand balls and ridottos were resumed, as well as marathon sessions of card-playing. One of his first actions was to evict his father's mistresses from their luxurious suites: the Duchess of Kendal's was given over to Lady Suffolk, the official mistress whom he had inherited from his father. She and the new Queen were on friendly terms, and George, like his father, ambled over occasionally.

Although he had many *amours*, George's great love was the 'blonde, sprightly and amiable' niece of Countess von Platen, the lovely Amalie Sophia von Walmoden whom he visited so often in Hanover that in 1736 a placard was affixed to the main gate of St James's Palace

> LOST OR STRAYED out of this Parish:
> A MAN who has left a Wife and six
> Children on the Parish.
> WHOEVER will give any Tidings of him
> to the Churchwardens so as he
> may be got again, shall receive Four
> Shillings and Six Pence REWARD
> NOTE: This REWARD will not be encreased,
> nobody judging him to deserve
> a Crown.

George II was a stickler for etiquette, commanding full attendance at his functions. Every Sunday there was a 'Publick Dinner' with the courses served on bended knee. It was said that those who were lucky enough to get a ticket 'could watch the Royals eating like the animals at the Zoo'.

However, not everyone was impressed with the new King – particularly that great lady of fashion Kitty, Duchess of Queensberry. Her *protégé*, John Gay, had had a prodigious success with *The Beggars' Opera*, until Sir Robert Walpole persuaded the Duke of Grafton to ban it. Gay then wrote a sequel, *Polly*, and the Duchess solicited everyone to subscribe, despite the King's disapproval. His Majesty thereupon sent her a message 'to forbear coming to Court'. Her answer is classic: 'The Duchess of Queensberry is surprised and well pleased that the King hath given her so agreeable a Command as to stay away from Court where she never came for Diversion but to bestow a great Civility on the King and Queen.' Her husband immediately renounced his office as Admiral of Scotland – and neither ever attended the Court again during

George II's lifetime. The Duchess lived to a very great age, remaining a most powerful figure in politics and fashion to her dying day.

George II, like his father, never had a good word for anything British but had learnt to speak broken English. His manners left much to be desired, particularly his habit of turning his backside to any Minister who displeased him by word or deed. The Whig opposition founded a Rump Club of those who had been favoured by the King's arse.

He intensely disliked his eldest son, Frederick Louis, who had been created Duke of Gloucester by George I, when still a child in Hanover. He was excellently educated and a quiet and polite young man. His father had wanted him to be Elector of Hanover – which he regarded as a much superior title, but Frederick Louis thought otherwise. Disregarding his father's wishes he came to Britain, taking a hackney coach all the way from Harwich, alighted at St James's Palace on 8 December 1728 and, unannounced, walked up the back stairs to his mother's apartments. The King's anger knew no bounds. Not until 6 January 1729, under intense pressure from Sir Robert Walpole, did he create his son Prince of Wales, and he deprived him of his proper revenues.

The young Prince was compelled to borrow money profusely, proving a very good investment for politicians and financiers. He spent the money on 'enjoyment in reprehensible circles', which included gambling and whoring. The Earl of Egmont observed that his investments included '. . . to buy, in *Fee Simple* for £1,000 the daughter of an *Hautbois* player . . . to pay a year's subscription to Madame Bartholdi the *prima donna* at the Opera House . . . to have an *affaire* with an Apothecary's daughter at Kingston . . . he has several Mistresses . . . is not nice in his choices. . . .'

The Prince was also rather sexually careless, as witness a Court announcement on 4 May 1732: '. . . the son of a lady much talked about at Court was christened in the Chapel as FitzFrederick . . .'.

Although in 1732 an admirer had given Frederick Louis Carlton House in Pall Mall, he could not afford to live there because he had no regular revenue of his own. Only marriage offered him a chance to get away from his father's palace, and he was ordered to marry Princess Augusta of Saxe-Gotha, a good-looking and affable young lady already known as 'Princess Prudence'. The wedding, in St James's Palace, was private because the King was not prepared to go to any expense for his son. More to the point, he could not afford to have a violent demonstration of support for his son outside his palace. Amongst the 'mob' who stood for the Prince were the Lord Mayor and Sheriffs of the City of London and the Liverymen!

There were Porteous Riots in Edinburgh and Shoreditch Riots in London. Any mention of the King was booed, and the Queen was hissed at the Opera House in November 1736.

There was talk of disinheriting Frederick Louis in 1737, especially when it was discovered that his wife was pregnant. He was frightened that his mother would have the baby poisoned! (The Queen wanted her younger son, William, to be heir to the throne.) When the birth was imminent, the young couple set off in a coach all the way from Hampton Court to St James's, at full gallop, reaching the palace at ten o'clock that night: 'Nothing had been prepared but the Midwife there within a few Minutes got busy. . . . Napkins, Warming-pans, Sheets etc., had to be borrowed from neighbouring houses . . . the Princess was put to Bed between two Tablecloths. At a quarter to eleven she was delivered of "a little Rat of a Girl" . . . on the ninth day Queen Caroline and her two Daughters went to see the Infant . . . the Prince spoke not a single word to them. . . . When she left, the Prince knelt and kissed her hand and at once went back leaving his Sisters to go through the mud and Mob to their Coaches . . . the Queen made no more trips and the King told her that "she was well enough served for thrusting her Nose where it had been shit upon already!" . . .'

Lord Hervey observed that, 'This expression of His Majesty – tho' not of the cleanest – is related just as the Queen reported it to me.' Later the King remarked, 'My Dear Son, my first-born, is the greatest Ass, the greatest Liar, the greatest *Canaille* and the greatest Beast in the world and I heartily wish he was out of it!'

Frederick Louis – thereafter known as 'Poor Fred' – was ordered to vacate his suite immediately and was not allowed to take a single piece of furniture. The suite was to be occupied by his brother, William, Duke of Cumberland. Poor Fred moved into Norfolk House in St James's Square and died there in 1751. He had a posthumous revenge – his son became George III in 1760. The Prince's life was succinctly celebrated in the verses attributed to Horace Walpole:

> Here lies Fred,
> Who was alive and is dead.
> Had it been his father
> I had much rather!
> Had it been his brother
> Still better than another,
> Had it been his sister
> No one would have missed her;
> Had it been the whole generation

Still better for the Nation.
But since 'tis only Fred,
Who was alive and is dead –
There's no more to be said!

The Queen died on 20 November. George's grief was sincere – but very brief! Asking Sir Robert Walpole how he might assuage his grievous loss, he was told to bring La Walmoden to Britain and overcome her unwillingness by creating her Duchess of Yarmouth. Subsequently she made an honest living selling peerages on the sound principle that, the less worthy the applicant, the more it would cost. She was ensconced in the suite of the former Duchess of Kendal, dislodging Lady Suffolk in the process.

All these glittering events masked a grimmer background caused by neglect of ordinary sanitary hygiene. Despite the hundreds of servants, the palace was too much of a warren to be regularly and properly cleaned. In 1740 Baron von Bielefeld, who went to the Court regularly, said it was 'a King's lodging-house, crazy, smoky and dirty'. Ventilation was poor, although there were many broken windows and persistent draughts, and there was a lack of washing and lavatorial facilities.

Personal habits were casual: Anthony à Wood was at the Court in 1665 in Oxford when the courtiers departed 'leaving their excrements in every corner, Chimneys, Studies, Coal-houses and Cellars'; Pepys while in Deptford the same year, finding that the maid had forgotten the chamberpot, 'did shit twice in the Chimney fireplace'. The use of toilet paper was unknown until in 1676 Lord Rochester urged his doxies to be clean and kind by 'using *paper* still behind and *sponges* for before', and in 1710 the broadsheet *The Lass with Velvet Arse* extolled 'a buxsome Lasse who always used Brown Paper'. Shells, bunches of herbs or feathers were the norm.

Although already used in France by 1710, the *bidet à seringue* is not mentioned in Britain until 1752, when it was called 'the machine the French Ladies use for ablutions'. Chamber-pots, not even put into 'closets' until the end of George II's reign, were universal but no secret was made of their use. When in 1724 the Duchess of Broglie, wife of the French Ambassador, was in the palace, Lady Mary Wortley Montague noted: '. . . she makes a great Noise but 'tis only from the Frequency and Quantity of her Pissing which she does not fail to do at least ten times a Day amongst a Cloud of Witnesses. . . .'

The Lords and Ladies of the Bedchamber had the unpleasant task of attending the royal evacuations and passing the filled

29

L'Après Dinée des Anglais, 1814
A satire on the English habit of separating the sexes after dinner: when the ladies had retired, the gentlemen were able to attend to certain pressing problems: the chamberpots were kept in the dining-room cupboard and then used for all excretory purposes

chamberpots down to the next person in pecking order to the Page of the Backstairs who had brought them up originally, although it was the Bedchamber *Woman* whose task was the most unpleasant, the Lady of the Bedchamber merely overseeing.

Incidentally, the Pages of the Backstairs were not young lads, but usually adults who by the nature of their office were often very close to the monarch, sometimes, like Will Chiffinch to Charles II, acting as *hommes de confiance* in tricky or delicate errands.

Society then was far less affected by smells than today. Most people hardly ever washed their bodies, being content to wash their hands, faces and necks and – very occasionally – their feet. In 1750 John Wilkes observed that 'the nobler parts are never in this island washed by women'. The smell of sweat or unclean linen was taken for granted. Women's stays were hardly ever washed, and men's wigs were usually full of lice. The prohibitive cost of good soap contributed to the general aversion to washing. The advent of the *bagnios* (public bath-houses) about 1680 helped to change sanitary attitudes amongst the wealthier class although in 1720 'most men would only bathe . . . before sexual enjoyment in the *bagnios*!' Even the fastidious Lady Diana Beauclerk who '. . . slept alone in a separate bed and changed her bedsheets daily . . . did not wash her body daily . . .' Bad breath was also taken for granted.

Moreover in the palace the stench from the enormous number of candles was overpowering – although the candle-ends later proved a very profitable 'perk' for a young footman named Fortnum.

One of the more pleasant tasks was that of Chocolate-maker to the monarch, a post mentioned as early as the first years of the reign of George I. John Teed, who was gazetted as Chocolate-maker to Queen Caroline – George the Second's consort – from 1735 until her death in 1737, stayed on as a part-time official as an 'Extraordinary Page of the Backstairs', and a man of the same name was still at Court in the reign of George III.

George III used the palace only to hold his Courts and to attend the Chapel on Sundays. He made a number of extensions and improvements but nevertheless it still had a neglected air. When King Christian VII of Denmark came in 1765 his Chamberlain Count Hokke commented that the rooms were very dirty and '. . . not fit to lodge a Christian . . .', although the suite had been specially refurbished at a cost of £3,000.

While Court functions were now sedate, with full protocol and seemly behaviour there were occasional small lapses, such as in April 1762 when: '. . . a Female Infant was dropped in one of the courts . . . His Majesty ordered a Nurse be provided and the child baptized Georgina Charlotte Sophia & three Ladies of the Bed-chamber to be Sponsors with one Lord of the Bedchamber'. Judging from the above protocol this was one of the Prince of Wales' bastards. Later that month the Chapel Book recorded: 'This evening a Female Child about four weeks old was baptized by the name of Frances Mary it being dropped in the Court. Miss Tryon and Miss Meddowes, Maids of Honour to the Queen . . . to stand as Godmothers by proxy . . .'.

The well-known actress Margaret Cuyler always declared she was the daughter of a maid of honour and to have played with the royal children, a claim supported by the fact that, despite her promiscuous and scandalous life, she was always accepted at Court. The little Elizabeth Ashe, 'a pretty creature between a Fairy and a Woman', claimed to be the daughter of the Princess Amelia and Admiral Lord Rodney, and was also *persona grata* at Court although known as a 'Courtezan'; nor did her lesbian friendship with Lady Harrington interfere with her social acceptance.

There was a cryptic announcement in 1762 in the Chapel Book: 'About fifteen years ago [i.e. in 1747] a Boy and a Girl were dropped

Attempt to assassinate King George III by Margaret Nicholson, on 2 August 1786 outside St James's Palace

in the Palace. The Princess Amelia and the Princess Caroline took the girl and H.R.H. the Duke of Cumberland the boy, who died soon afterwards. The girl is still living and the Princess Caroline left her a Legacy. . . .'

A most disturbing incident occurred on Wednesday 2 August 1786: as King George III, after attending a *levée*, was stepping out of his carriage at the gate of the Palace, one Margaret Nicholson tried to assassinate him while presenting a petition: '. . . suddenly without any warning she drew a knife from her bosom . . . made a plunge forward aiming at the King's heart . . . the King stooping to receive [the petition] the knife passed between his coat and waist-coate . . . she was about to make a second thrust when she was seized by one of the Yeomen of the Guard. . . .' She refused to give any account of herself, was examined by 'competent medical authorities' and was sent to Bedlam 'where she remained upward of forty years'. The King remained calm, calling to the crowd, 'I am not hurt. This poor creature is mad! Do not hurt her!'

The next incident to disturb this tranquil Court was the fire which occurred in the kitchens in January 1807. Two years later another fire destroyed the whole of the east wing, just missing the 'German Chapel'. A more serious incident was the violent row in 1810 between the Duke of Cumberland and his Corsican valet, Sellia. When the valet was found with his throat cut, it was alleged that the Duke had made homosexual advances, taunting him with being a Catholic and accusing him of adultery with the Duchess.

It was at this time that Sir Richard Phillips observed, '. . . with great concern . . . the neglected appearance of the Park, the seats old and unpainted, and gaps in the line of trees . . . the Palace in ruins after the fire . . . which should ordinarily have been restored in a few weeks . . . it is now a chaos of ruins . . .'. However, there must have been some unruined parts, for a visiting American, Richard Rush, remarked on 'his splendid reception . . . given by the Prince Regent . . . where there were Golden Urns for Tea and light Refreshments . . .'.

George, Prince of Wales, was born in the palace in 1762, and it

A Ceremony at Court, 1782, introducing a lady to Queen Charlotte. On the right, top to bottom, the Prince of Wales (the future George IV), George III and Queen Charlotte

was the scene of many of his amorous escapades until in 1783 his father gave him Carlton House, on condition that he paid all the expenses and taxes and the upkeep of the garden. He was, however, married in the palace on 8 April 1795, being so drunk that he collapsed into the fireplace of the bridal chamber and did not awaken till the next morning.

From about 1765 onwards George III was subject to recurring fits of insanity, and the Prince was appointed Regent on several occasions until in 1788 he was permanently entitled Prince Regent. He put St James's firmly on the map for pleasure, luxury and debauchery, summed up by a contemporary: 'This Town degenerates hourly. Honesty and Virtue are almost dwindled to Nothing. Roguery, Folly and Vice are constantly increasing, growing ever more Publick and Insolent.'

The Prince was a patron of the arts and architecture, bringing London and St James's into the modern world. He encouraged the demolition of ancient noisome alleys and streets and their replacement by broad avenues and squares, ousting hundreds of small shops and eating-houses and promoting *inter alia* the many exclusive clubs.

His predilection for the King's Place 'nunneries' was well-known, as was his fondness for such 'fast' and handsome drivers of phaetons as Letitia Lade and the Misses Watson.

Letitia Lade (*née* Smith) was a woman 'of low birth and education, a buxom extrovert with a ready bawdy wit, 'educated' by the famous 'Sixteen-string' Jack Rann, the highwayman. She had been briefly involved with the second son of George III, Frederick Augustus, Duke of York, and after he had been sent abroad she took up with Mrs Thrale's nephew, Sir John Lade, who married her.

The Prince's amours were facilitated by his factotum John (later Sir John) MacMahon and his equally rapacious wife, who amassed a fortune by introducing into the royal circle not only useful moneyed toadies but also light ladies. 'Supplicants came to MacMahon for jobs and titles, Money in hand.' Mrs MacMahon died with £14,000 in a drawer; her husband in the end got 'too boozey', and the Prince had to discharge him in case, when drunk, he spilt too many royal beans.

Even more useful was the egregious Louis Weltje, a Westphalian cook who had wormed his way into the Prince's graces and was to serve him in many secret ways. One prime function was to keep the Prince's creditors at bay as well as introducing likely financial saviours.

A cherryseller at the Palace Gate, at the corner of St James's Place

After his accession, in 1820, George IV provided his brother the Duke of York with York House (the present Lancaster House), and another brother, William, Duke of Clarence, with Clarence House; both houses within the palace precincts. The State Apartments at St James's were used only for accreditation of foreign ambassadors as they are to this day.

Clarence House had originally been built as an annexe to St James's for the occupation of 'Poor Fred'. The new occupant described his former apartments as 'dirty, wretched and inconvenient for a Hanoverian!'. When he became in turn King William IV, in 1830, he moved back into St James's.

William was popularly known as 'Jack Easy'. In Hanover he had 'pursued him amours with the Ladies of the Town, up against a wall or in the middle of a parade ground . . . he lamented for the pretty girls of Westminster who would never clap or pox him'. He had 'an insatiable sexual appetite and a vast repertoire of dirty stories' and in May 1787 had two onsets of venereal disease for which he received the mercury treatment.

In 1790 William fell in love with the actress Dorothy Jordan and fathered a large number of children upon her all of whom bore the surname FitzClarence and who made 'good marriages'. In 1818, on the instructions of his brother George IV he married Adelaide of Saxe-Meiningen but failed to produce the required legal heir for the dynasty. This last of the Hanoverian kings was an easy-going man, causing considerable embarrassment at Court, where 'his foul-mouthed intemperance and speech became a byword in Georgian Drawing Rooms', but his entertainments brought the old palace back to life during his seven-year reign.

Walter Savage Landor's epitaph aptly sums up the Hanoverians.

> George the First was always reckoned
> Vile, but viler George the Second.
> And what mortal ever heard
> Any good of George the Third?
> When from the earth the Fourth descended,
> God be praised, the Georges ended!

The young Queen Victoria ascended the throne in 1837. In 1839 she was married in St James's Palace but she refused to live there. However, her daughter, the Princess Victoria, was married there, as also her grandson, the future George V.

The accession of a new sovereign is still proclaimed from St James's, and all Privy Councillors assemble there when convened. Many officials of the royal household have their lodgings there but

The Guards parading at St James's Palace, 1790

none of the rooms is open to the public. The Changing of the Guard still takes place for the delectation of the public and tourists.

No chronicle of St James's is complete without a reference to Buckingham Palace, the focal point of the nation, albeit a few hundred yards from the parish boundary.

In the time of King James I, it was the site of the Mulberry Garden, specially established for the cultivation of silk-worms. The Head Gardener, a royal appointee, was Jasper Stallenge. In 1628 Charles I appointed Walter, Lord Aston, to be 'Custodian of His Majesty's Mulberry Gardens . . . for Silk Worms', for which he was to receive a fee of £60 per annum for his lifetime and that of his son; he was also allowed to build some houses. The venture was a failure: on 10 May 1654 John Evelyn reported: 'My Lady Gerrard treated us at Mulberry Garden, now the only place of Refreshment about the Town for Persons of the Best Quality to be exceedingly cheated at. Cromwell and his partisans have shut up and seized on the Spring Gardens which 'til now had been the usual Rendezvous for the Ladies and Gallants at this Season.'

After the Restoration it became a very popular place of resort, Dryden often went there with his mistress, Anne Reeves, to eat tarts. The poet Mathias wrote of this foible

> Nor he, whose Essence, Wit and Taste approv'd
> Forget the Mulberry Tarts that Dryden lov'd.

This patch of land was incorporated into Goring House, built by George Goring, later Earl of Norwich, but in 1662 his son sold it to Henry Bennet, later Earl of Arlington. Evelyn was not impressed with this house, saying that, '. . . it was ill-built but capable of being made into a pretty Villa'. In 1674 it was burnt to the ground, with its wealth of pictures, plate and fine furniture, and when it was rebuilt it was renamed Arlington House.

In 1698 it came into the possession of John Sheffield, known as 'Comte Orgueil' because he was so proud and arrogant, and when he was created Duke of Buckingham in 1702 he demolished the mansion. The new building was called Buckingham House, occasioning a verse:

> A princely Palace on that space doth rise
> Where Sedley's noble Muse found Mulberries.

Dr Johnson had a poor opinion of Sheffield, remarking that, '. . . his sentiments with regard to Women he had picked up at the Court of King Charles . . . his Principles concerning Property were such as a Gameing-house supplies . . .'. Sheffield's third wife was the illegitimate daughter of James II and Catherine Sedley, and when her husband died in 1721 the Duchess of Buckingham stayed on, 'giving herself the airs like as to one of the Blood Royal' – which in fact she was. On the anniversaries of the execution of Charles I, 'she would sit . . . dressed in deep mourning, in the great Drawing Room in a Chair of State attended by her Women . . .'. This daughter of James II was for a time considered the head of the Jacobite movement, mainly because of her labours on behalf of her brother, James Stuart, the Old Pretender.

On the Duchess's death Buckingham House came into the possession of Sir Charles Herbert Sheffield, one of Buckingham's bastards, who sold it to George III in 1761 for £28,000. The King and Queen Charlotte took up residence in May 1762, and in 1775 it was settled upon the Queen for life and became known as 'the Queen's

House'. All their children, with the exception of the Prince of Wales, were born in that house, and after the Queen's death in 1818 the Prince rebuilt it, since when it has been known as Buckingham Palace and the seat of the monarchy.

It must not be confused with Buckingham House in Pall Mall, the residence of George Grenville when he was created Marquess of Buckingham in 1784: it was still known by that name till he died in 1813.

3 St James's Park

St James's Park extends to about one hundred acres bounded by the Mall on the north, Birdcage Walk on the south, with the Horse Guards' parade ground as its easterly border and Queen Victoria's memorial as the western limit.

In the Middle Ages it was the marshy bog on which the leprous maidens' sheep browsed and their hogs fed, for sustenance or sale. Henry VIII drained these bogs, raised deer on the new meadows and made room for a bowling alley and a tilt-yard. The trees were gradually cut down during the reigns of his children but it was still large enough for his daughter Elizabeth to hunt in. Her successor, James I, laid it out with formal gardens and a small menagerie of 'strange beastes' and gave the liberty of access to the public.

On his way to execution on 30 January 1649 James's son Charles I was escorted through the park by a Guard of Halberdiers with, 'before and after', drums beating and his dog, Rogue, running after him. In Oliver Cromwell's time the park was neglected, and most of the remaining trees were cut down for firewood.

King Charles II played a significant part in the park's restoration, repairing the neglect and vandalism. New trees were planted, the deer were re-introduced and the beautiful avenue, the Mall, was constructed. A new road, Catherine Street (better known as Pall Mall), started the development of St James's as a highly desirable residential district for the nobility and gentry.

Nell Gwyn's house stood on the south side of Pall Mall, its garden going down to the park, divided only by a low wall. The King often walked in the park with his spaniels, to stop and chat with her. One day when both were sitting quietly and their child playing nearby, Nelly called to it, 'Come here, you little bastard!' When the King expostulated, she replied that, although all his other bastards had been given titles, this child, Charles Beauclerk, so far had none. The King at once created him Duke of St Albans.

Several small ponds were converted into a beautiful canal, along which the King could be seen with one or other of his mistresses, feeding the ducks and occasionally swimming in it. The park was stocked with wildfowl, including two pelicans presented by the Muscovite Ambassador. Stags and roebuck roamed around the thirty-six extra acres by which Charles had enlarged the space.

His Majesty would often stop and speak to ordinary folk; on one occasion Richard Harris was committed to Bedlam for throwing an orange at him, and in 1677 Deborah Lyall was also sent there for throwing a stone at the Queen.

The park soon became less pleasant. The best contemporary description is Lord Rochester's *A Ramble in St James' Park* (1672):

> Much Wine had pass'd, with grave Discourse
> Of who fucks who, and who does worse. . . .
>
> And nightly now, beneath their shade
> Are Buggeries, Rapes and Inceasts made . . .
> Great Ladies, Chambermaids and Drudges
> The Rag-picker and the Heiress trudges.
>
> Carmen, Divines, Great Lords and Taylors
> Prentices, Poets, Pimps and Jaylers,
> Footmen, fine Fopps do here arrive
> And here – promiscuously – they swive. . . .*

Sodomy, although still a heinous crime under Henry VIII's draconian law, was discreetly tolerated in Court circles. As early as 1590 John Donne in one of his *Satyrs* wrote:

> . . . thou dost not only approve
> But in rank, itchy Lust, desire and love
> The nakedness and bareness to enjoy
> Of thy plump muddy Whore or prostitute Boy.

The poet Thomas Shadwell reported that Dryden, when in company with 'Persons of the Quality' at Windsor Castle, being asked how they might pass an afternoon, scandalized them by suggesting, 'Let's bugger one another now, by God!', although he also wrote of Dryden:

> He boasts of Vice (which he did never commit)
> Calls himself *Whoremaster* and *Sodomite*
> Commends Reve's Arse, and says he buggers well. . . .

---

* The unexpurgated version can be read in my *Collection of Bawdy Ballads* (Penguin, 1982).

The greatest scandal was the arrest and trial of Captain Charles Rigby RN, who in 1698 importuned young William Hinton one evening in St James's Park. Minton told his master who, with a Justice of the Peace, laid a trap. Rigby defended himself by saying, '. . . it was no more than was done in our forefathers' time . . . the French King did it and the Czar of Muscovy made a carpenter, one Alexander, a Prince for that purpose. . . .' One of Rigby's defence witnesses was disallowed because '. . . that Gentleman stood indicted for aiding advising and assisting him in the commission of this crime.' Rigby was fined £1,000 and sentenced to a year in prison and to stand thrice on the pillory at St James's, as well as having to give sureties for later good behaviour. It was reported: 'Captain Rigby stood today upon the Pillory but not with his Head in it and dressed like a *Beau* but so many attended with Constables and Beadles that nobody could throw anything at him.' Further representations were made 'at a high level', and in December 1700 he was ordered to be released from Newgate in June 1701 so that 'he might seek his Fortune abroad'.

The park was long a haunt of prostitutes, from the starving 'Bunters', earning just some food and drink, to the glamorous 'Toasts' in their coaches whose starting price was a gold piece. In addition, as early as 1708 the satire *Allmonds for Parrotts* mentions that, '*Cundums* were sold openly in St James's Park, in the Mall and Spring Gardens.' Amongst other diversions in 1772 a man ran naked round the park for a wager of 30 guineas, and two women were found wrestling there, stark naked, the prize being a lace handkerchief. To get the real contemporary flavour, the chapbook *A Trip Through the Town* (1735), later reprinted as *A Tripp from St James' to the Exchange* (1742), is worth quoting: 'The *Great Men* at the Court-end of the Town are peculiarly distinguished by refusing to do anything to serve others, and by a great number of tall powder'd *Animals* with two Legs . . . at the hind part of the Chariot embracing one another in an indecent Posture. . . . Here is *The Mall*, famous as the rendezvous of the *Gay* and the *Gallant* . . . the *Ladies* to shew their fine *Clothes* and the product of their *Toilet*; the *Men* to

(Opposite) *This is not the Thing* or *Molly Exalted*
In October 1762, 'a respectable tradesman aged about sixty' was exposed in the pillory for the offence of buggery. 'The populace tore off his Coat, Waistecoate, shirt, hat, Wig and Breeches and pelted and whipp'd him, leaving him naked and covered with Mud.' Public Advertiser, 9 Oct. 1762
'I am now in the Hole,
Indeed come all in my Friends.'

A man at Shadwell in the Pillory Ap. 1763. was killed by the populace.

This is not the T H I N G :

O R,

M O L L Y   E X A L T E D.

Tune, *Ye Commons and Peers.*

I.
YE Reversers of Nature, each *dear* little Creature,
  Of soft and effeminate sight,
See above what your fate is, and 'ere it too late is,
  Oh, learn to be—all in the *Right*.
          Tol de rol.

II.
On the FAIR of our Isle see the Graces all smile,
  All our Cares in this Life to requite;
But such Wretches as YOU, Nature's Laws wou'd
  undo,
  For you're *backward*—and not in the *Right*.
          Tol de rol.

III.
Can't Beauty's soft Eye, which with Phœbus may vie,
  Can't her rosy Lips yield ye Delight?
No:—they all afford sweets, which each Man of
  Sense meets,
  But not *You*,—for you're not in the *Right*.
          Tol de rol.

IV.
Where's the tender Connection, the Love and
  Protection,
  Which proceed from the conjugal Rite?
Did you once but know *this*, sure you'd ne'er do
  amiss,
  But wou'd always be—all in the *Right*.
          Tol de rol.

V.
The *Sov'reign* of ALL, who created this *Ball*,
  Ordain'd that each Sex should unite;
Ordain'd the soft *Kiss*, and more permanent Bliss,
  That ALL might be—all in the *Right*.
          Tol de rol.

VI.
But a Race so detested, of Honour divested,
  The Daughters of *Britain* invite,
Whom they leave in the Lurch, to well flog 'em
  with Birch;
  Shou'd they flay 'em they're—all in the *Right*.
          Tol de rol.

VII.
Press ye *Sailors*, persist, come ye *Soldiers*, inlist,
  By *Land* or by *Sea* make 'em fight,
And then let *France* and *Spain*, call their Men
  home again,
  And send out their WIVES—to be *Right*.
          Tol de rol.

VIII.
Now tho' many good Men, have so frolicksome been,
  Our Pity and Mirth to excite,
Yet may these worthy Souls have the uppermost
  Holes
  In the PILLORY;—all is but *Right*.
          Tol de rol. &c.
          Ap. 1763.

To be had at the *Bee-Hive*, Strand; and at all the Print and Pamphlet Shops in *Great Britain* and *Ireland*.

From Dunton's The Women-Hater's Lamentation, *an anti-homosexual broadsheet published in 1707, showing two men embracing while in prison*

shew their *Toupees*, observe the *Beauties* and fix on some Favourite to toast that Evening at the Tavern. . . . Company is not sought here for the benefit of *Conversation* . . . for they talk only to be taken notice of those who pass by.'

The author describes a lady pointing out the sights: 'She pointed to a goggle-eyed Jew of the Tribe of *Mordecai*; that Fellow . . . is a constant Frequenter of *The Mall* three or four times a Week particularly on *Sundays*. He is remarkable for his upright *Gait*, morose *Speech* and pretty smooth *Countenance*; he makes love to almost every Woman he meets. . . . On their Sabbath he is very formal and precise, but will whore, go to a Play, or Tavern in the evening without scruple . . . that jolly *Dame* that walks by him is Wife to one of his Dependants, she dresses in so elegant a manner that she's envied by all the Women in her Neighbourhood and admired by the Men. . . .'

That 'dour Dutchman' William III built a bird sanctuary at the east end of the lake, still known as Duck Island, and could be seen there smoking a huge pipe. By Queen Anne's time the Park had deteriorated further, from the disturbances caused by aristocratic hooligans known as 'Mohocks'. It was, moreover, a favourite place for duels.

The gates were locked at nightfall, but hundreds of people had 'unofficial' keys, so that there was no lack of company at any time in the twenty-four hours. Macky, in 1724, said it was a pleasant place to stroll in after breakfast. Alexander Pope gives a different vignette in the 1740s, in his second book of Horatian Satires:

The Royal Cockpit in the Reign of Charles the First, c.1640
Cockfighting was a recognized entertainment from Tudor times; the Cockpit Royal was situated on the south-west side of St James's Park. From 1731 there were regular advertisements in the press for 'This repair'd and Beautified, very Handsome' place for these Great Mains of Cocks, the prizes ranging from Thirty to Two Hundred Guineas for the winners. They were still being advertised in 1806, by persons calling themselves Feeders

My Lord of London, chancing to remark
A noted Dean much busy'd in the Park
'Proceed' he cry'd, 'proceed my Reverend Brother
'tis *Fornicatio Simplex* and no other;
Better than lust for Boys, with Pope and Turk
Or other Spouses like my Lord of York'.

William Hickey recorded that he had lost his virginity in the park, and James Boswell, while living in Downing Street, 'overlooking the Park', diarized for 20 March 1763: '. . . I felt a carnal inclination . . . I went into St James's Park and picked-up a Whore.

A view of St James's Palace from the Park, 1741

For the first time I did engage in *armour* which I found but a dull satisfaction.' His next encounter was rather fraught. On 24 June, the King's Birthday, '. . . I went into St James's Park and picked up a young *Brimstone* . . . I agreed with her for Six Pence: we went to the bottom of the park arm-in-arm . . . I dipped my *Machine* in the Canal and then perform'd most manfully . . . then I went along to the Strand and picked-up another . . . for Six-pence. . . .' However, this girl resisted him, and her screams alerted some soldiers who came running up and threatened him. He avoided a fracas by pulling rank, and the soldiers made off.

There were of course some lighter moments. One concerned the glorious Kitty Fisher.

One day George III spotted her, wonderfully dressed and glittering with diamonds, on the arm of his equerry, General Ligonier, who saluted his sovereign and – for the sake of protocol – introduced Kitty as a foreign lady, a 'Duchess de N'. The King was of course not taken in, but thought he would have a joke on William Pitt who was just passing by. He told Ligonier to present the lady to the Chief Secretary, which he did: 'Mr Secretary Pitt – Miss Kitty Fisher.' The Great Commoner, no whit embarrassed, told the astounded girl that if he had met her when he was a young man he would have hoped to have succeeded in winning her affections, '. . . but now that I am old and infirm I have no other way of avoiding the force of your beauty but by flying away from such temptation' and he hobbled away.

The next Sunday Casanova was introduced to George III, 'who spoke to him softly but appeared not to have caught his name' – which much upset the Count. Casanova then went into the park 'to watch the Great Beauties parading, riding and driving' but told Pembroke that 'he had seen . . . six or seven people shitting in the bushes with their hinder parts turned towards the Publick . . .'. He thought it disgusting, but Pembroke shrugged it off as common occurrence.

In the park Casanova had seen Kitty Fisher, 'magnificently dressed and glittering with diamonds worth at least a hundred thousand francs', but Pembroke told him he could spend an hour with her for 10 guineas, which he offered her only to be met with withering scorn – her minimum price at this time was a piece of paper – a £50 note.

In these matters the Italian was given some useful advice by 'the Stable Yard Messalina', the Countess of Harrington – granddaughter of Charles II and one of the *haut ton*'s most profligate Toasts. He told her that he was paying his *amoureuses* in gold but she told him that '. . . this was a solecism only pardonable in a Stranger. . . . Gentlemen were expected to pay by Bank-note.'

During the Regency St James's Park was 'cleaned up' but it was still a prime place for prostitution. The most beautiful women in the kingdom were to be found there – the 'Great Impures' were the setters of fashion, and the King's Place 'abbesses' paraded their 'best Pieces'. The pure mixed with the impure to copy the fashions.

Round the park the Prince's favourite lady friends would career in their phaetons or race madly – but skilfully – about in their two-wheeled chariots known as *Vis-à-Vis*. Prominent amongst this group were such dare-devils as Lady Letitia Lade and the 'Bird of Paradise', Gertrude Mahon, and the Watson twins from Berkeley Square. The Prince could often be seen with one of his mistresses, surrounded by servile courtiers. In the background were growing numbers of affluent middle-class people aping 'the Quality' and scheming to join their privileged ranks.

There were still, as late as 1765 cows tied to posts, 'to swill passengers with milk' drawn from their udders on the spot and served in little mugs, and still, in 1766, there were 'the men running in races stark naked round the park on the Sabbath Day'.

Later the park was utilized for all sorts of national celebrations, and during this period a seven-storey Chinese pagoda was built across the canal on a bridge painted yellow. It caught fire in 1825 during a fireworks display, killing a lamplighter and injuring several workmen. In the following year the canal was remodelled, trees were planted and walkways laid out. Best of all the park was lighted by gas, making it much safer for law-abiding citizens to enjoy an evening stroll. A refreshment pavilion was built on Duck Island, which became a very popular resort of 'people of the middle sort', as well as the light ladies from King's Place and elsewhere in St James's parish.

4 St James's Square

This beautiful and prestigious enclave got off to a shaky start on 27 March 1662 when the Queen Mother, Henrietta Maria of France, widow of King Charles I, '. . . dimised to John Harvy and John Coell Esquires all that feilde or close called the Pall Maile ffeilde . . . comprising forty-five acres from her Jointure, with all the houses thereon for twenty-five years'. The fee was £6,000.

On 1 April 1665 King Charles II granted the freehold of 'the site of St James's Square' to Henry Jermyn, Earl of St Albans. The King's Warrant was for '. . . thirteene or fourteene greate and goode houses . . . Wee being informed that Men are unwillinge to buylde suche greate houses [only] for Inheritance . . .' – they would want long leases which only a freeholder could grant. There were then only four or five houses which had been erected.

The new houses were to be 'palaces fit for the dwellings of Noblemen and Persons of Quality', the rooms to be spacious and the stairs wide and easy of ascent, and the façades were to be of plain red brick dressed with stone, three storeys high, plus attics to a general design of Sir John Denham, the Surveyor-General. In 1669 it was stipulated that each tenant should pave the piazza sixty feet in breadth in front of his house 'with square Purbeck stones' but all that transpired was the construction of a raised pavement for pedestrians walking round the square, protected by posts and chains from the so-called carriageway. The whole of the centre of the new square was left waste and was neither paved nor lighted. All the offal and cinders, dead cats and dogs of Westminster were being thrown there. At one time a squatter built a shed for rubbish '. . . under the very windows of the gilded *salons* [in which] the First Magnates of the Realm, the Norfolks, the Ormondes, Kents and Pembrokes gave banquets and balls . . . it was the dunghill and dustheap of the parish . . . Bullies were allowed to take up their station without let or hindrance. . . .'

The open space was also used for public fireworks displays – a truly magnificent display celebrated William III's victory at the Battle of the Boyne in 1695, and another celebrated the Peace of Ryswick in 1697, when several people were killed by falling rocket-sticks. It was proposed that 'the King's statue in brass be set up in St James's Square'.

In 1726 the residents successfully petitioned Parliament to be allowed to make a rate upon themselves 'to cleanse adorn and beautify and maintain in good repair' their square, and levy fines on any who deposited filth or committed a nuisance. They also ruled that no hackney coach should ply for hire in the square and that coachmen must set down their fares and drive off immediately. In May 1727 a contract was made for an ornamental basin of water 'about 150 ft in diameter and 6 or 7 ft depth' of octagonal design with an iron railing round it, and 'at each angle a 9 ft stone pillar surmounted by a lamp' and a gravelled walkway around it. Originally there was supposed to be a fountain but by 1735 a plinth intended for the statue of William III was substituted. Footpads and highwaymen often robbed people returning home or passing through at night. The square was used as a doss-house for vagrants

St James's Square in 1754

– in his early, poverty-striken years Dr Johnson once walked all night with the poet Richard Savage round and round the pond, for want of money for a lodging!

In 1734 there were 'four Dukes, eight Earls, one Baron and a Prime Minister' living in the square, and it was regarded as 'the most fashionable address in all London'.

The later numbering started with the house cornering with Charles Street on the northern side, a large double house occupied in 1676 by Sir John Bennett, afterwards Lord Ossulston, who hired it out for balls and masquerades. At one such the Duke of Monmouth's guests consisted solely of 'debauched men and lewd women'. In January 1677 Robert Villiers, Viscount Purbeck, hired it for a similar purpose. Charles Bennett was created Earl of Tankerville, and his successor, the second Earl, Master of His Majesty's Buckhounds, was prominent in the sporting world, racing at Ascot and Newmarket and encouraging cock-fighting. Shortly before he died he sold Ossulston House for £6,000. It was demolished and when rebuilt in 1753 the houses were separated, No. 1 coming into the possession of William Legge, second Earl of Dartmouth. It was to remain in the Dartmouth family until 1841, when it was taken over by the London & Westminster Bank.

No. 2 was bought by Hugh Boscawen, second Viscount Falmouth, Captain of the Yeomen of the Guard at the Tower of London, and was to stay in the Boscawen family until 1890. His son Hugh, the third Viscount, was the notorious 'commodious persistent Whoremonger and Drab' popularly known as 'Lord Pybald'. The gallant Admiral Edward Boscawen, 'Old Dreadnaught', demonstrated a better facet of this famous family in the great naval battle off Finisterre in May 1747. Another sort of fame came to the family with Evelyn, the sixth Viscount, who won the Two Thousand Guineas race three times, the Derby twice, the Oaks four times and the St Leger thrice, all with horses bred in his own stables.

The Rent Roll of 1676 mentions that the house (which is today No. 3) was held by Edward Shaw, by an Assurance dated January 1763, but 'now My Lord Cavendish'. This was William Cavendish who later became Duke of Devonshire and who was a son-in-law of the Duke of Ormonde, whose name first appears as the tenant in 1686. Devonshire was described as 'a Libertine in principle and practice . . . an ambitious and revengeful man.' He was, however, a pillar of the Protestant religion, a staunch anti-Papist and a turbulent Parliamentarian, active in bringing William of Orange over to the kingship.

A succeeding tenant was Isabella Bennet, daughter of Lord Arlington, who had been married at the age of five to Henry, Duke of Grafton, then aged nine (he was King Charles's son by Lady Castlemaine). The marriage of these infants created some comment and they were re-married in 1679 when she was twelve and he sixteen. He was described as a 'Very handsome young man, brave, quick-tempered and honest'.

In February 1685, in consequence of some disparaging remarks made by Jack Talbot, younger brother of Charles, Duke of Shrewsbury, about the Princess Anne and her husband, George, Prince of Denmark, Henry challenged him to a duel. The difference between these two young men could not have been greater, John Talbot was a catamite – indeed, the scabrous satire *On the Ladies of Honour* (probably composed by Pope) says:

> Thrice fortunate Boy
> Who can give double-Joy
> And every Turn be ready;
> With Pleasures in Store
> Behind and Before
> To delight both My Lord and My Lady.

The satire *The Court Diversion* (by Pope) asserts of Talbot:

> In France he was the Town and Court's *Salt Itch*
> Each Page and Footman knew him by his Breech.

The duel took place in Chelsea Fields on the morning of 2 February 1685 and Jack Talbot was killed, the Duke wounded. A verdict of manslaughter was returned but no further action was taken. The result was celebrated in *The Duel*:

> And now the Duke bugger'd the Sodomite;
> Such fatal Providence his hand did rule –
> He slew an *Atheist* to preserve a Fool!

The 'fool' was George of Denmark, known to be a particularly stupid man – but the line is also thought to refer to King James II.

Grafton was killed in action at the siege of Cork in 1690. His young widow – who had become Countess of Arlington in her own right when her father died in July 1685 – moved into No. 3 but stayed only a year.

By a quirk of fate, in 1695 Jack Talbot's brother, Charles, Duke of Shrewsbury, moved into No. 3, staying for a year before going over to No. 5. To lighten this grim story, there is the amusing anecdote about his Duchess, who was a foreigner not quite familiar with

Norfolk House

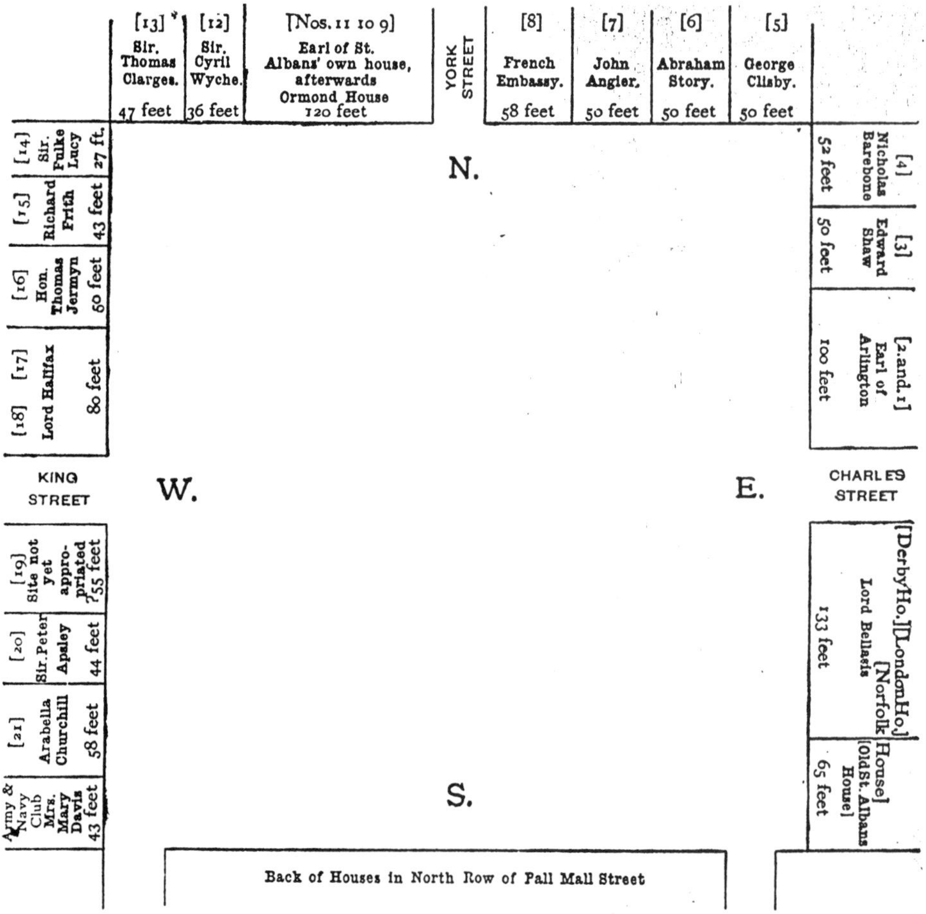

Top row (north side):

| [13]* Sir Thomas Clarges. 47 feet | [12] Sir Cyril Wyche. 36 feet | [Nos. 11 10 9] Earl of St. Albans' own house, afterwards Ormond House 120 feet | YORK STREET | [8] French Embassy. 58 feet | [7] John Angier. 50 feet | [6] Abraham Story. 50 feet | [5] George Clisby. 50 feet |

N.

West side (left):

[14] Sir Fulke Lacy 27 ft.
[15] Richard Frith 43 feet
[16] Hon. Thomas Jermyn 60 feet
[17] [18] Lord Halifax 80 feet

East side (right):

[4] Nicholas Barebone 52 feet
[3] Edward Shaw 50 feet
[2 and 1] Earl of Arlington 100 feet

W.   E.

KING STREET   CHARLES STREET

West side (lower):

[19] Site not yet appropriated 55 feet
[20] Sir Peter Apsley 44 feet
[21] Arabella Churchill 58 feet
Army & Navy Club Mrs. Mary Davis 43 feet

East side (lower):

[Derby Ho. London Ho.] [Norfolk House] Lord Bellasis [Old St. Albans House] 133 feet
65 feet

S.

Back of Houses in North Row of Pall Mall Street

Allocation of building sites in St James's Square, 1676

No. 22. Moll Davis's House

No. 55. Earl of Strafford

No. 4. Earl Cowper

London House

English. Talking one day with the rather pious Lady Oxford, she said, 'Madam, I and my Lord are so weary of talking politics! What are you and your Lord?' Lady Oxford replied that she knew only 'the Lord Jehovah', whereupon Lady Shrewsbury answered, 'Oh! Dear! Who is that? I suppose it must be one of the new titles, for I never heard of him before!'

The fourth house was built in 1676 by Nicholas Barebone, a son of the famous Puritan 'Praise-God' Barebone, and bought in the following year by Anthony Grey, tenth Earl of Kent, founder of a great and noble house of politicians. Most remarkable was Jemima, Marchioness de Grey, 'a Great Lady to her fingertips' who was fond of reminding visitors that she was born in the year in which 'the great Duke of Marlborough died [1722], married at seventeen and was twenty-four when the rebels were defeated at Culloden . . . when our house caught fire in 1725 . . . the Prince of Wales directed the efforts of the firemen and ordered the Guards into the square to keep off the mob . . . my household was startled by the roar of an angry Mob which surged through the square during the riots caused by that madman Lord George Gordon. . . . I even hear wild dreams about steam providing us with new powers of locomotion!' By the time her long life ended, in January 1797, she had witnessed unbelievable transformations of the London scene, considering that her Prince of Wales was 'Poor Fred', that the Gordon Riots were in 1780 and the first steam locomotive only a few years after her death.

No. 5 was built by another speculator, George Clisby, who disposed of it at once to Henry Hyde, second Earl of Clarendon, a grandee who became Lord Privy Seal but, because 'he would not speak for King William', was thrust into the Tower of London in 1690 as an unrepentant Jacobite. By 1679 the house was briefly occupied by Meinhardt de Schomberg while Schomberg House was being built in Pall Mall. About 1712 it belonged to Thomas Wentworth, Baron Raby and Earl of Strafford, who, with his paramour William Bentinck, Earl of Portland, was dubbed a 'raving homosexual', creating a scandal by their behaviour. Strafford died in exile in Paris in 1739. The mansion, which was rebuilt in 1749, was to be occupied by Georg Byng, an MP who assumed that title in 1795. It is Strafford House to this day.

The next house has a more interesting history. It was built in 1676 by another speculator, Abraham Storey (his name is commemorated in Storey's Gate nearby), and occupied in the following year by John Hervey, the Queen's Treasurer and, after his death in 1679, by his widow. After short sub-lets, in 1699 John, first Lord Hervey and later Earl of Bristol, became the occupier. He married the beautiful actress Molly Lepell, praised by Lord Chesterfield: 'She has been bred all her life at Courts . . . she has acquired all the easy good-breeding and politeness without the frivolousness . . . she understands Latin perfectly well altho' she conceals it wisely . . . she has *le ton de la parfaitement bonne compagnie, les manières engageants et le je ne sais quoi qui plaît!'*

It was her son, Augustus John Hervey, who, as a penurious captain, married Elizabeth Chudleigh secretly and kept it quiet when she married bigamously the Duke of Kingston. He lived in this house between 1776 and 1779, when his brother Frederick, fourth Earl and Bishop of Derry, succeeded him. In 1807 the fifth earl, Frederick William resumed occupation for the family, in whose possession it remained until it was demolished in 1955.

No. 7 was built for that extraordinary character Richard Jones, Earl of Ranelagh, a poor Irish peer with the gift of the blarney and the luck to become one of Charles II's closest cronies. He '. . . rais'd himselfe from noe greate Estate . . . to greate Riches . . .', despite the fact that as Paymaster-General he had embezzled more than £100,000 and was several times castigated in Parliament for his peculations. The only punishment he received was the loss of his offices by Queen Anne many years later. Bishop Burnet reluctantly admitted that, '. . . he had the art of pleasing masters of very different tempers . . . so that he was enabled above thirty years to hold great Positions'.

In 1712 John Macky described him as '. . . very fat and very black . . . and hath spent more Money, built more fine Houses and paid out more on House-hold Furniture & Gardening than any other Nobleman in England . . . a bold Man very happy in Jests and Repartees . . . of very little Religion . . . but with an Head for Projects form'd for Intrigue, Artful Insinuating . . . Greedy of Money . . .'. He eventually over-reached himself and by 1711 was bankrupt, petitioning the Treasury for a pension and concluding, '. . . Fayre Wordes will neither paye Clerkes . . . while the Grasse is growinge the Horse may starve . . . I have neither Place nor Pencioun, with seventy Yeares and manie Debtes upon my Backe . . . [I have] . . . nothing but a small Irish Estat ill payde. . . .'

He will always be remembered for his aristocratic playground at Ranelagh in west London.

Another inhabitant between 1757 and 1760 was 'the Battersea Baron', Frederick St John, second Viscount Bolingbroke, '. . . a profligate tawdry fellow . . . appears in Society and swears that he will seduce any Innocent Girl whatsoever . . .'. His amorous adventures included the far from innocent 'Toasts', the beautiful Nelly O'Brien and the reigning 'Impure Beauty' Kitty Kennedy. His wife, the lovely aristocratic Lady Diana Spencer, 'with a mind for Love' after ten years of marriage had an affaire with Topham Beauclerk, a grandson of Charles II. After a messy divorce, she married him, although he was well known as 'a wastrel Man-about-the-Town, a Gambler, a heavy Drinker' who used even to borrow money from the waiters at Brooks' Club. Lady Diana pursued a promiscuous career almost until she died in 1808.

Henry Jermyn's Rent Roll for 1676 for St James's Square has the following revealing information about No. 8: 'His Excellency Monsieur Courtin the French Ambassador payeth for His Lordship's house situate on the north side of the Piazza . . . by the year by quarterly payments.' But His Excellency M. Antoine Courtin failed to pay the rent of £400 a year, and his successor Honoré Courtin had to rectify the omission when he came in 1686. His successor, Paul Barillon, found himself faced with a disorderly riot during the anti-Papist demonstrations in December 1688 which preceded the flight of King James II. His call for military protection actually prevented the pillage of the whole square, the Florentine Embassy in the Haymarket being set on fire and ransacked.

From 1694 to 1699 the house was the refuge of Anne, Duchess of Buccleuch, widow of the unlucky Duke of Monmouth, King Charles's bastard, whose Protestant *putsch* had failed and who had been executed by his uncle, James II. She was followed by the Dukes of Queensberry and Norfolk, but of more interest is the occupation between 1772 and 1784 by Sir Sampson Gideon, Bart., son of the great Jewish financier Sampson Gideon, *né* Abudiente, of an eminent family of Portuguese descent. After a series of violent quarrels with the Elders of the Synagogue in Bevis Marks, Sampson *père* had all his children baptized, gaining the sobriquet 'The father of many Christians', although he never left his ancient faith and was buried in the Jewish cemetery. As a Jew he could not be given a peerage – he would not take the oath as a Christian – but as a sop his son was created a baronet. After his father's death he was created Earl Eardley.

Josiah Wedgwood the Younger, in 1796, after the death of his father, moved the firm's showrooms into No. 8, where they remained until 1830.

The story of numbers 9, 10 and 11 is more complicated. They were originally a large mansion built for Henry Jermyn's occupation, and he lived in it from 1677 until 1683, selling it to James

Butler, Duke of Ormonde, in the Irish peerage. In that year, having been given an English dukedom, his son urged him to move into the square, saying, 'How ill it would look now that you are an English Duke to have no house there!' Thereafter it was known as Ormonde House.

The second Duke had the misfortune in 1715 to fall foul of the 'Whig Ascendancy' and was (*vide* Dasent) 'condemned unheard, his estates confiscated, his family honours extinguished and a price of £10,000 set upon his head': he died twenty-five years after his fall, in exile. His brother, the Earl of Arran, 'an inoffensive old man', was followed by his sister, 'a young heiress of ninety-nine', who survived him until the middle of 1719. The property was then bought by James Brydges, who was nicknamed 'Princely Chandos' when in 1720 he was created first Duke of Chandos. This was a *magnifico* of the old school. He had made a vast fortune as an army contractor and by property developing, his show-piece being the huge estate at Canons, in Edgware. By 1735 what with horse-racing and heavy gambling, he was forced to sell the mansion to another property-speculator, Benjamin Timbrell, who promptly demolished it and built three houses on the site. (Chandos Street and Brydges Street in Covent Garden are the Duke's memorials; the Canon's estate was later bought by Charlotte Hayes's husband, the egregious Denis O'Kelly.) From this point there are three separate histories.

At No. 9 there were a number of short occupancies, including the Austrian Ambassador, Count Christian de Seilern, between 1765 and 1769, and the Captain of the Yeomen of the Guard, Heneage Finch, Earl of Aylesford. In 1790 the first of the great banking family of Hoare took over, their reign ending with Mrs Anne Penelope Hoare who died at the age of one hundred in 1887, after which the Portland Club became the occupiers.

As soon as No. 10 was completed in 1737, Sir William Heathcote, Bart., took possession and the house remained in this prominent political dynasty until 1819, although from time to time the family leased it out. The most famous lessee was William Pitt, the great Earl of Chatham, after whom the house is called to this day. He lived there from 1759 to 1762, giving way then to Sir Charles Sheffield who had just sold Buckingham House to be the new residence of King George III. No. 10 was briefly the home of the select literary group called the Windham Club. In 1737 it housed Edward Stanley, fourteenth Earl of Derby, who was to be Prime Minister three times and who was – after a short let to Lord Tollemache – to be succeeded in 1790 by an even more famous

Prime Minister, William Ewart Gladstone, who later caused Queen Victoria such aggravation.

No. 11 has a more dignified history. It was occupied in 1737 by George Parker, second Earl of Macclesfield, who was responsible for the Bill for the Reformation of the Calendar in 1752, when eleven days were dropped, whereupon his carriage was pursued by an angry mob clamouring for the eleven days by which their lives had been shortened. The only other incident of note was the installation of a swimming bath in 1865 by Mr Henry Hoare – a great rarity at that time.

By contrast, the happenings in No. 12 were much more colourful. It was originally built for Sir Cyril Wyche, who became President of the Royal Society and at one time Lord Chief Justice of Ireland. By 1678 it was in the tenancy of Aubrey de Vere, twentieth Earl of Oxford, 'a Man of loose Morals but of courtly Manners', though he was certainly no gentleman in the Victorian sense. He had married the little Lady Anne Bayning, who was only ten years old, and she had died in 1659. Then in 1661 he fell hopelessly in love with the ravishing actress Hester Davenport – she was, says Antony à Wood, 'the kind of woman who made men take ill courses'. She was then twenty years old and already famous as 'Roxalana' in Davenant's play *The Siege of Rhodes*. Oxford was forty-four, a childless elderly widower, and beseeched her to become his mistress, but she held out for marriage, then unthinkable between a belted Earl and a commoner, let alone an actress. Pepys on 20 May 1662 says that, 'she was owned by my Lord Oxford'. Eventually they went through some form of marriage. Hester left the stage and bore a son, baptized on 17 April 1664 as Aubrey 'son to the Right Honorable the Earl of Oxford'. They seem to have led a normal married like until in April 1673 '. . . in obedience to the King's command . . . [he married] . . . a shop-worn Court Lady, Diana Kirke', daughter of George Kirke who had been Gentleman of the Robes to Charles I and Keeper of Whitehall Palace under Charles II. Diana was at that time Lord Romney's mistress.

The couple took up residence at Derby House in St James's Square, moving to No. 12 in 1678, living there until 1683. There are frequent mentions in the parish records about the Rates: 'refused to pay', 'out of town', 'won't pay more' and 'gone away and won't pay'.

Lord Oxford died in 1703 without a legitimate heir. Four months later, Hester married one Peter Hoett, describing herself as 'Dame Hester, Countess Dowager of Oxford' in the register. When she died in 1717, she was registered as 'Dame Hester, Countess of Oxford' and she had signed her Will 'Hester Oxford', though there was great dispute about the validity of her marriage.

Then in 1754 came Frederick Calvert, seventh Earl of Baltimore, immensely rich – his father had owned the American province of Maryland. He was a libertine *par excellence*, on intimate terms with the most famous 'Courtezans' including Kitty Fredericks, Elizabeth Armistead and the lovely Swiss Jewess known as 'La Charpillon', to mention but a few. Indeed, he might have married Kitty Fredericks had not she flounced out of his house and his life after a bitter quarrel.

Baltimore maintained a harem of 'five white and one black women', and his wife, Lady Diane Egerton, daughter of the Duke of Bridgewater, '. . . acted as the Mistress of her husband's *harem* . . . chaperoning the girls in their outdoor excursions . . .' in St James's Park.

The Earl ran into great trouble in 1768 when he kidnapped the sixteen-year-old Sarah Woodcock from her father's shop on Tower Hill. When by fortuitous circumstances she was rescued and complaint was made to Sir John Fielding, the Earl and his housekeeper, Elizabeth Griffenberg, her husband, Dr Griffenberg, and a Dean Street procuress, Mrs Harvey, were sent for trial before Lord Chief Justice Mansfield 'for a rape'. Although Lord Baltimore was cleared by a technicality of the rape charge, the judge had harsh words to say to him, and he 'thought it prudent to retire to Paris'.

The next inhabitant was Henry Herbert, tenth Earl of Pembroke, a Lord of the Bedchamber, 'a man well acquainted with every Den of Vice in London' as well as 'Toasts' such as Mrs Kendal (later his mistress), the Countess La Rena, Miss Anne Reynolds of Newman Street, who claimed connection with Sir Joshua Reynolds and was known as 'a painter in crayons' (she also passed upon occasion as 'Miss La Roche' when attending to gentlemen in the Diplomatic Service) and Lady Dorothy Worseley. He was Casanova's guide and mentor, putting him wise to the tricks of the trade as well as pointing out the best brothels and introducing him to La Charpillon (who was to cause Casanova much grief) and into Mrs Cornelys' charmed circle.

The Honourable Mr Laurence Hyde had taken possession of No. 13 in 1676 and leased it the following year (having meanwhile been given John Wilmot's earldom of Rochester) to Sir John Williams, Bart., in whose family it stayed until 1684. Lady Williams was at one time an intimate of James, Duke of York and on easy terms with Nell Gwyn. She was also suspected of harbouring Papists.

R. Ackerman's view of Nos. 7–16 St James's Square, supposedly about 1760, though the statue was not erected until 1812. The cattle are put in for effect

In 1690 Evelyn Pierrepoint, soon to become Duke of Kingston, stayed in this house, but between then and 1698 there were several sub-lets, including Jonkheer van Citters, the Dutch Ambassador. He was followed by one of Lady Castlemaine's sons, George, Duke of Northumberland, who stayed from 1699 until his death in 1708.

No. 14, which was built for Sir Fulke Lucy in 1676, was by 1694 in the possession of John Vaughan, third Earl of Carbery, an eccentric of eccentrics. Although a very rich man, he was so miserly that he lived 'in excessive and habitual penury', starving his dependants as well as himself. As Governor of Jamaica he increased his fortune but did not improve his disposition. He was accused of having taken with him 'several shauntlemen of Wales' and sold them as slaves – he actually sold his private chaplain to a local blacksmith to save himself the cost of his fare back to England at the expiry of his governorship.

Another noble resident was General David Colyear, who married Catherine Sedley, King James II's ex-mistress, being created Earl of Portmore. A more worthy resident was General Sir Jeffrey Amherst, who captured Montreal and secured Canada for the Empire; he came on retirement in 1789 but had to wait until 1796 to be given his Field Marshal's baton, by which time he was in his dotage. In 1845 it became the London Library, which exists to this day.

The story of No. 15 is much more exciting. It was erected by the builder-architect Robert Frith – after whom Frith Street in Soho is named – and occupied in 1678 by 'La Belle Stuart', Frances Theresa, Duchess of Richmond, over whom Samuel Pepys often rhapsodized: '. . . but above all Mrs Stewart in this Dresse with her Hat cock'd and a red Plume, with her sweete Eye, little Roman Nose and excellente Taille is the greatest Beauty I ever saw in my life . . .'.

King Charles was greatly taken with her. For a while Lady Castlemaine's nose was out of joint when she discovered that Lord Sandwich, the Duke of Buckingham and Sir Henry Bennett 'were trying to get her for the King'. However, this young lady was under the protection of the Queen Mother, and although the King 'was besotted upon her', young Frances fended him off. The King was always giving her presents: one day 'he ordered a Jewel, a new Gold Medal with her Face to represent Britannia by'.

In April 1667 young Charles Stuart, third Duke of Richmond and Earl of Lichfield, '. . . did fetch her to *The Beare* at the Bridge foot (old London Bridge) where a Coach was ready, and they are stole awaye into Kent without the King's leave' to be married.

John Evelyn averred: 'Mrs Stewart is as virtuous as any Woman . in the World . . . she could no longer continue at the Court without prostituting herself to the King . . . she had no other way but to marry or leave the Court. . . .' She was comparatively poor, '. . . having but £6000 in Jewels . . . a Necklace of Pearls worth £1000, jewels, as Valentines from the Duke of York £800 and a Ring from Lord Mandeville £600 . . . the King of France gave her jewels . . . to prove that she had been Honest to the last . . .'.

The King was furious for a while, but even after January 1668 when Frances had had the misfortune to have her beauty marred by smallpox, he pursued her again. The young Duke of Richmond was angry, but he could do little except persuade the Queen to make his wife a Woman of the Bedchamber to protect her. To counter this, the King appointed Richmond Ambassador to Denmark, where he died in 1672. Frances moved from Somerset House to St James's Square and died there in 1702.

In the intervening years No. 15 was inhabited for fairly short periods by such as John Fitzgerald, eighteenth Earl of Kildare – whose wife Elizabeth was also considered one of the great beauties of the age, Henry Hyde, fourth Earl of Clarendon, the unfortunate Marquise de Gouvernet, one of the Protestants who had to flee after the Revocation of the Edict of Nantes in 1685, and Thomas Thynne, later first Marquess of Bath.

In 1745 the house sheltered Admiral George, Lord Anson, popularly known as 'Little Ben' and reputed to have been a great wencher – although Horace Walpole claimed he was actually impotent, for which reason his wife Elizabeth was known as 'the Mere Maid'. In 1791 a later Anson, Thomas, Earl of Lichfield, rebuilt the house, from which time it was known as Lichfield House.

No. 16 also has a flamboyant history. It was occupied in 1676 by Robert Villiers, Earl of Purbeck, and was the highest rated of the dozen then standing, at £10 per annum (Lady Newburgh was rated at £2, and Madam Davis at £2.6s.). Purbeck was 'a wild young Rake' who, when the house was hardly finished, held a *bal masqué* to which none but debauchees of both sexes – 'the Blackguard Quality' – were invited. From 1679 to 1680 it was the residence of the Swedish Ambassador Johan Barkman Leijonbergh. From 1691 it was occupied by 'that extreamly handsome but indolent and dissolute man' Henry Viscount Sidney, on the occasion of his being granted the earldom of Romney. He played an important part in securing William of Orange's accession to the throne – he was given some important roles, despite the opposition of Government Ministers, being at one time Master of the King's Ordnance. William had no illusions about him, saying, 'He will do until I find a fit man.'

However, Sidney's private life was nasty. He was a heedless and uncaring wencher. For almost twenty years Mrs Grace Worthley, a gentlewoman of good family whose husband had been killed in action against the Dutch in 1665, had been his mistress and she had borne him a son. She had averted her eyes from his numerous affaires, and particularly from his meanness – he allowed her only £50 a year. When he started his violent affaire with Diana Kirke, Countess of Oxford, he left Grace Worthley destitute, despite her constant pleas for help. He complained that, 'he was pestered by acrimonious correspondence about his numerous bastards', for whom he had failed to provide.

On the accession of Queen Anne Sidney was deprived of all his offices and died 'an unrepentant bachelor' of smallpox in August 1704, leaving his estate to some nephews and nothing to Grace. Despite her frequent petitions to the Treasury for a pension, this was never granted and she died in abject poverty.

From 1705 the house was occupied by Sir John Germain, a somewhat stupid but brave soldier of fortune of Dutch extraction who had served under William of Orange. He had married Lady Elizabeth ('Betty') Berkeley, daughter of Charles, second Earl, and because she had married so far 'beneath her' Sarah, Duchess of Marlborough, was much incensed – forgetting her own plebeian origin, asserting that 'Elizabeth had married a butcher's son . . . because she had no Portion . . . and had had an unlucky accident with one of her servants . . .'. Elizabeth, a real patrician, cared nothing for such criticisms and had never hidden her unorthodox sexual activities. Germain was created a baronet just before he died in 1718, and later Elizabeth inherited a vast fortune. She entertained much – her card parties were famous – and her guests included George II's superannuated mistress Henrietta Howard, Countess of Suffolk, various diplomats and Horace Walpole. Lady Betty was in old age fond of repeating that she was born in the same year as good King Charles (the Second) was on the throne and 'that she had seen five sovereigns on the throne of England'; she died in 1769 having survived her husband fifty years, having 'outlived all the irregularities of her youth and was much esteemed for her kindnesses and charity'.

The house was pulled down in 1790, and the site lay undeveloped until 1807, when it was rebuilt for a rich merchant, Edward Boehm, whose wife had great social pretensions. She reached the pinnacle of her ambition on 21 June 1815 when entertaining the Prince of Wales to dinner. Suddenly 'a dirty bloodstained officer' arrived to inform the Prince of the victory at Waterloo, and George, after promoting Major Henry Percy a colonel on the spot and showing pleasure and relief at this news, '. . . looked sad and with much feeling said . . . it was a glorious victory and we must rejoice, but the loss of life has been fearful and I have lost many friends . . . while he spoke the tears were running down his cheeks'. He then left and the party broke up. Mrs Boehm later complained that he had spoilt her party!

Mr Boehm's tenure ended in 1819 when he went bankrupt.

Numbers 17 and 18 were for many years regarded as one house, the home of the Saviles, Marquesses of Halifax, the first of whom occupied what can be called No. 17 from 1673 until 1695. George Savile was Lord Privy Seal and Lord President of the Council, two of the highest offices of State. For his great and agile political skills

(Overleaf) *The Loss of the Faro Bank* or *The Rooks Pigeon'd*
A Servant who had stolen £500 was charged by Lady Buckinghamshire. In revenge he informed on her Faro Table *in St James's Square: it was raided and she and three of her noble companions were in their turn brought before Lord Justice Kenyon, who threatened them with the pillory for this illegal activity*

stole, my Lord? — it in the Housekeepers — this comes of admiting e house! — Ah! the Cheats! gone smack; - without of the Cards!
Bank stole? — why I had a Gold snuff box stole last night from my Table in Grafton Street
O! if they come to the Mount, if I don't tip them Shelalee
Zounds! I hope they don't smoke me!
nor me!
Stole! — bless me why a Lady had her Pocket pick'd at my House last Monday

he earned the sobriquet 'The Trimmer' – an early Talleyrand, living to serve three kings. He was a pioneer of fashionable Society, his house being the focus of the political world for upwards of twenty years. His eldest son, Lord Elland, married the daughter of the Marquis de Gouvernet, who had a fortune worth 200,000 crowns.

Halifax House was rebuilt in 1725 as two houses, No. 17 being occupied briefly by Mary, Countess of Bradford, who was involved in the scheme to install the centre pond. She gave way to Sir Orlando Bridgeman, Bart., whose amorous adventures would fill a book. His most famous *protégée* was the Covent Garden beauty Lucy Cooper. He was a member of Sir Francis Dashwood's madcap Hell-Fire Club and a cheerful source of revenue to a whole bevy of whores, who bemoaned his early death in 1764.

In 1790 Sir Philip Francis, reputed author of the *Junius Letters* which created political havoc, became the lessee. His widow lent the house to Queen Caroline during her trial, when crowds accompanied her as she drove to the House of Lords daily, cheering her vociferously.

No. 18 was occupied by Philip Dormer Stanhope, the famous Lord Chesterfield, whose *Letters to his Son*, instructing him in good manners and civilized behaviour, caused Dr Johnson to assert that, '. . . they inculcate the Morals of a *Strumpett* and the Manners of a Dancing-Master'. ('Dancing-master' was a pseudonym for a whoremonger.) This self-proclaimed arbiter of civilized behaviour was wont '. . . when he went to stool, to take a book and when finished tear out pages' to wipe his behind. According to the Harris *List of Covent Garden Cyprians*, his particular peccadillo with his doxies was 'to have his eyelids licked by two naked whores'.

In September 1733 he married Melusina von der Schulenberg, the illegitimate daughter of King George I, who had a dowry of £50,000 cash down and an income of £3,000 a year for life from her mother's immense estate. Chesterfield claimed that George II had defrauded them by burning the Will, and when he threatened to sue, the King gave him £20,000 'as a quietus' and then revenged himself on the importunate Earl by dismissing him from Court for offending the Queen because he had paid court to Lady Suffolk, the King's *maîtresse en titre*. (Henrietta Howard was by then long past any mistressing and in any case had been installed by the King's ministers because she was 'harmless' and 'no threat to Her Majesty'.) George II described him as 'a little gossipping Tea-table Scoundrel'.

From 1773 to 1781 the Dutch Minister-Plenipotentiary, Jan Waalraad, Count van Welderen, had his offices at No. 18, and after him could be found Lord Edward Thurlow, passionate defender of Warren Hastings, twice Lord Chancellor and 'the worst-mannered man ever to hold such a high position'.

Three years after his departure came Robert Stewart, Viscount Castlereagh, who became the most unpopular Minister of the time, mainly because he was held responsible for the troubles in Ireland. He has been immortalized in Shelley's famous couplet,

> I met Murder in the way
> He had a Mask like Castlereagh.

The Viscount lived next door to the house from which Queen Caroline went daily to her trial. The mobs hooted him, on one occasion, smashing the drawing-room windows. He was a courageous man, as was proved during the Westminster election when he left the hustings at Covent Garden and insisted on walking back, although jostled by an angry mob all the way to Whitehall. At the Admiralty Gate he stopped, doffed his hat and bowed to the crowd, saying, 'Gentlemen, I thank you for your escort!' In 1822 – by which time he was Marquess of Londonderry – he became deranged and was ordered to go and rest at his mansion

The Manner, in which the Queen proceeded daily from Lady Francis's House, St James's Square, to the House of Lords
Queen Charlotte was facing an action for divorce and the crowds were thereby demonstrating their dislike of George IV

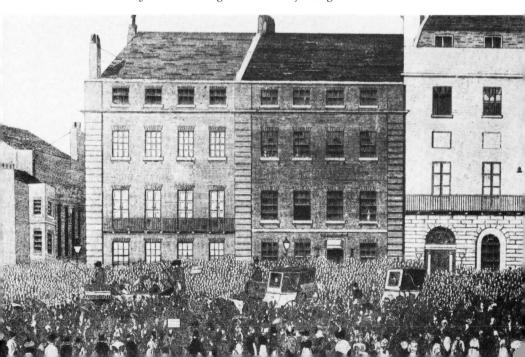

in Kent. There, despite the removal of every potential weapon, including his razor, he committed suicide by cutting his carotid artery with his little nail-paring knife.

No. 19 was first held by the ill-fated Arthur Capel, Earl of Essex, who was implicated in the Protestant scheme to assassinate Charles II and his brother James, Duke of York, for their alleged pro-Catholic sympathies – the so-called Rye House Plot. He was sent to the Tower of London on 28 June 1683 and cut his throat 'almost to the back vertebra of his Necke' with a razor.

From 1716 to 1719 the Venetian Ambassador, Tron, lived at No. 19, and he caused a scandal by refusing to pay any rates, which some years later occasioned an Act requiring that 'empty houses occupied by Ambassadors or Ministers from any foreign state' were to have the rates paid by the landlord or owners.

No. 20 came into the possession of the Bathurst family in 1693, with Sir Benjamin, who was Treasurer to Princess Anne – the future Queen Anne – but his son Allan, who inhabited the house from 1705 to 1771, was more notable. Described as 'an extremely gay and lovable Man fond of dancing, who begot many children at home and abroad', he was also famed for keeping a harem in his London mansion.

> Fair *Coursers*, Vases and alluring Dames
> Shall then *UXORIO* – if the Stakes he sweep
> Bear Home six Whores – and make his Lady weep!

Lady Bathurst was generally thought to be only his house-keeper, acting as duenna to his harem. He died at the age of ninety-five, in this house, still cheerful and dancing, and greatly mourned by all who knew him. It was said of him that, 'At eighty he had all the Wit and Principles of a man of thirty; at ninety-one unimpaired by his love of Pleasure.'

The house was rebuilt by Robert Adam in 1775 and came into the possession of yet another eccentric, the immensely rich Welsh magnate Sir Watkyn Williams Wynn, fourth Bart. and MP. An ardent nationalist, he paraded his Welshness to such an extent that he was nicknamed 'Prince of Wales'. He was a constant visitor to the King's Place 'nunneries' and to the Berkeley Square establishment of Elizabeth Weston.

'Old Watkyn' was fond of the theatre and at one time was in partnership with Thomas Sheridan – they were known as 'Bubble and Squeak', Watkyn being 'Bubble'. He died in 1789, at the age of forty, worn out by all his political and sexual activities. The family were still in occupation as late as 1890, with the seventh baronet,

Sir Herbert Lloyd Watkyn Williams Wynn. Today the premises are part of the Distillers' House – which also subsumes No. 21, which has a much longer and even more interesting pedigree, having harboured two royal concubines.

There were actually two houses, one as No. 21 and a smaller one, next to it, part of the same demesne but never designated by a number. In fact, this smaller house must have been the very first to have been erected in the square, with an entrance from Pall Mall, since it was designated for the King's mistress Mary ('Moll') Davis and to give immediate access to His Majesty when walking from his palace in Whitehall.

Lord St Albans' Rent Roll of 1676 has the following entries:

(21) Robert Werden, Esq., holdeth by Assurance dated June 14 1673 in trust for Mrs Churchill. [This had a 58 ft front.]
(–) Edward Shaw holdeth by Assurance dated (blank) 1672, now Mrs Davis. [This had a 43 ft front.]

Arabella Churchill, 'a tall Creature, pale of Face, nothing but skin and bone', at the age of twenty became a maid of honour to the Duchess of York, soon becoming mistress to the Duke. She moved into the house in 1675 and stayed till 1678, when one of the King's factotums, Sir Joseph Williamson, known as 'Arlington's tool', became the tenant. In 1678 he had married the wealthy sister of the Duke of Richmond and with her money had bought the house for £8,000. In 1685 he gave way to Catherine Sedley, mistress of the Duke of York, who was compelled to move out of her apartments in St James's Palace when the Duke became King.

Catherine was the daughter of King Charles II's favourite, Sir Charles Sedley, and had inherited her father's spirit and wit. A 'lean and ugly girl', her wit made amends for her ugliness, and her good nature and sense of humour made up for any other blemishes, for she was 'none the most virtuous'. She was later created Countess of Dorchester, which, says Evelyn, 'the Queen took very grievously . . . she hardly ate one morsel nor spoke one word to the King nor any about her . . .'. Sedley's own caustic rejoinder was, 'King James hath made my daughter a Countess and I have been helping to make his daughter a Queen!', referring to his support of Princess Mary and her husband William of Orange. Catherine later married David Colyear, Lord Portmore.

Upon his accession to the throne, William promised his wife to give up his mistress, Elizabeth Villiers, and for a while she lived in this house. After her marriage to George Hamilton (who had been created Earl of Orkney), she moved over to Park Place to become –

The Whore's Last Shift, 1779
A woman, naked except for her shoes is washing her last shift in a broken chamber-pot. Although her hair is dressed as a most fashionable courtesan's the room is poverty-stricken. The two pill-boxes on the floor contain 'Leake's Famous Pills', a well-known quack remedy against venereal disease and other ills. The picture is thought to refer to Lady Dorothy Worseley after her divorce, although her period of hardship was of very short duration

unwittingly perhaps – a neighbour of Mrs Elizabeth Needham, the notorious procuress.

Lord and Lady Portmore were at No. 21 again from 1711 until Catherine died in 1717, when Lord Portmore moved over to No. 14, but he returned in 1724, staying till 1730, when his son took over until 1739. In the following year Thomas Osborne, fifth Duke of Leeds, His Majesty's Cofferer, took up residence in 1742. In 1790 he had the house rebuilt to the design of the famous architect Sir John Soane. From 1829 to 1875 it was the London residence of the bishops of Winchester, then it became a branch of the War Office. It was demolished in 1934 to allow for an extension of the Distillers' offices.

Far more famous was the inhabitant of the unnumbered No. 21, the sprightly, lovely and 'divine dancer' Moll Davis, bastard daughter of Colonel Howard, who had captured King Charles's heart with her rendering of the song 'My Lodging is the cold, cold ground'. In October 1666 Evelyn included her in 'the foul and undecent women who had seduc'd the King'. By January 1668 the King was much in love with her, although Pepys voiced Mrs Pierce's criticism: 'Moll Davis . . . is the most impertinent Slut in the World . . . the more so that the King do shew her Countenance and she is reckon'd his Mistress even to the Scorne of the whole World . . . the King hath given her a Ring of £700 whiche she shews to Everybody . . . he hath furnish'd a House in Suffolk Streete most richlye . . . whiche is a most infinite Shame . . . she dances beyonde any thinge in this Worlde. . . .'

At this house, No. 11 Suffolk Street, Moll gave birth to the King's daughter, Lady Mary Tudor. In 1674 Charles paid £8,000 for the house in the square, giving her a pension of £1,000 a year. She made a single appearance on the stage in February 1675, but by this time the King's affections had veered elsewhere. In 1686 she married the French flautist and composer, Jacques Paisible, and after 1687, when she sub-let the house to John Bennett, Lord Ossulston, the square knew her no more. Eventually No. 21 was pulled down to make way for the Army and Navy Club.

So far as can be ascertained, the building on the western corner with Pall Mall was a very ancient hostelry, the Bell Tavern, in existence long before the game of *paille-maille* was known. Ingress to the new square was originally through its stable yard or perhaps by way of a narrow alley that was later called George Street, which then became a proper entrance to the west side.

The development of the eastern side was quite different. Lord St Albans had already built himself the so-called Old St Albans

House, with a sixty-five-foot frontage at the corner with Pall Mall. The entrance was from Pall Mall, perhaps through some stables. Later a little street called John Street was cut, matching George Street on the other side. The rest of the space up to Charles Street, measuring 133 feet, was assigned by an agreement dated 24 March 1669 to his friend Lord John Bellasis to develop. By 1676 three mansions had been completed, Norfolk House, London House and Derby House.

As early as 1669 St Albans House was lent to the Grand Duke of Tuscany, who provided the populace with a grand fireworks display and free wine and beer. Not until 1684 were the Norfolks first associated with it. Lady Isabella Wentworth's description in 1708 is very amusing: 'I have been to see a very good hous in St Jamsis Squair. It has thre large Rooms forward & two little ones backward, closetts & marble chimney-peicis, and harths to al the best rooms & iron backes to the chimneys. Thear is twoe pretty clossets with chimneys and glas over them and picturs in the wenscoat . . . bras locks to al the Doars, wenscoat at the bottom and top . . . thear wil want little to be dun to it. Thear is back stairs twoe coach housis & stable for 11 horsis, rooms over for sarvents, very good offissis, a yard for the drying of cloaths and leds for that purpas . . . & a back gate whiche I forget the streets name that it goes into. Thear is a handsom roome al wenscoted for the steward to dyne in & another for the sarvents to dyne in, even with the kitchin belowestairs under the hall and parlors . . . tomorrowe the man comes to tell me the prise. . . .'

Thomas Howard, eighth Duke of Norfolk, acquired the house in 1721, paying £10,000 for it. In 1737 the Prince of Wales, 'Poor Fred', having been summarily ejected from the palace by his father, George II, was offered the house as a refuge and moved in at once with his wife and children, paying £1,200 a year rent. In the following year he bought the three houses adjoining, thus extending it to Pall Mall. His son, the future George III, was born in Norfolk House.

Norfolk House became a centre of fashionable life, with masques and balls and gambling. The Prince was particularly fond of music. He was '. . . a gay little gentleman, a pleasant host altho' a poor shot; a good Master but a bad Debtor, he never did anyone any harm. He was especially happy with his children, especially his eldest son George altho' his second son Edward was his favourite . . .'. He used to walk the streets unattended, chatting familiarly with working men and Thames fishermen, and would 'enter the cottages of the poor and listen to their tales and partake of their fare

. . .'. Although deprived of money, he nevertheless had considerable prestige as Prince of Wales and in consequence was surrounded by toadies and other place-seekers and, of course
moneylenders. George III later paid his father's immense debts.

'Fred' was proud to be regarded as the first English-speaking
Hanoverian. He was also a very compassionate man. He saved the
life of that 'little woman of genteel appearance . . . whose name
will live in history for ever', Flora MacDonald, because, said the
Prince, his own wife would have acted as Flora had to save *his* life in
the like circumstances – although in fact Princess Augusta was
much put out about Flora's '. . . riding about Scotland in company
with that young Man [Prince Charlie] with thirty thousand pounds
upon his Head and her maid's petticotes around his legs'. The
Prince collected £1,500 from a number of Jacobite ladies and sent
Flora back to Scotland, thus earning the hatred of Tories but
increasing his political status with the Opposition.

He left Norfolk House in 1748 for his new mansion in Leicester
Fields – now Leicester Square – and died there of pleurisy on 20
March 1751. His son George almost fainted with shock but his
father, the King, said he was glad and went off to visit his new
mistress in Hanover, Countess Walmoden.

On retaking possession, the Duke of Norfolk built a magnificent
palace, and from 1756 the Duchess's card parties and extravagan-
zas were constant subjects of scandalous conversation in high
society. Edward Howard, the ninth Duke, died in 1777 at the age of
ninety-two – he boasted that he had known six sovereigns. One of
his family, the eleventh Duke, was described as 'having all the
Habits and Attributes of a Hogg . . . he rarely wash'd but when he
was drunk and then by his servants . . .'.

Norfolk House was demolished in 1938, and the present building was General Eisenhower's Headquarters for the Normandy
invasion which put an end to the Hitler menace.

The house next door, London House, was first occupied by
Anne, Countess of Warwick, from 1676 to 1685, and later, in 1718,
by the profligate Henry Fiennes Clinton, Earl of Lincoln, who
fancied himself a stallion of the calibre of Charles II, fathering
several children upon a Covent Garden prostitute, Peggy Lee, and
causing much anguish to his friends thereby; he stayed for ten
years. The mansion's future was secured when in 1771 Richard
Terrick, the hundredth Bishop of London, took it over. It remained
an episcopal residence until 1886, when the bishops moved to
Fulham Palace. The house, now No. 32, is still called London
House.

Derby House was built for Aubrey de Vere, twentieth Earl of Oxford (see the story of No. 12), on ground leased in 1669 to that staunch old Cavalier Lord John Bellasis, after whom it was called Bellasis House for many years. By 1687, as a suspected Papist, he found himself in the Tower of London before dying in St Giles in 1689. Between 1732 and 1735 it was used by Sir Robert Walpole, and then by the Captain of the King's Bodyguard, John Hobart, first Earl of Buckinghamshire – a title which his successors brought into ill-repute, particularly George, third Earl, at one time stage-manager at the King's Theatre in the Haymarket, whose wife Albinia was the notorious Faro-table expert who incurred the wrath of Lord Chief Justice Kenyon, who threatened her with carting!

Derby House gained its name when, in 1854, Edward Stanley, fourteenth Earl of Derby and one-time Prime Minister, took up residence. The house remained in the family till well into the twentieth century.

A great deal of gambling took place within most of these great houses. It was ruled illegal, so it was prudent to play only in 'closed clubs' and in private residences, not taverns. Inhabitants of the square who just wanted a normal convivial drink could go to the old Bell Tavern or to the Crowne Tavern. For another kind of sin, King's Place was within a few yards, and there were also facilities for 'that most heinous crime', homosexuality, at George Whitwell's 'Mollies House', the Royal Oak, which stood at the junction with Pall Mall and John Street.

In 1726, during the famous trial of Mother Clap for keeping a house for sodomites, one of the young catamites, Edward Courteney, informed on James Whitwell. He deposed that there were rooms at the back of the Royal Oak '. . . used by *Mollies* acting as married couples . . . [and that] Whittle had put the bite on him . . . to go with a Country Gentleman who promised to pay him handsomely . . . he stayed all night but in the morning he gave me no more than a sixpence . . .'. James Whitwell was sentenced to Newgate prison and also to stand in the pillory, but nevertheless was still the occupier as late as 1738.

From about the middle of the eighteenth century, most of the houses were rebuilt (many because of the shoddiness of the original constructions) and then occupied by wealthy tradesmen or politicians and quite a few ambassadors. In 1776 it was noted: 'Altho' the appearance of the Square hath an Air of Grandeur yet that by no means resulteth from the Pomp and Greatness of the Structures . . . but rather from a prevailing Regularity throughout, joined to the neatness of the Pavement. . . .'

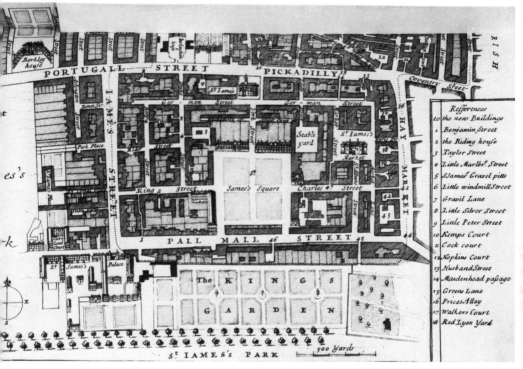

A section of Strype's map of 1742 showing Pall Mall and its environs

Thereafter the square began to lose caste. The nobility and gentry moved further westward, to Mayfair and Belgravia. Their places were taken by *parvenus* and 'tradesmen and those of a lesser sort'. The square was physically deteriorating; in 1808, when at long last William III's statue was being erected, the elegant pool was now 'slimy and stagnant'. A further half century was to elapse before this eyesore was replaced by the present pleasant garden – and then only because of a cholera scare!

The south side of the square never acquired any prestige as a residential area. The earliest reference to it is as 'the back of the north row of houses in Pall Mall Street' – the back gardens and stables. Not until fairly late in the nineteenth century were they overbuilt with unpretentious houses, at least three of which were lodging-houses. All were cleared away at the time when the Junior Carlton Club was being built between 1866 and 1868.

77

5 Pall Mall

One of the more believable legends about the reason for the construction of Pall Mall was that the carriages bowling along to the Court at Whitehall in summertime raised such clouds of dust that the *paille-maille* players could not see what they were doing. Pepys remarked on 2 April 1661 that this was the first time he had ever seen the sport. Later he asked 'the Keeper of the Pell-mell', while he was sweeping the floor, about the type of earth needed 'to floor the mall': and was told '. . . over it is cockle-shells powdered', spread to keep it fast, though in fine, dry weather it turned to dust 'and deads the ball!'

After that Pepys saw the game quite often, noting on 4 January 1664: 'A Gallant, lately come from France did swear mightily at one of his companions for suffering his man . . . to be so saucy as to strike a ball while his Master was playing!'

There had been a number of dwellings along the old road for many years previously, the best known being the Old Bell Inn. In 1665, during the Great Plague, Pepys remarked that he saw the house shut up in which 'in Cromwell's day we young men used to keep our weekly clubs'. This was Wood's Coffee-House. In 1630 one David Ballard, 'Shoemaker to the King', had erected a dwelling 'previously taken by M. Jean Bonneale under pretence of building a *pall mall* . . . but the house was pulled down the following Candlemas'.

Dr Thomas Sydenham, the eminent Court Physician, lived from 1658 'in the seventh house on the north side'. This was the house let to Nell Gwyn while she was nagging Charles II to give her a bigger, better one on the south side.

At the Restoration in 1660 the King was naturally pestered to give presents to supporters and to reimburse for old wrongs. In 1660 Mr Samuel Morland petitioned for the '. . . restoration of a House, Garden, and Stables . . . whereon he had spent £500, and

The earliest illustration of the game of Pall Mall, c. Charles I

forced by the coming of the Rump Parliament to part with to Colonel Berry for less than £100 . . .'. At the same time the King gave '. . . to Daniel ONeale, Groom of the Bedchamber . . . a piece of ground 1400 feet in length and 23 in breadth between St James Street and Pall Mall, to be called Catherine Street . . .'.

The King had named the new street after his Queen, but the name never stuck and very shortly afterwards it became known as Pall Mall. It stretched, on the south side, from the Spring Gardens at Charing Cross up to the Palace of St James; on the north side from Colman-Hedge Lane (now Whitcomb Street) to St James's Street. Both sides were quickly built up with small shops, coffee-houses, taverns and private dwellings. The south side was the more favoured because it bordered upon the royal gardens, and the nobility and gentry vied with each other to buy or rent a house or a lodging there. The north side quickly became full of shops geared to women's wishes, such as milliners, mantua-makers, dressmakers and, particularly, peruke-makers.

The upper storeys on both sides harboured a mixed multitude of attendants and servants and by 1700 were *the* place for lodgings for foreign visitors as well as a large number of light ladies and mistresses. Dean Swift lodged hereabouts in 1710.

A small section on the south side at the Charing Cross end was left open for an ingress to the Royal Gardens, known as Stonecutters' Alley. Fronting this was a splendid mansion built by the fervent Royalist Sir Philip Warwick, who stood close by the King during the battle of Edgehill. Punished for this 'disloyalty' by the Commonwealth by a fine of £447, at the Restoration in 1660 he was rewarded with a knighthood.

Warwick House was to have a long association with the royal family, although in 1800 the Prince Regent asked for Stonecutters' Yard to be closed because 'it was noisy and of ill-repute', only to be refused because it was an ancient public right of way.

From the very beginning Pall Mall was a busy fashionable, popular thoroughfare, thronged night and day by men and women

View of Pall Mall and St James's Palace in 1753. Marlborough House can be seen with the Lutheran Chapel just behind. There is a sedan-chair rank in front of the Palace

of the highest and the lowest status. It was always brightly lit, not only from the compulsory lamp over each front door but also from the glitter of innumerable candles inside the windows. However, the bright lights hid the mass of poverty and human misery in the many dark and noisome alleys leading off the thoroughfare, as highlighted by John Gay's famous panegyric:

> O! bear with me the Paths of fair *Pell-Mell*
> Safe, on the pavements, grateful for thy smell. . . .
> At distance rolls along the gilded Coach,
> Nor sturdy Car-men on thy Walks encroach:
> No *Lets* would bar thy ways, were Chairs deny'd –
> The soft Support of Laziness and Pride.
> Shops breathe Perfume, thro' Sashes, Ribbons glow –
> The mutual Arms of Ladies and the *Beau*.
>
> Yet e'en here, when Rains the passage hide,
> Oft, the loose stone spirts-up a muddy Tide:
> Beneath thy careless Foot: and from on high
> where Masons mount the Ladder, Fragments fly. . . .

Colman-hedge Lane – mentioned as early as 1505 by Wynkyn de Worde in *Cock Lorells Bote* – supplied the multitude of poor prostitutes who lived in a poverty unbelievable today. Pall Mall harboured pickpockets and con-men, ruffians and drunks bent on assault and mayhem, even murder – although the earliest public killing was due to quite other circumstances.

On Sunday morning 12 February 1682 the peace and quiet of Pall Mall were shattered by the sound of five gunshots, marking the last stage of a vendetta which had ended with the death of a dissolute rake and adventurer, Thomas Thynne, Squire of Longleat.

Elizabeth Percy, daughter of the eleventh Earl of Northumberland and his lovely wife, Elizabeth Wriothesley, daughter of the Earl of Southampton, was three years old when her father died in 1670. Her mother, then only twenty, went to Paris and married there, leaving the child in the care of the grandmother, the immensely rich and powerful Dowager Countess of Northumberland. At twelve Elizabeth was immensely rich, with a dowry of £10,000, and thus a natural target for every adventurer, so the grandmother arranged for her to marry the thirteen-year-old Lord Ogle, heir to the Duke of Newcastle. Unfortunately, within a few months little Lord Ogle died and the little widow was once again a great prize.

The old Dowager chose, from amongst a number of suitors, Thomas Thynne MP, a well-known, well-born character-about-town, but she did not know that Thynne had paid a commission for the introduction to her to a shady financer, Richard Breet, 'for the sale of Lady Ogle'; nor did she know that he had already been involved in the seduction of another young lady 'under promise of marriage'. The little girl was terrified of this much older man but the marriage took place in 1681, 'when suddenly she disappeared from her grandmother's home . . . to avoid Mr Thynne to whom she had been married in the summer . . . but the marriage was not consummated'. Thynne, having received the money, was nicknamed 'Tom of Ten Thousand'.

A complication was that Elizabeth preferred the dashingly handsome young Swedish adventurer Count Philip Christopher von Königsmarck, who had squandered a great fortune in gambling and wenching and high-living. A rich marriage would solve his problems. Grandmother Northumberland, however, spiked his guns by getting the marriage annulled by the King's Bench and marrying off her grand-daughter in May 1682 to the nineteen-year-old Charles Seymour, sixth Duke of Somerset – of such overweening arrogance that he was dubbed 'the Proud Duke'. The union lasted forty years and produced thirteen children.

In the course of his wooing Königsmarck had fallen foul of Thynne, who sent a posse of six men to Paris to murder him, but they failed. In revenge, the Count, with his aide Colonel Vratz and three retainers, waylaid Thynne on that fateful Sunday morning at the junction of Pall Mall and St Albans Street, killing him with five shots from a blunderbuss. The assailants were apprehended and charged with murder, but by some judicious bribery Königsmarck and Vratz were acquitted and the three retainers were hanged.

Nemesis overtook the Count in due course. He became the lover of Sophia Dorothea, wife of Prince Georg Ludwig of Hanover but, being surprised more or less *in flagrante delicto*, had to flee, and his *inamorata* was immured in Ahlden Castle for the rest of her life by her vengeful husband, who was later to become Britain's King George I. Königsmarck was found dead in Stade, in Germany, in 1694, almost certainly assassinated on the orders of Georg Ludwig.

At the point where Thynne was murdered, on 7 January 1668, the mail-coach from France was held up and robbed 'almost under the eyes of the Palace Guard'.

(Opposite) *The Murder of Thomas Thynne Esq. in Pall Mall, 1668, at the corner with St Albans Street by Count Königsmarck and his friends Colonel Christopher Vratz, Captain John Stern and Karl Georg Borovsky. Stern and Borovsky were hanged. Königsmarck was hacked to death in 1694*

The Thynne family, as Viscounts of Weymouth and Marquesses of Bath, were to have a long association with Pall Mall. A wit was to observe, 'Although Thynne by name they were not thin on the ground!', and most of them were to carry on the tradition of gambling and wenching.

By 1720 John Strype could write of Pall Mall: 'It is a long fine street with Houses on the south side having a pleasant Prospect into the King's garden . . . greatly disfigured by several meane houses of the lowest Mechanicks interspersed. . . .'

Amongst these 'meane houses' were the inns and taverns and coffee-houses. Apart from the Old Bell, there were now Ye Croune in Pell Mell (from *c.* 1660 to 1690), Ye Goatte atte ye foote of ye Hay-market (from 1666 to 1672) and the King's Head Tavern, next to the gate of Marlborough House, established in 1686 by Will Threeves and even then 'of ill-repute'.

Of coffee- and chocolate-houses there was a plethora. The earliest was Wood's; then came Gaunt's (1686–1702), the Cocoa-Tree and the Smyrna (both from *c.* 1680) and Ozinda's. Soon afterwards there were the Hanover (on the corner with the Haymarket) established in 1701, the Pall Mall (1702–14), Power's (1702–14) and Giles' (1702–44). In East Pall Mall, 'over against the King's Mews', was The British, and in the Spring Gardens the Old Man. On the corner with St Alban's Street there was the Carv'd Balcony Tavern, originally built in 1666 as a private residence for Sir Thomas Clifford, but by 1686 a wine-house run by the licensed vintner Thomas Rugeley. On the other corner was the equally old St Alban's Tavern and Coffee-House. Later in the century there was also to be the famed Star & Garter.

John Macky, on his 1724 visit to London, called Pall Mall 'his Winter Quarters' – he spent his summers in the City: 'I am lodg'd in the Streete call'd Pall Mall, the ordinary Residence of all Strangers because of its vicinity to the King's Palace, the Park, the Parliament House, the Theatres and the Chocolate and Coffee-houses where the best Company frequents. . . .'

For the next hundred years or so, distinguished and not-so-distinguished visitors found lodgings there, but of the inhabitants of Pall Mall, such as shopkeepers and artisans in the earliest period, very little is known, except in the case of such celebrities as Nell Gwyn, Peg Hughes and other royal favourites.

(Opposite) *The Carv'd Balcony Tavern on the corner of St Alban's Street and Pall Mall, erected in 1666 and originally occupied by Thomas Rugeley, a Wine Merchant*

The earliest Rates Books show that the south side was crammed with minor aristocrats and many knights created by King Charles after 1660. Included in this tally appears the name of Solomon de Medina, 'a Jew', living in the eleventh house from Stonecutters' Yard. A Portuguese *Marrano*, fleeing to Holland from the Inquisition, he became an army contractor to William of Orange and gave him great assistance when he was called to take the throne. Medina reverted to his ancient faith and became a highly respected and very important member of the Jewish community, then based at the synagogue in Bevis Marks. He was dubbed a knight by William at Hampton Court Palace in June 1700, being excused the formal oath – he was, in fact, the first Jewish knight. He lived in Pall Mall from 1686 till 1700.

Curiously enough, somewhat further westward and contemporaneously there was another distinguished Jew, Moses David de Chaves, of an ancient family of Italian rabbinical scholars – David de Chaves, as he was known in England, was a poet of distinction. The only other Jewish ratepayer was Isaac Norsa of the Cocoa-Tree. By 1725 young Jewish *beaux* were to frequent Pall Mall in search of love and adventure together with their gentile friends, distinguished only by the fact that they did not wear their swords on their Sabbath.

Best known of the earliest residents is Nell Gwyn, King Charles's 'Protestant Whore', who from about 1671 was lodged on the north side, but she went to the Secretary of State, Sir Joseph Williamson, who told the King that, 'Madam Gwinn complains that she has no House yett.' She was quickly moved to a more commodious residence on the south side, but when she discovered that it was only under a Crown lease she returned the Conveyance, saying that, '. . . she had always Conveyed Free under the Crown and always would, but would not accept it [the house] till it was Conveyed to her by Act of Parliament.'

Whatever the truth of this anecdote, on 1 December 1676 Charles conveyed the freehold to his valet and factotum, Will Chiffinch, and Martin ffoulkes, a trustee of the Earl of St Albans, who in turn on 6 April 1677 conveyed (with Sir Walter Clarges as her trustee) the freehold to Nelly 'for her life . . . and thereafter upon her younger son James Lord Beauclerk . . . with Remainder to her eldest son, Charles, Earl of Burford . . .' (later Duke of St Albans). In compensation Henry Jermyn was granted the freehold of 3½ acres of land 'on the west side of Colman Hedge Lane'.

James Beauclerk died in 1680 and Nelly in 1687, so that Burford inherited the house, leaving in 1694 when he had to assign the leasehold to his creditors – the house remains the only independent freehold in Pall Mall to this day.

From 1699 to 1716 the house was occupied by Robert, first Earl Ferrers of Oakham in Rutlandshire – a title going back to pre-Norman times, when the Barons de Ferrer '. . . held the tenure of Oakham . . . by taking off a Shoe from every nobleman's horse that passes with his Lord through the street unless redeemed with a piece of Money . . .'. The last such payment was made as late as 1788 by Prince Frederick Augustus, Duke of York, second son of George III, who tendered a silver shilling.

Another bright star to illuminate Pall Mall was Nelly's neighbour Margaret ('Peg') Hughes, who first appeared in 1666 in the King's Company of Comoedians under Tom Killigrew's management. She came from a family of actors. Apart from her charm and 'flashing black Eyes', she had very lovely legs, which showed to great advantage at this period, when women in breeches enjoyed a vogue. On 7 May 1668 at the King's Theatre Sam Pepys '. . . did kisse the prettie woman newly-come, call'd Pegg that was Sir Charles Sidley's mistress . . .'. He saw her again the following February playing Desdemona in *Othello*. It was on this occasion that the King's cousin, the brave and dashing Prince Rupert, fell in love with her; by the end of the year she had left the stage to become his mistress.

In 1673 Peg gave birth to a daughter, Ruperta, and she did not return to the stage until March 1676, playing for the Duke's Company regularly until May 1677. She and her daughter were then living 'in a fine house . . . bought for Mrs Hews . . . from Sir Nicholas Crispe for £25,000' by the Prince. He died in November 1682 leaving in his Will £6,000 each to Peg and his daughter. Peg quickly gambled her inheritance away and moved in 1684 'to a small house not far from Mistress Gwynn's'. Indeed, Nelly reproached her '. . . for losing by Gambling what she had acquired by Whoredom'. Luckily, Ruperta had made a good marriage to General Emanuel Scroope Howe and was able to support her mother until 1699, when Peg moved to Lee in Kent, where she died on 1 October 1719, aged about seventy.

On 10 June 1666 the Queen told Lady Castlemaine that she might catch cold 'by staying so late abroad'. Castlemaine replied that the King had not stayed so late with her, '. . . and he must stay somewhere else . . .'. The King overheard this remark, took Castlemaine aside, told her 'she was a bold impertinent woman' and ordered her out of the Court until he sent for her, whereupon, 'She went to a Lodging in Pell Mell, kept there for a few days and then

One of the Tribe of Levi going to Brakefast with a Young Christian, 1778 A scene in a King's Place Nunnery. *The Bawd lounging on the sofa is most probably Charlotte Hayes. The young courtesan has been brought in for the inspection of the elderly Jewish gentleman. The surroundings are very luxurious; the little black servant serves breakfast on a silver tray*

sent to ask the King whether she might send for her things . . . the King sent for her . . . they are all friends again. . . .'

Dryden's beloved mistress Anne Reeves ('who had more beauty than talent') was also a player in the Duke's Company under Killigrew. Her first appearance was in 1670 as 'Esperanza' and later at Lincoln's Inn Fields Theatre in *Marriage à la Mode*, and she played at various places until 1675 when 'she went to become a *Nun* in a foreign country' (meaning a 'nun' in the King's Place sense – see p. 197). The vicious attack upon Dryden in *The Medal of John Bayes* (1682) made many gross references, including the verse:

> His Prostituted MUSE will become for him
> As his mistress *Reeverie* was – upon whom he spent
> So many hundred Pounds – and of whom
> (to show his Constancy in Love)
> He got three *Claps*, and she was a Bawd.

The location of Anne Reeves' lodgings in Pall Mall is not known.

Even more famous was the actress Anne Oldfield, the illegitimate child of a trooper in the Royal Horse Guards, born in lodgings in Pall Mall in 1683. A lively, witty, precocious and lovely girl, she taught herself to read and write. While working for her aunt, Mrs Voss, in the Mitre Tavern in St James's Market, she was 'discovered' by the rather disreputable Captain Farquhar. She was then only fifteen but already known as a beauty with a musical voice. Soon afterwards Colley Cibber put her on the stage at Drury Lane, where she was an immediate success. She was also a success with many gentlemen, including General Charles Churchill, George Bubb-Dodington and Arthur Maynwaring MP, Collector of Customs, who proved her most constant and reliable lover. She was also an intimate of 'that swaggering nobleman but arrant knave in common Dealings' Richard Savage, Earl Rivers. Amongst 'the twenty paltry Whores' to whom he left legacies when he died in 1712 was 'Nance' Oldfield, who received £500. She proved a good friend to his son by Lady Macclesfield, the poet Richard Savage – a bitter, jealous, disappointed and angry man who constantly sponged off the warm-hearted Anne.

The tally of beautiful residents must include the famous but errant Hortense Mancini, Duchess of Mazarin, niece of the famous Cardinal. She came to London in 1676 at the invitation of Charles II and occupied a magnificent suite in the nearby palace. She was ousted in 1685 when James II fled precipitously, losing at a stroke her income of £4,000 a year and all her friends, though she still maintained her immense pride and arrogance. Hortense lived in lodgings in Pall Mall for several years but died in June 1699 in poverty in a Chelsea lodging-house, her death, said Evelyn, 'being hastened by the intemperate drinking of strong spirits'.

The combination of princely and proletarian pulchritude in the public houses quickly ensured Pall Mall's development as a fashionable parade ground, aided by the fact that much of it was paved, making perambulation much easier and more pleasant. There were also *divertissements*, such as the day in 1733 when four women, half-naked, raced down Pall Mall, the prizes being a Holland smock, a cap, a pair of check stockings and a pair of laced shoes.

In September 1634 Sir Sanders Duncombe secured '. . . a fourteen year License . . . for the Sole Privilege of using putting-forth and letting for hire within the Cities of London and Westminster & the Suburbs and Precincts thereof of certain Covered Chairs the Like where of being used in many Parts beyond the Seas for carrying of People in the Streets . . .'. The preamble said that the people 'were pestered and encumbered with the unnecessary multitude of Coaches whereby HM Subjects were exposed to Peril and Danger'. A sedan-chair was a single-seater borne by two men, entered by a front door – later ones were hinged so that the entire front opened to allow for the elaborate clothes and head-dresses of men and women – accompanied by link-boys, carrying torches at night to show the way and discourage footpads. (They were, however, in use in Covent Garden as early as 1632, when Rich opened his theatre.)

There were official sedan stands in Pall Mall outside Will Threeves' King's Head Tavern, White's Chocolate-House and the Cocoa-Tree – as late as 1812 a half-dozen could be found outside White's Club in St James's Street. (The last sedan was seen in Mayfair in 1841.) The chair-men were always in great demand for assignations and messengering, as well as pimping, and played a most colourful part in London's life.

The King's Head Tavern, was opened by one William Threeves about 1683, when it was known as 'Will Threeves's' place. It never had high repute and at times was little more than a brothel, but its location was excellent, being almost outside the gate of Marlborough House and only a few yards away from the entrance to St James's Palace, at the junction of Pall Mall and St James's Street.

In 1700 it was known as Will Threeve's Coffee-House, and four years later it secured a licence as a public house. Between 1716 and 1740 the proprietors were members of the well-known Arnold family, but from 1740 the name of Brackley Kennett appears.

A man of poor and obscure parentage, Kennett had been a waiter at another Pall Mall tavern, the King's Arms, which Horace Walpole named 'a notorious house of ill-fame', and thereafter kept a brothel of his own before taking over the King's Head. By this time he was trading as a wine merchant and becoming very wealthy and involved in the politics of the City of London. He was elected a Common Councilman for the Cornhill Ward and Sheriff in 1765–6. In 1767 he was admitted to the Vintners' Company and became the Master the following year. He finally became Lord Mayor in 1779 and was unlucky enough to be involved in the Gordon Riots, over which 'he displayed a querulous ineptitude' – effectively immortalized in Dickens's *Barnaby Rudge* – for all that he was then Colonel of the Orange Regiment! He was still a Common Councillor for Cornhill Ward in the City when he died in 1782.

Much more informative as to the manners and morals of the inhabitants are the histories of some of the contemporary coffee- and chocolate-houses.

The Cocoa-Tree Chocolate-House

Sometime about 1650 chocolate – as a drink – was introduced into England. By 1657 *The Publick Advertiser* was able to refer to 'an Excellent new West India Drincke call'd Chocolate'. In April 1661 Samuel Pepys reported that he took his 'morning draught in chocolate' to settle his stomach after the drunken upset of the previous day's coronation of King Charles II.

There was a small house on the south side of Pall Mall (the site is now covered by the Royal Automobile Club) which about 1680 was occupied by Sir Thomas Gault and by 1684 Lady Elizabeth d'Arcy, the newly married fourth wife of the aged Conyers d'Arcy. She did not long enjoy either married bliss or aristocratic status for she died in May 1689, the new tenant being Solomon de la Foy – founder of the famous eighteenth-century firm of diamond merchants – who traded 'at the Sign of the Cocoa-Tree in Pell Mell'.

When in 1702 Isaac Nursa became the occupier, the name was changed to 'The Cocoa-Tree Chocolate-House', and the house was to enjoy a long, exciting and often turbulent history. Isaac Nursa was an Italian Jew, a scion of a well-respected rabbinical family who had originated in the Middle Ages in the Umbrian city of Norcia and later become bankers in Milan. Isaac and his elder brother Abraham came to England to escape the vicious Inquisition, and both of them married English-born Jewesses of Spanish ancestry.

Isaac's establishment quickly became 'a place . . . where the *Beau Monde* were wont to assemble in the Mornings to drink their favourite Beverages and exchange the latest News'. Daniel Defoe went there in 1703. There was another side to this *bonhomie*, not then generally stressed, for about this time Roger North, 'Roger the Fiddler', Attorney-General to Queen Mary (of Modena) described as 'an honest Lawyer', remarked that the chocolate-houses were for the benefit of Rooks and Cullies of the Quality, where Gameing is added to all the Rest!'

There are numerous general references: the *Tatler* of 5 September 1709 advertised 'Two Irish DOGGS lost from the Cocoa-tree in Pall Mall' and Joseph Addison in the first issue of *The Spectator* on 1 March 1711 admitted that, 'My face is likewise very well-known at . . . the Cocoa-tree and in the Theatres.'

For Isaac himself there was to be a much closer involvement with the 'Highest Quality'. In this house in January 1714 he married Esther de Chaves, and later that year the union was blessed with a daughter. This lovely and talented child grew up to become the famous singer and actress Hannah Norsa making her *début* at Drury Lane Theatre in 1732 and scoring an immediate success. Four years later, at the Haymarket Theatre, she met Sir Robert Walpole, then First Lord of the Treasury – effectively Prime Minister – and became his mistress. She went to live with him at his country seat at Haughton in Norfolk, being known as 'Mrs Haughton' and nicknamed 'Lady W's Vice-Regent' because it was assumed that, upon the death of the ailing Lady Walpole, Sir Robert would marry her.

The liaison was quite open. Horace Walpole wrote that, 'he had met his brother's concubine and her father . . . an Old Jew, Issachar . . . and was well impressed with his wit humour and manner . . .'. Since Isaac was a highly educated man and only an inn-keeper because it was one of the few occupations open to immigrant Jews, Walpole's remark was rather patronizing. The actual situation was rather sad.

Lady Catherine Walpole died of dropsy after a long illness in August 1737 at the age of fifty-five. Within a few months Sir Robert married his long-time mistress Maria Skerrett, but she died of a fever on 4 June 1738. Moreover, his political career had ended when he stepped down from the prime ministership in February 1742 so that Hannah had every expectation of becoming Lady Walpole – she was behaving haughtily, like an imminent peeress.

It is possible that the £3,000 which she later alleged had been a loan which Walpole had never repaid, was in fact her dowry in expectation of her marriage. However, Sir Robert, who in his last years was very ill of gallstones and was to die in great agony from this disease on 18 March 1745, had not bothered about such legitimation of his relationship. Certainly in 1746 Hannah was in serious financial straits and 'dependent upon the charity of Charles Macklin', the actor-manager, because her stage career had been for so long interrupted. She was to make a triumphant come-back later as a singer, dying forgotten in 1785.

Between 1702 the Cocoa-Tree was often referred to as 'the Great Chocolate House of Queen Anne's reign' when '. . . a *Whigg* will no more go to the *Cocoa-Tree* or *Ozinda's* than a Tory will be seen at the *St James' Coffee-House* . . .'.

In 1717 Isaac Norsa moved to Brydges Street in Covent Garden, running a tavern with his brother Abraham. By 1721 they had taken over the Punch Bowl in Drury Lane where they were still to be found in 1736 when Abraham died. The Cocoa-Tree was taken over by Matthew Field, and the only notable incident in his time was on 4 January 1723 when 'Captain Lloyd.R.N. was seiz'd with an Apoplectick Fitt while drinking a Dish of Chocolate and fell down and died upon the Instant.' Matthew died in 1727, and his widow Martha in 1729, when John Cartier became the incumbent.

Sir Robert Walpole opined that clubs and coffee-houses were centres of traffic where bribery and venality were rampant and men were bought and sold, and indicated that the Cocoa-Tree was one of the hotbeds. It was certainly well enough known to be a fixed point of reference. In January 1727 *The Daily Post* advertised that the dwelling-house of the late Earl of Essex 'neare unto the Cocoa-Tree in Pall Mall' was to be let, and in April there was an advertisement for a gold repeating watch, splendidly enamelled, which with other jewellery 'had been lost at Newmarket . . . WHOEVER brings it to the Cocoa-Tree Chocolate House in Pell-mell . . . shall have TEN GUINEAS reward . . . and No Questions ask'd'.

In June 1735 the *London Daily Post* advertised: 'A LOSS at the ASSEMBLY in the HAYMARKET of a small Gold and Diamond Pendant . . . if taken to Mr Cartier at The Cocoa-Tree will get a Guinea Reward'. This plea being unsuccessful, it was advertised again in the same terms in March the following year.

As a resort of Jacobites, the house was under surveillance by the Hanoverian authorities, and when in 1744 Count Charles de Soleirol took over, their worst fears were confirmed – in the following year, with the Young Pretender's rebellion, it was clear that it was a centre of the Stuart faction. The Soleirol family were wine merchants – James and Andrew de Soleirol had been admitted to the Worshipful Company of Vintners as early as 1722, and Charles (who claimed to be a French Count) was admitted in 1745.

When, in 1757, the Duke of York decided to build a new mansion which would incorporate three houses, Soleirol moved the Cocoa-Tree over to the north side of the street, two doors away from the equally famous Star & Garter Tavern. He converted his new house into a most luxurious premises, this time to be a private club. One of the most bizarre frequenters was the well-known French spy, Florence Hensey, a doctor of medicine with practices in London and Paris, both operating in incredibly open fashion – undoubtedly with the knowledge of both powers. In 1758 Dr Hensey was arrested, found guilty of treason and sentenced to be hanged – only quite inexplicably to be released and pardoned the following year.

The new premises, ready in 1760, were designed, said Soleirol, '. . . for more Aristocratic and less Seditious Persons . . .'. It then became known as the Ministerial Club, politically favourable to the Prime Minister, then John Stewart, Earl of Bute. Edward Gibbon, a member, described it as 'a respectable body . . . which affords every Evening a sight truly English . . . twenty or thirty of the First Men in the Kingdom . . . of Fashion and Fortune, supping at little tables covered with a Napkin . . . upon a bit of cold meat or a Sandwich & drinking a glass of Punch . . . Bribery, High Play and Foul Play . . . were common . . .'.

William Hickey recorded that between 1762 and 1765 Robert Mitford lost a great fortune at the Cocoa-Tree. Heavy gambling was to be the club's hallmark throughout its existence.

Lord Bute's activities thrust the Cocoa-Tree almost daily into the limelight, occasioning hundreds of vicious satirical caricatures. For example, great play is made with 'The Cocoa-Tree Letter' and 'Jack Boot' (one of Lord Bute's nicknames), being a letter allegedly addressed 'To the Gentlemen . . . of the Cocoa-tree . . . being Jacobites, supporters of the Stuarts, Enemies of Freedom . . . [publishing] Stuart Doctrines . . .'. On 3 December 1762 the Government ordered that No. XLV of *The North Briton* should be publicly burned by the common hangman. A huge crowd assembled to prevent this, and Mr Sheriff Harley was injured by a billet of wood thrown through the glass of his coach. The report continued: 'By zeal of the Officers the paper was partly burnt but the crowd rescued the remainder and made a great Bonfire of it at the Temple Bar, burning also a large Jackboot.'

The fact that Lord Bute was a Scotsman and the lover of Augusta,

Dowager Princess of Wales (mother of King George III), compounded all his political failures.

In 1764 Charles Soleirol was succeeded by Thomas Griffiths, with gambling now the main activity. In 1770 Lord Stavordale 'not yet twenty-one' lost £11,000 at Hazard but eventually won it back 'by one hand', and in 1780 an Irish gambler, Mr O'Brien, won £100,000 at one sitting. Another reckless gambler was Charles Howard, eleventh Duke of Norfolk, as great a glutton as a gambler.

In 1787 Griffiths moved the Cocoa-Tree over to No. 64 St James's Street which had been the home of Lady Anne Bateman until 1755; and had served as a casual whorehouse until in 1774 it was taken over by that extraordinary character Ludwig Weltje, an immensely gross and uncouth Westphalian who had started life as a cook in the kitchens of the Duke of Brunswick. In Britain he made his first appearance as an itinerant street musician. He then opened a gingerbread stall, gaining a reputation as a very good pastrycook and as an excellent catering organizer, which brought him to the attention of the Prince of Wales. A good financier and an excellent 'fixer', he eventually became the Prince's Comptroller at Carlton House – his many enemies called him 'Clerk to the Kitchen'. An assiduous toady, his services to the Prince were invaluable. He dealt with all problems 'too vulgar for the Equerries', such as bribing where necessary, placating pressing creditors and outraged husbands, supplying His Highness with nubile, willing ladies and, most important, suborning the Press.

Weltje's arrogance became a byword. When, in May 1778, an Installation Supper of the Knights of the Bath was to be held at the Pantheon, at which the Prince and the Duke of York were to be present, Weltje refused to cater for the projected magnificent banquet, saying that '. . . for the one thousand guineas offered he could supply only sandwiches'. The prince shrugged off all complaints.

The club at No. 64 was run with the connivance of the Prince and his brothers as a most exclusive and extremely expensive gambling house. It had the additional advantage of being two doors away from Betty's Fruit Shop with all its varied facilities. Weltje increased his income by arranging introductions into the royal circle and speculation on the Stock Exchange on 'insider' information. His *tour de force* was gaining control of *The Morning Post* to be the Prince's mouthpiece, which earned him the sobriquet of 'the Curse of Carlton House' and elicited an attack by *The Times*, advising him, '. . . to go back to keeping your Gingerbread stall . . an itinerant German Music-Grinder, raised from earning halfpennies . . . to a

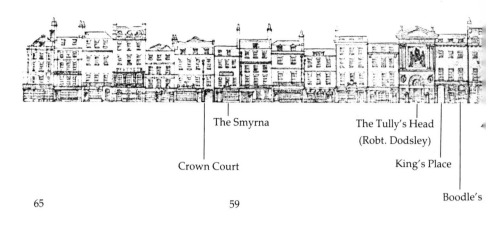

The Smyrna   The Tully's Head
(Robt. Dodsley)

Crown Court   King's Place

Boodle's

65   59

Pall Mall, north side, in the eighteenth century (not to scale)
The locations of the principal establishments in the eighteenth century, when
there were no numbers, but corresponding approximately to today's num-
bers. From St James's Street, the 7th was the Smyrna; the 14th was the
Tully's Head (Robert Dodsley); Almack's occupied three premises, the
westernmost being run by Boodle until he moved in 1770 to St James's
Street; and the Cocoa-Tree was midway between the Star and Garter which
was the 22nd house. The illustrations are based upon Coney's drawings

Great German Toad-eater who has amassed a great Fortune by dubious Practices . . .'. In all the years he lived in Britain he never bothered to learn to speak English.

From 1785 to 1787 the club was known as 'Weltjies' and was managed by his son Christopher, while Louis was conducting arcane financial matters for the Prince in Brighton. By 1810, when he died, he had gambled away his fortune, leaving his widow penniless. The Prince granted her a pension of £90 a year, which she supplemented by running a fruit shop in Pall Mall.

After Griffiths moved to No. 64, the proprietor was James d'Aubigny, from which time it was known as 'the Cocoa-Tree in St James's Street'. The Prince and his cronies, who included 'Old Q', continued to support it with their reckless gambling – indeed, *The Times* in February 1793 mentioned that it was one of the six 'Faro-Banks' in the neighbourhood. In 1803, under d'Aubigny's successor, William Newton, it was called 'The Cocoa-Tree Subscription-house . . . frequented by Members of Parliament and Others . . .'.

In 1810 Newton was succeeded by his head waiter, Robert Holland, who was to raise himself to become Sir Robert Holland Bart., before he died. During his time there was an amusing incident: '. . . when the Waiter, known as Sam, took it upon himself to write a note to the Prince, using the formula "Sam

96

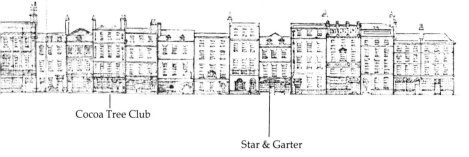

George Street

Cocoa Tree Club

Star & Garter

43

presents his Compliments to H.R.H. etc.,". The next day the Prince said to him "Sam! this may very well do between me and you, but it won't do for the Norfolks or the Arundels!"....' Such grandees would have been outraged by such presumption from a servant.

From 1832 to 1835 the proprietor was John Parton Raggett, after which the club fades from history.

The Smyrna Coffee-House

In 1688, at the time of the Great Revolution, Henry Mordaunt, second Earl of Peterborough, '. . . had a minde to be well with My Lady Sandwich' (Lord Rochester's sister) and, knowing that she was fond of curious objects, he approached '. . . the Woman who kept a great Coffee-house in Pall Mall . . . who had a Miraculous Canary-bird that pip'd twenty Tunes. . . . But shee woulde not part with it!' His lordship, by 'guile, switched the bird' and went off to make Lady Sandwich happy. Somewhat later, being curious about the outcome, he went back and '. . . remarked to the Proprietess that she must be very sorry to have refused his Offer seeing that the Canary did not now sing. "No!" she replied "No! nor ten times, Your Lordship, for that dear little Creature has mop'd and never once open's its pretty Lips since the Day the poor King [James II] went away" . . .'. The landlady was the redoubtable Widow Arnold whose husband Robert had opened this coffee-house in Pall Mall in about 1686, and she was still there in 1699. (The Arnold family later had an interest in Will Threeves's tavern.)

In 1702 it was taken over by Richard Martin, a member of a large family of Smyrniote wine merchants who had settled in England many years previously. By 1686 six of the brothers were Freemen of the City of London Company of Vintners, but Richard was not a

97

Freeman Vintner, nor did he have a publican's licence. He could only sell tea, coffee and chocolate.

From this time the Smyrna Coffee-House was to become well known. The third Earl of Peterborough – the first aristocrat to shock Society by marrying an actress, Anastasia Robinson – wrote in 1703 to his friend Dr John Arbuthnot: 'I would fain save Italy and yett drincke Tay with You at *The Smirna* this Winter.'

Dean Swift and the poet Matthew Prior patronized it regularly. *The Tatler* of 8 October 1709 advised: 'ALL who wanted to be instructed in the noble Sciences of Musick, Poetry and Politicks . . . go to *The Smirna* between eight and ten o'clock at Night . . . where they can instructed *gratis* [so long as] . . . they had a couple of Cups of Bohea and some pinches of Snuff . . . the Cluster of Wise-heads sits every Evening . . . from the left-hand side of the Fire to the door.'

A few months later 'the Seat of Learning' had been moved to a round table in the middle of the room but also near the fire, and while the move satisfied the brains, the porters and sedan-chairmen were unhappy because they were wont to view the proceedings through a pane of glass 'that had remain'd broken all last Summer'.

In the early years of George I the Smyrna was a resort of Jacobites and from time to time a swoop on potential troublemakers was made, but there were also other incidents, such as when in 1718, Catherine Edwards, convicted of petty larceny, '. . . was ordered to be stript naked upwards from her Middle and whipt at a Cart's Tail from and against . . . *The Smyrna* in Pall Mall . . . to the lower end of the Hay Market'.

At this period the Smyrna was situated on the north side of Pall Mall, on the eastern corner of the Pav'd Alley (now Crown Passage), having a frontage of twenty feet. It stood directly opposite Marlborough House. For some, as yet unexplained reason, it was then moved over to the south side adjacent to Schomberg House, next door to the rich Dutch merchant Abraham van den Bempde (whose grand-daughter was to become Marchioness of Annandale and live in the same house till she died), who had his letters addressed to him as 'neere unto the Smirna Coffehouse in Pell-Mell'.

In 1722 Daniel Defoe remarked that in fine weather he would take a turn in the park, 'but if it be Dirty . . . talk Politicks at *The Smyrna*' and two years later John Macky observed that 'a mixture of all Sorts go to the Smyrna'. It was a resort of the literati and intelligentsia.

In 1727 the Smyrna went back to its old home on the north side and now had a very large window facing Pall Mall. In 1742 'Beau' Nash would wait a whole day to get a bow from the Prince or even the Duchess of Marlborough when they passed by, '. . . and then would look round for Admiration and Respect . . .'.

After a series of managers a Thomas Martin, a licensed vintner, appears in 1731. Richard had died on 9 March 1750, aged ninety, 'the Oldest Coffee-man in London'. From 1740 to 1742 the place was known as the Giles & Smyrna – as early as 1699 Marmaduke Giles had his coffee-house further along the street, his widow dying in 1740, but it quickly reverted to the old name of the Smyrna.

The 'French Spy' Dr Hensey was a frequent visitor, 'gathering intelligence and gambling'; Sam Derrick, Boswell's mentor for London's sin-and-sex scene, was to be seen there after 'Beau' Nash died in 1760. When the Rules for Almack's Club were being drawn up in 1762, Almack 'was authorised . . . to order Food without any direction from anybody . . . the Prices were not to exceed those at *The Smyrna*'.

In 1751 the Widow Martin sold the business to Talbot Condon, who had a publican's licence 'for selling alcoholic Liquors', and in 1768 he moved the Smyrna over to his premises in St James's Street, although still paying the rates on the Pall Mall house until he died in 1772. (The Smyrna's further history is described under William's Coffee-House.)

Ozinda's Chocolate-House

When Pall Mall was originally laid out, it stretched on the southern side to a point about a hundred yards short of St James's Palace, so that a short piece of the ancient highway still remained in front of the palace. About 1670 several small 'meane' houses and shops were put up and, despite some protests from such as the Duke of York, remained for many years, being referred to as 'at the foote of St James Street'.

Sometime before 1690, a French immigrant, Domenico Osenda, described as 'a Merchant', opened up a 'Chocolate House'; by 1702 it was listed as Ozenda's Coffee-House. It was a place of refreshment ordinarily used by Tories, and amongst its most fervent supporters were Jonathan Swift, his friend Dr John Arbuthnot and members of their 'Brothers' Club'. The food was regarded as 'Mighty fine', but according to Swift, the dinner '. . . was dress'd in the Queen's kitchen . . . [and] we were never merrier nor better Company and did not part until gone eleven . . .'. Since Queen Anne's kitchen was immediately behind Ozinda's and her *cuisine* was French, cooked by Frenchmen, there was clearly some understanding between the French restaurateur and his fellow-countrymen, at least as far as victualling on certain occasions.

Domenico's place being much patronized by Jacobites, he was suspected of Jacobite sympathies, and suddenly in 1715 he, Sir Richard Vyvyan Bart., and Captain John Forde were arrested by the Guards 'and carried away captive' during an anti-Jacobite raid.

He died in 1722, bequeathing 'the residue of his property' to his brother Honoré. In 1724 the Scottish traveller John Macky, in his *Journey Through England*, observed: '. . . the Parties have their different Places, where however a Stranger is always well receiv'd, but a *Whig* will no more go to *The Cocoa-tree* or *Ozinda's* than a Tory will be seen at the Coffee-house of St James . . .'. but the American tobacco-planter William Byrd remarked that, 'Drinking, betting and reading the newspapers were the main attraction there.'

Honoré Osenda seemingly had no great desire to remain in Britain, for on 28 March 1724 the following advertisement appeared in *The Daily Post*'. 'Mr. OZINDA, keeping the Chocolate-house joining to St James' Gate, being dispos'd to return to France intends to sell by Auction all his household Goods and Pictures . . . and likewise his Shop Goods, consisting of severall sorts of Super-fine Liquors of his own making, as *Egro de Cedro*, Cinamon-water, *Piercico* &c with a quantity of *Hermitage* Wine, which will be lotted-out by Dozens . . . the House is likewise to be Lett.' These disposals seem to have taken some time for early in 1725 *The London Journal* reported the death of a small child '. . . who had fallen into a Vat of boiling Chocolate at Ozinda's . . .'. This probably hastened Honoré's departure, for from 1726 the occupier was George Lodge, who had been a servant to Domenico Osenda. (There may have been a connection between him and the well-known Jermyn Street procuress to the nobility Sarah Lodge.) He continued trading until 1748, when the house was demolished for the completion of Pall Mall's roadway 'in front of the palace'.

The St Albans Tavern and Coffee-House

One of the first streets to be built by Henry Jermyn is that recording his title as Lord St Albans. He built his mansion on the western side of the street – on the site now covered by Norfolk House.

On the opposite corner with Pall Mall there was a hostelry known as 'the St Albon's Tavern in St Albon's Streate'. Its history is closely bound up with the remarkable Carv'd Balcony Tavern next door, which was originally built in 1666 as a private residence for Sir Thomas Clifford. From 1670 to 1685 it was occupied by Sir Hugh Cholmondeley, founder of a dynasty which was still famous in the days of Edward VII.

In 1685 it was taken over by a wine merchant, Henry Rugeley, who called it the Carv'd Balcony Tavern, and seemingly it already included the older St Albans Tavern for under the latter name it was reported in 1692 that 'the Person that keeps this tavern is Butler to the Prince of Denmark' (Princess Anne's husband).

The St Albans was much frequented 'by men and women of St Jeames' Market' as well as cut-purses and prostitutes, but from 1702, when John Manneux took over, it became more respectable, since he was not only a Freeman of the Vintners' Company but also a vestryman in St James's Church. From about 1740 the St Albans Lodge of Freemasons met regularly until 1777, celebrated for political dinners and fashionable gatherings. On 3 May 1749 there was a meeting between '. . . the Prince's Party and the Jacobites . . . which was opened by the Duke of Beaufort . . . one hundred and twelve Lords and Commoners were present to voice their views against the Government . . .' (the Prince was 'Poor Fred').

The proprietor then was Mr Chaeuvel, who is undoubtedly that murky character James Chauvel, son of good 'Old Mother' Chauvel who in 1719 kept a whorehouse in St Martin's Lane. He had been a waiter in the tavern but by dint of saving money and some peculation had secured a vintner's licence. He was well known in O'Kelly's racing circles, although considered a 'blackleg' – a petty racecourse swindler and tipster, but had managed by 1765 to become a successful property speculator in St James's Street and St James's Place, where he died in March 1786. He became a colonel in the Middlesex Militia through his racing contacts.

Whatever Chauvel's social status, the tavern was esteemed by 'Persons of the Fashion'. In September 1771 '. . . a Set of young Men dining there found the Noise of the Coaches unbearable and ordered the street to be littered with Straw . . . as is done for Women that lie-in . . . it cost them fifty shillings each . . .', and William Hickey gave a dinner there in 1781, where '. . . altho' one or two Snarlers found fault . . . all admitted the Wines were exquisite, the Champagne especially . . .'.

In June 1812 the Roxburghe Club was founded there, Lord Spencer being elected President. Under its aegis the remarkable volumes known as *The Roxburghe Ballads* were published. The tavern is last mentioned in 1813, after which it disappeared in Nash's construction of Regent Street and Waterloo Place.

The Orange Tavern

This tavern was originally established as a coffee-house about 1686, on the site of an older hostelry on the corner of Pall Mall and Haymarket and was named 'The Prince and Princess of Orange Heads Coffee-House'. It was quickly shortened to 'The Prince of Orange' and then by the turn of the century to 'The Orange'. It was much patronized by the players from the adjacent theatres as well as by light ladies from Suffolk Street.

One day in April 1737 the famous violinist Michael Festing, then director of the Italian Opera House, was standing in the doorway of the Orange talking to the oboe-player Thomas Vincent when he noticed the destitute orphan children of their colleague, the oboeist John Kytch, who had been found dead a few days earlier in St James's Street by a passer-by. Moved by pity, they went inside and made a 'subscription' for the children. Realizing that there were very many 'decay'd players whose widows and children were in like case', they enlisted the help of the eminent German-born flautist Karl Friedrich Weidemann (later tutor to George III) and by their efforts, in April 1738, was founded the Society of Musicians, '. . . to relieve indigent members of the Profession & assist their distress'd Widows and Orphans'. In 1790 this became the Royal Society of Musicians, and George III directed that Handel's *Messiah* be performed annually for its benefit.

Among the most famous visitors was Count Casanova, who arrived in London in September 1763 and immediately found a suite of rooms in Pall Mall, '. . . fully furnish'd and complete with domestick Staff including a French Cook . . . for twenty Guineas the Week . . . excluding food . . .'. He arranged to be introduced to the social and sexual life of London High Society, using a letter of introduction to Charles Wyndham, Earl of Egremont, who at once recommended him to a nearby bagnio, '. . . where a rich man can sup, bathe and dine and then sleep with a most fashionable Courtezan . . . making a magnificent Debauch which only costs six Guineas . . .'. His mentor advised '. . . that this expense can be reduc'd by one hundred francs', which suggestion Casanova indignantly rejected because '. . . economy in Pleasure is not to my taste'. As he had about £15,000 credit with London bankers, he had no need to be thrifty.

Casanova found a bosom companion in the profligate Henry Herbert, tenth Earl of Pembroke, who knew every haunt of vice and dissipation in London. He recommended the Star Tavern, renowned for the prettiest girls in London. The landlord told him that girls were available for his inspection but each one he rejected must be given a shilling in recompense. Casanova rejected some twenty and complained later to Pembroke, who explained that these 'tavern plyers' were kept in a back room 'like sheep in a fold waiting to be let out', and the least personable were sent in turn, the landlord getting his cut. Pembroke then told him he should have asked on entry 'for a Woman at four, eight or, the very best, at twelve Guineas' and would have been spared his ordeal!

On Pembroke's advice the Count went to the Orange Tavern, recommended as being 'one of the most disreputable Coffee-houses in all London', which recommendation is supported by an advertisement in 1770 in *The General Advertiser* by one 'H.H.Esq.': TALL WELL-FASHION'd handsome young Woman about eighteen, with a fine Bloom on her Countenance, a Cast in one of her Eyes scarcely discernable; a well-turn'd Nose and dark brown uncurl'd Hair flowing about her Neck . . . walk'd past last New Year's Day about three o'clock in the After noon . . . met a young Gentleman wrapp'd up in a blue Roccoco Cloake whom she look'd at very steadfastly. IF SHE will send a Line . . . to be left at the Bar of the *Prince of Orange Coffee-house* intimating where she can be spoke with, she will be inform'd of something Greatly to her Advantage . . . there was a Footman following close behind seem'd to attend her. . . .' Unfortunately there is no record of the result.

In 1793 *The London Pocket Pilot* reported that, '. . . *The Orange Coffee-House* . . . is chiefly us'd by Opera Dancers and *Castratas* . . . it is crowded with Foreigners and *Dancing-masters* . . . there are good Breakfasts, Dinners and Beds . . .'. The latter advantages were repeated in an advertisement in 1803. It became Ransom's Bank shortly afterwards.

The Star & Garter

There were originally two establishments of this name in Pall Mall, opened at about the same time. One was on the south side roughly on the site of the present Royal Automobile Club, the other on the north side. It is difficult at times to disentangle their histories but the one that eventually became famous was that on the north side, which started life about 1680 as a coffee-house run by Samuel Hillson. By 1699 it was being run by James Youill as a coffee-house because he had no liquor licence. Nevertheless, under his skilful administration it quickly became popular with men of letters, and by the time his son Thomas took over in 1707 it could boast such luminaries as Jonathan Swift and Richard Steele. Swift, although praising its 'moderate charges', liked to haggle over the bill, and complained in 1711 that for 'four Dishes and four First and Second Courses, without Wine or Dessert' he had been charged £21.6s.8d.

The premises remained in the Youill family for many years, although the running of the establishment devolved on others, such as Mrs Thorpe, her husband Joseph and their son Edward, who until about 1722 had their own business two doors away. In 1724 Joseph Thorpe was granted a liquor licence and from that time it was known as 'The Star & Garter Tavern'. In 1740 Alexander Fraser, 'a Brandy-seller', was 'mine host', his partner being that John Venables who in September 1750 was to take over the notorious Bedford Arms Tavern in Covent Garden, an event chronicled in *The General Advertiser* of 28 September. From 1743 The Society of Dilettanti met there, and from 1752 'the Nobility and Gentry of The Jockey Club'. In 1751 Fraser sold out to Thomas Dew, a licensed vintner, whose partner James Fynmore, or Finnimore, also a vintner, traded as a wine merchant from a shop on the south side a few doors away from the newly-built Pall Mall Court which was filled with 'People of the Quality'.

The Star & Garter became renowned for its fine meals and for the outstanding quality of its claret, although this fame was to be obscured by the events of January 1765 when an argument developed over dinner where William Chaworth, a former High Sheriff of Nottinghamshire and a considerable landowner, Lord William Byron (the poet's uncle) and several other gentlemen differed about the preservation of the game on their estates. Chaworth was for more severity against poachers and Byron disagreed. Both men became very heated and when they left the room were guided into an empty room to cool down. 'The next heard was the ringing of a Bell and the Waiter found Mr Chaworth mortally wounded: both had drawn their swords but Lord Byron had stabbed him in the abdomen.'

Lord Byron was charged before his peers but was acquitted of manslaughter although the verdict was badly received by Society in general: Byron however 'far from feeling remorse kept the sword hanging in his bedroom until he died!'

Perhaps of greater importance to posterity was the gathering in

1774 'of a Company of Gentlemen interested in Cricket' under the presidency of Sir William Draper, at which 'a Mr Thomas Lord offered his ground in Mary-le-Bone' for the game to be played. (This piece of ground is preserved today in Balcombe Square, hard by Marylebone railway station, although the present site of Lord's is now in St John's Wood.) It was still a popular resort when Thomas Loach was running it in 1779 but by 1815 the site had become a shoe-blacking factory. After the Battle of Waterloo in 1815 it became a museum displaying relics from the battlefield such as helmets, sabres, breastplates and rifles.

The British Coffee-House

For some time before 1699 there existed 'opposite Suffolk Street . . . over against the King's Mews . . . in East Pall Mall' a highly respectable place of refreshment called 'The British'. In 1700 it was managed by 'the Widow Phenick' – Mrs Anne Fenwick, and it was known for its close connection with Scotland. John Macky in 1724 noted that, 'About twelve, the *Beau Monde* assembles in several Coffee-houses . . . [including] *The British*. We are carried to these places in Chairs [sedan-chairs] which are very cheap . . . a Guinea a week or a Shilling the Hour, and your chair man will serve as a porter to run your Errands as do the Gondoliers at Venice . . . the Scots go generally to *The British*.'

The esteemed proprietress, 'the famous Mrs Fenwick, Mistress of The British Coffee-House . . . was buried in the church of St Martin-in-the-Fields on July 4th 1728', but her successors were Scottish ladies of the same redoubtable calibre who maintained the highly respectable character and Scottish ambience.

The British was the venue for meetings of masonic lodges, as well as for auctions of pictures and other *objets d'art*. Tickets for all sorts of functions, including the theatres, could be bought there, demonstrating that its respectability was not endangered by such frivolity. It was also well respected for its *cuisine* – in March 1739 John Perceval, first Earl of Egmont, noted: 'We dined at *The British* in great number' and much enjoyed their repast.

But above all it was a place for expatriate Scots, and it was here that they heard of the disaster of Culloden, which smashed the powers of the Jacobite lairds and led to the Act of 1748 which ended those lairds' 'heredical jurisdictions' and swept away the tribal ethos of 'the kilted warrior with his broadsword' fighting for his patriarchal chief. As G. M. Trevelyan said, 'The Scots were now free men' – although perhaps at the British in 1745 they rightly mourned their countrymen massacred by 'Butcher' Cumberland.

In 1759 the proprietress, Miss Douglas, was the sister of the bishop of that name, and she was followed by Mrs Anderson, 'a Woman of uncommon talents and most agreeable Conversation' and, like her predecessor, 'a Person of excellent Manners and Abilities'. Scottish peers were to be found there in great numbers, so that the Hanoverian authorities kept a close surveillance while Jacobitism was suspected.

The premises were rebuilt in 1770 under the direction of the architect Robert Adam, and afterwards the Scottish ambience was much diminished, though the food remained good. It was particularly esteemed for its 'remarkably fine Breakfasts and Jellies'.

Another famous and welcome visitor was Charles James Fox. In January 1813 *The London Chronicle* reported: '. . . that a number of Noblemen and Gentlemen dined there at *The Fox Club* to commemorate the Principles of that most Enlightened and Liberal Statesman . . . his relation, Lord Holland, was in the Chair . . .'. Not present however, was his widow, the former Elizabeth Armistead, although still very much alive and received in royal society – she could not enter this male preserve, even to see her famous husband's memorial.

It was at the British that on 24 March 1827 Captain J. E. Johnson proposed the establishment of the Junior United Service Club, and on 17 May 1830 Lord Palmerston presided over the gathering which decided to establish the Oxford & Cambridge Club. For some weeks they used a room in the coffee-house for their meetings until they found premises nearby.

There was, of course, no lack of curious and eccentric characters in Pall Mall in the course of its history.

There was George Bubb-Dodington, son of a Weymouth apothecary, Jeremiah Bubb (himself the son of William III's Court Usher), whose brother-in-law was a wealthy West Country landowner and building speculator, John Dodington, who about 1716 came into possession of the magnificent mansion built by Sir John Perceval on a site now covered by Waterloo Place. George was lucky enough to inherit all his uncle John's estates when he died in 1717, willingly assenting to the proviso that he adopt his name. As George Bubb-Dodington he moved into the Pall Mall mansion in 1729, immediately converting it into an even more large and palatial residence. Not everyone was pleased – the surveyor Robert Seymour observed: 'The new house of Mr Dodington, built after the Italian style . . . has . . . the aspect of a Bottle-glass . . . house.'

George, who was educated at Winchester, became a Member of Parliament and was a Lord of the Treasury from 1724 to 1740. He was described as having '. . . some idea of correct public principles . . . accurate and good-natured . . . [but] . . . a most avid and unabashed political Harlot, unsteady, treacherous, vain and without regard for the truth'.

He was the laughing-stock of his contemporaries for his pseudo-grandeur. When he gave 'an audience' to his friends, he would sit in his Court dress 'with his star' – a mixture of ostentation and slovenliness accentuated by his great bulk. He would drop off to sleep and suddenly wake up and fire off witty remarks or read out some highly indelicate matter which would embarrass some of the ladies, although most of them enjoyed it – Lady Hervey thought him 'a delightful companion'.

He was, however, best known as an obese and obsequious toady to the Prince of Wales – 'Poor Fred' – to whom he lent vast sums of money without expectation of or wish for repayment. He wished only to be in the royal circle and eventually to get a peerage, but the Prince died in 1751 while George was suffering from a bad hernia and was away in his Villa La Trappe in Hammersmith. Poor Fred's son, George III, bestowed a barony on him in 1761 as a reward for his kindnesses to his father, and he died, as Lord Melcombe, the following year 'in great agony' from his rupture.

His private life was also extraordinary. He had married in 1725 a rather simple woman, Kathleen Behan, who kept the mansion in Pall Mall, though she was always thought to be his mistress. His real mistress was the beautiful black, haughty and jealous Nico Strawbridge whom he kept in a house in Russell Street, Covent Garden. She died in 1742 without ever knowing that he was married. Kathleen died in 1756 and is buried in St James's Church.

In 1772 Poor Fred's widow, Augusta, Dowager Princess of Wales, demolished the house to include it in her enlargement of Carlton House. George's only memorial is Melcombe Street next to Marylebone railway station.

At the other end of the street, in about 1728, romance was blossoming for the young and very beautiful Dorothy Clement (daughter of the Postmaster at Darlington), who was living as an apprentice to Mr and Mrs Rennie, who had a second-hand clothes shop. Upstairs lived Edward Walpole, son of Sir Robert Walpole, 'young, impetuous, passionate and a viol-player'; he was then twenty-eight, and she about fifteen. He could not marry her because of Sir Robert's opposition but he fathered five children on her, setting her up in a house in nearby Ryder Street. Their three daughters were reckoned to be among the most beautiful creatures in all Britain: Maria became Countess Waldegrave and later the wife of Prince Henry, Duke of Gloucester, brother of George III.

Charlotte married the Earl of Dysart, and Laura Dr Frederick Keppel, who became Dean of Windsor. When he died, Sir Edward Walpole left his house in Pall Mall to Laura and her husband, 'who were the most in need'. Keppel later became Bishop of Exeter, and their son Frederick lived in this same house until 1830.

Next door was a house originally built in 1664 and occupied by Dr Thomas Sydenham, who later moved over the road. By 1670 the house and those on either side had been telescoped into a mansion for the Dowager Duchess of Portland, after whom it was known as Portland House until she died in 1694. It was then bought by Meinhard von Schomberg, third Duke of Schomberg, son of the Marshal Frederick, William of Orange's second-in-command in 1688, who was later killed at the Battle of the Boyne in Ireland. On 3 November 1698 it was reported that, 'Portland House is rebuilt and will be richly furnish'd for duke Schonberg' – new drains had also been installed. Schomberg House remained in the possession of the family until it was rebuilt in 1769, when it was divided into three parts. Each has a separate history. One part was then occupied by another Thomas Thynne, Viscount Weymouth.

Another Dutch immigrant to Pall Mall was the scion of a distinguished Amsterdam family of burgomasters, Abraham van den Bempde (the Rate Collectors had great trouble over this name, 'Bender' and 'Benden' being most commonly used until they got it right), who married an English girl, Mary Spilman. He became very wealthy and their daughter Maria married Lord William O'Brien, son of the Earl of Inchiquin; their son Jan married Temperance Packer, and of their three children only the daughter, Charlotte, born in Pall Mall in 1699, survived as a very wealthy heiress. In November 1718 she married William Johnstone, first Marquis of Annandale. The second Marquess died in 1792, being certified insane, leaving the immense fortune of £400,000. The family had occupied the same house in Pall Mall for more than a century.

In 1734 Pall Mall Court was built. It was then described as '. . . a very neat place with fair new-built houses fit for Gentlemen, the back windows opening onto the Prince's Garden . . . [which] . . . hath a handsome freestone Pavement. At the entrance are Iron Bars with a Door to shut at Nights for the security of the Inhabitants . . .'.

The houses on the south side were, by the middle of the century, being demolished to make room for the larger, luxurious mansions of the greater – and richer – noblemen; the shops on the northern side became increasingly fashionable. In 1749 there were four apothecaries, two wine-merchants, two booksellers and two chandlers all on the north side, with a haberdasher, a sword-cutler and a grocer – and two gentlemen. On the south side were two-cheesemongers and two shoemakers, and one each of vintners, tailors and hatters, a china-man, a toy-shop, a perfumier and Dr Squire Carey, the surgeon. There were only three peruke-makers – most of these were now to be found in Piccadilly. The vintner was Brackley Kennett, and the haberdasher Melchior Wagner, whose family had opened their first hat shop in 1720 and were now Haberdashers to the King; they were still in business in the same premises well into the next century. Wagner's neighbours then were the King's jeweller, Mr Bellard, and John Winckles, His Majesty's jelly-man. Eight gentlemen were listed – these apart, of course, from the noblemen – and included George Dodington (not yet ennobled), Francis Godolphin (later also to be ennobled) and Edward Walpole who got his knighthood in 1753.

One of the two booksellers on the northern side was Robert Dodsley, who had started life as a footman to Charles d'Artiquenave but who had already produced two plays which had been staged at Covent Garden in 1735 and 1737. In 1738 he took over 'the fourteenth house from St James St corner' from Sir William Young (half way between the Star & Garter Tavern and the Smyrna Coffee-House) and set up as a bookseller and publisher. Over the door was the sign 'The Tully's Head'. The literary giants of his day, including Samuel Johnson, and Oliver Goldsmith, were his friends and he published many works of poetry as well as the important *London and Its Environs* in 1761. The other bookseller was Robert Wilson.

Two doors away (towards the market) was Nicholas Sprimont's Chelsea China Shop. In the following year he advertised that, 'The Quality and Gentry may be assured that I am not concerned in any shape whatsoever with the Goods for Sale at the "Chelsea China Warehouse" in St James Street.' At the eastern end could be found from 1726 the surgery of Dr Robert Rigg, whose father, Dr Richard Rigg, had opened up in 1707. Dr Robert was in his day a much sought-after surgeon.

The royal perfumier was John Crook, who had started in 1729 – another John Crook was running the business well into the next century.

One of the very few surviving firms is Justerini & Brooks, the well-known wine-merchants, originated by a young Bolognese, Giacomo Justerini, nephew of a wealthy distiller of Bologna. The business was started at No. 2 Pall Mall, under the colonnade of the Italian Opera House, in which Giacomo's ladylove, the opera singer Margherita Bellino, was appearing. The legend is that the young man had followed her to London; nevertheless, he came with some letters of recommendation, a pocketful of golden ducats and sheets of parchment on which were some 'secret recipes' of brews distilled by his grandmother.

The fair Margherita introduced him to one of the theatre's *habitués* Samuel Johnson (not the famous Doctor), who had started life in Cheshire as a dancing-master and fiddler. By the time he came to London, he was known as a composer, actor, dramatist and theatrical producer. He took a fancy to the Young Italian and introduced him to his nephew, George Johnson. The theatrical *ambiance* was the making of the new venture. The times were propitious; there was plenty of money about for those who wished to sample their special apricot wine and nectarine gin, their *aqua mirabilis* and other strong waters. One untoward occurrence was

The burning of His Majesty's Theatre in the Haymarket in 1789. Justerini's premises round the corner in Pall Mall were saved, but the cellars were flooded

on 1 November 1755, when the shop shuddered, glasses rattled and bottles quivered in their racks – it was the repercussion of the great earthquake which destroyed Lisbon. Another was in July 1789, when the Opera House caught fire. The shops under the colonnade in Pall Mall were saved but much damage occurred from flooding. By 1760 Giacomo had retired, very rich, to the sunshine of his native land, and no more is heard of him or of his beautiful Margherita, but Johnson and his son Augustus continued trading as Johnson & Justerini. In the following year George III granted them their first Royal Warrant. In 1831 Augustus Johnson II disposed of the business to a young man of good connections and fortune, named Alfred Brooks, from which date the firm became known as Justerini & Brooks (hence the famous initials 'J & B Rare' for their own brand of whisky), remaining in Pall Mall until 1954, when they moved to their present address at No. 61 St James's Street.

Next door was Thomas Butler's shop, originally a bookseller's and stationer's but his real interest was in painting animals. In March 1756 he advertised in *The Whitehall Evening Post* that his paintings of 'horses and dogs, fruit, fish and game, was so en-creas'd that' that he was prepared to let off 'to a suitable Gentle-man' the bookselling and stationery part of his business and '. . . one side of the shop, with a Counter and other Conveniences, and there is no better Situation any Person of tolerable acquaintance can't fail to get a genteel Living'.

Amidst all these successful traders there was at least one pro-letarian, Ralph Taylor, 'Bricklayer to the Prince of Wales', with a speciality that 'he cureth smoakey Chimneys'.

The greatest of the Great Houses on Pall Mall was Marlborough House, built in 1709 for Sarah Jennings, who had married John Churchill, Duke of Marlborough. She was at the time the intimate friend of Queen Anne and desired to have a palace next door. Her husband was not enthusiastic about it. In 1733 she wanted to improve access by making a new entrance from Pall Mall and had already erected the gateway when she discovered that in 1725 her arch-enemy, Sir Robert Walpole, had bought the leases of some houses fronting Pall Mall to spite her. She had to buy four old houses at the western end to build the entrance. She died there in 1744.

Then came great changes, the south side being particularly affected by the demolition of many of the old – and by now decrepit – houses and shops. One of the first was Old Schomberg House, which in 1769 was divided into three premises. The eastern part became the shop of Gregg & Lavie, mercers and textile merchants who gave way in 1782 to a well-known firm of lace-men, Robert Dyde & Co, and in 1796 to Hardy & Co, furriers to the King, who stayed till 1857.

The centre section was taken over by John 'Lucky Beau' Astley, a poor boy who had been a fellow pupil with Reynolds at art school and had made a name as a portrait painter and then had the good fortune to marry a rich lady who died soon afterwards, leaving him an estate with an income of £5,000 a year. He turned his shop into an art gallery, building a penthouse with a private staircase, and entertained largely 'in great Style with a splendid Table'.

Undoubtedly the next occupier was more popular and bizarre. This was the notorious 'Doctor' James Graham, son of a poor Edinburgh saddler. A highly intelligent lad, he studied medicine and practised as an oculist in Bristol where he was reputed to have made some wonderful cures. He moved to London about 1775, where he found a friend in Catherine Macaulay, the feminist and 'a great Enthusiast for Liberty'. She scandalized Society by sharing bed and board with the Reverend Thomas Wilson, Rector of St Stephen's Walbrook, in the City of London. She was a friend of Dr Johnson and of the famous politician John Wilkes; she was also a heavy gambler. (She later married Graham's younger brother, William.) Graham opened his 'Temple of Health' at No. 4 Adelphi, advertising his 'remarkable Medical-Electric Machines' and the 'Grand Celestial Bed, with pink Sheets and Mattresses filled only with the Hair of English Stallions'. Most popular, however, was his Chamber dedicated to Apollo, with the very young and very nubile Emma Lyon – later to become Lady Hamilton – posing in the nude as the attendant goddess. When the pace grew too hot, in the spring of 1781, he moved to Schomberg House, where he opened his 'Temple of Health and Hymen', charging £50 a night for the use of the Celestial Bed with high-class copulation 'guaranteed to produce perfect Babies even to the Barren!' Everything was going well, but his error was to allow the illegal game of 'E & O' to be played, and in August 1782 a posse of constables led by Justices Hyde, Wright and Addington raided the premises. Addington, known as 'the Amorous Justice' because of his brazen affaire with the actress Jane Lessingham, was hit on the head with a bludgeon by one of the furious gamblers. Graham got away with a fine and, no whit discomfited, carried on, though now stationing two husky footmen in scarlet Livery with long staves at the door, who 'invited the Patients to enter'.

The principal attraction was the Lecture 'by the Rosy Goddess of

Youth and Health, HEBE VESTINA', who would discourse on Love while standing nude on a pedestal. Not surprisingly, this was Emma. Once more the Law came after Graham, and in August 1783 he fled to Edinburgh and was arrested and confined in the Tolbooth prison, dying eventually in a lunatic asylum in June 1794.

Graham's premises were then occupied by the celebrated portraitist in miniatures Richard Cosway who accumulated a fortune by his paintings as well as a large collection of Old Masters. His beautiful Italian wife, daughter of a Livorno hotel-keeper, Maria Cecilia Louisa Hadfield was a great beauty and a gifted painter, but of a very religious nature. She came to Britain in 1781 to exhibit at the Royal Academy and married Cosway the same year. There were some *frissons*: 'Her manners were so foreign that he kept her secluded until she could speak English', but she was a great success later in high society, becoming friendly with the fashionable leaders Lady Cecilia Johnstone and the Hon. Mrs Damer. When Cosway 'found spiritualism', she left him in 1804 to go into a nunnery in Lyons returning only once to place a monument over Cosway's grave.

After him in 1792 Thomas Goddard established his Polygraphic Society there, and from 1796 to 1804 the noted picture-dealer Michael Bryant was to be found there. In the eastern wing from 1774 until 1788 the famous painter Thomas Gainsborough, 'an agreeable man full of fun and frolick', had his studio. During the nineteenth century the building was part of the War Office. In 1956 it was completely reconstructed behind its original façade – it is the only reminder of Pall Mall's earliest glories.

There was also Cumberland House and Buckingham House, the latter not to be confused with the other Buckingham House further west which later became the Palace. Cumberland House was built about 1710 for Thomas Pitt, Governor of Madras, grandfather of the great Lord Chatham. From 1737 Richard Grenville (Earl Temple from 1752) lived there till he died in 1779, and his son, George Nugent Temple Granville, bought the house next door. It was included in the rebuilding, and the subsequent mansion became known as Buckingham House, when he was created Marquess of

(Overleaf) *E.O.* or *The Fashionable Vowels, 1781*
E and O (Evens and Odds) became the rage in gambling circles, high and low. Like Faro, it was illegal. It was a primitive form of roulette, played on an octagonal table for eight players, originally in the houses of the nobility and gentry but it spread rapidly down to inns and taverns and 'houses of Resort'. The soldier placing his bet is Captain Edward Topham

Buckingham in 1784. The Grenvilles were still there when it was sold to the War Office in 1854. The Royal Automobile Club now occupies the site.

There is a curious story connected with Cumberland House and Lady Henrietta Grosvenor, who in 1769 was having an affaire with Henry Frederick, Duke of Cumberland, in the nearby house of the widow Mary Rede who kept a milliner's shop and let out the upstairs rooms to 'the Best People'. They were spotted by the blackmailing 'Countess Dunhoff' – Camilla Bennet, daughter of the Earl of Tankerville – which resulted in the Prince's being involved in a case of *crim con*, and a great scandal.

All this was at a time when women were still being transported for sexual offences and being burnt at the stake for coining shillings as well as murdering their husbands. On 27 October 1779 Isabella Condon was burnt at the stake, and likewise Margaret Sullivan on 25 June 1788, although both had been the victims of brutal sadists. The last case was on 18 March 1789, though Christine Bowman was strangled before being burnt. Public indignation was so great that from that time death was by hanging, although juries now preferred to press for transportation to the American colonies.

There is a curious incident which involved Lady Grosvenor's sister, Miss Vernon, who was a Maid of Honour at Court in 1771. Her lady's maid, Sarah Wilson, on an errand to the royal apartments, filched a valuable jewel and was sentenced to death, but at Miss Vernon's intervention the punishment was commuted to transportation to Maryland: 'In August 1771 she was expos'd for Sale and bought by a Planter, but decamp'd to Virginia and then to South Carolina. . . . She assum'd the title of Princess Susannah Caroline Matilda – a sister to the Queen – wore the most fashionable clothes and a Medallion of the Queen which was among the jewels which she had stolen. She was invited into the Homes of the Best Gentry – many had the honour to kiss her Hand . . . until a "RUNAWAY SLAVE" advertisement appeared, and she was recognised . . . a Messenger came . . . she was convey'd back to the plantation near Charleston to serve out her time.'

By the 1760s Pall Mall was becoming a place of residence of artists, writers and booksellers, as well as of 'foreign-quality Salesmen' such as Italian perfumiers, French hairdressers and the like. The street itself had been improved from 1761 by the Commissioners of Paving, Cleaning and Lighting, who levied a special rate on householders, although many narrow alleys off the main streets were still unpaved a hundred years later!

By 1760 too there had been some slight improvements in sanitary conditions in the houses, mainly through the use of special closets which contained commodes. Horace Walpole, visiting Lady Almeria Chudleigh, saw '. . . a great mahogony Commode with Holes and Brass Handles . . . it was the loosest Family I ever saw . . .'; and coaches now had chamberpots under the seats 'which were pierc'd so that it was necessary only to move the Cushion'. (The first to have a 'primitive Water Closet' was the Duke of Bedford in 1771.) Ventilation was still poor, and 'the smells of unwash'd Aristocracy tended to persist' – although there were very many servants, most houses were never thoroughly cleaned regularly. There were, of course, no public lavatories – these were not to appear in Westminster before the middle of the nineteenth century – but there were men (called 'flyters') with large, wide cloaks who for a small fee would supply a pail and shield anyone from public gaze while they did their business in some corner.

A small revolution in social behaviour was due in part to a Scotsman named Almack – although some aver that he was a Yorkshireman from Thirsk. His real name was William Macall and he had at one time been a valet to the fifth Duke of Hamilton and had married the Duchess's waiting-maid, Elizabeth Cullen. Almack took over the Thatched House Tavern in 1755 from Benjamin Frere, did well and opened up a 'club' at No. 49 Pall Mall in 1759, amongst his patrons being the Dukes of Hamilton, Portland and Roxburghe, the Earl of Strathmore and Charles James Fox. In September of that year he received a victualler's licence to keep 'a common ale-house' (he already had a licence to keep a coffee-house in Curzon Street as early as 1754). His club differed from the others in that ladies were also admitted to the gambling tables.

Adjacent to his premises was a narrow alley, then known as Bingham's Yard, which in 1764 was transmogrified into a passage containing five spacious new houses, all of which were immediately taken over as high-class brothels. A narrow opening into Pall Mall made it a thoroughfare with King Street, and the famous Golden Lyon Tavern. In 1764 Almack bought four houses in King Street abutting Bingham's Yard (which was now known as George Court) and built a magnificent ballroom as the headquarters of the most highly exclusive and expensive club in London. It had one great innovation: it was run by a committee of ladies of the highest rank, and admission was granted only to those who had been introduced and approved by the committee.

'Almack's' was inaugurated in February 1765 by the Duke of Cumberland, 'while it was still dripping wet' (Walpole), in a great ballroom which could accommodate no fewer than 1,700 persons.

Marvellous fancy-dress balls were organized, and only members of 'the upper ten' were admitted. In February 1765 it was announced that, 'A new Subscription of Ten Guineas has been inaugurated at Almacks for which, in three very elegant, new-built Rooms, one can attend a Ball and Supper a week for twelve weeks.'

This 'Female Almack's' caught on. Fourteen Great Ladies constituted the committee and laid down a set of rules that were draconian in their application – at first even the Duchess of Bedford was blackballed, and though she was later admitted the Countesses of Rochford and Holderness were not. 'Old Q' was also blackballed. It was said that 'three-fourths of the Nobility knock in vain for admission' – in 1814 the great Duke of Wellington was not allowed in because he came late for the supper, which always started punctually at 11 p.m.

Almack acquired great wealth and retired to Hounslow, where he died on 3 January 1781, leaving the Assembly Rooms to his niece, who had married James Willis, then running the Thatched House. Although after 1772 the newly opened Pantheon in Oxford Street proved a stiff competitor, Almack's – by now known as Willis's – successfully survived until about 1850.

On the south side of Pall Mall there were 'stars' of a different magnitude but certainly of no less worth to civilization. Justin Vulliamy came to England from his native Lausanne in 1704 to study the construction of English clocks and watches under Benjamin Gray, who had been appointed Crown Clockmaker as early as 1742. In 1764 Gray moved from St James's Street to No. 68 Pall Mall – Justin having in the meantime married his daughter.

His grandson, Benjamin Lewis Vulliamy, erected public clocks in many famous locations, including Windsor Castle. He was appointed Queen's Clockmaker and was five times Master of the Clockmakers' Livery Company. In 1840 he was asked to design 'a Great Clock for the new Palace at Westminster' (the Houses of Parliament), but though his design was at first accepted, after some very curious manœuvres the work was given to E. J. Dent, Vulliamy's design being described as 'only a village clock of a superior nature'. Nevertheless, it is Vulliamy's design that is now world-famous as Big Ben. The Vulliamy family occupied the same house until 1854, having then been Crown Clockmakers for 112 years.

At the end of the eighteenth century Pall Mall was still 'a stately aristocratic-looking street . . . occupied by private mansions fit for . . . the wealthy and noble', although at the east end it was 'bordered with filthy alleys inhabited by abandoned characters'. Meanwhile Pall Mall was to become the first street in London to be

The Good effects of Carbonic Gas, 1807
*Friedrich Albrecht Winzer, known as Winsor, a German inventor living in
Pall Mall, first introduced gaslight outside his house and later, in 1807, lit
up Pall Mall. The innovation was not popular at first, even the great Sir
Humphry Davy declaring it would not work. Winzer went bankrupt but
his successor, the Gas Light and Coke Company thrived until the end of
World War I, when it was nationalized*

illuminated by gas, through the endeavours of a German immigrant, Friedrich Albert Winzer, born in Brunswick, who had come to Britain in 1803 to demonstrate the new idea of gas-lighting. He had his house and workshop at No. 93 Pall Mall and, despite the opposition of such as Sir Humphry Davy, who thought it could not work, set up four lamps outside his house in April 1807. Then, to demonstrate that it was not a fluke he set up a line of lamp-posts to celebrate the King's birthday on 4 June: 'The Mall continued to be crowded with spectators until near twelve o'clock and they seemed much amused and delighted by this novel exhibition.'

At the end of the year Winzer got permission to erect thirteen lamp-posts along Pall Mall, but he had to get permission each time before they were lit by four men, each of whom was paid a guinea to keep watch on the lights. In 1814 the Gas Light and Coke Company was formed, and thereafter all London was to be lit by gas until a century and a half later electricity was introduced.

Pall Mall still continued to be a centre of social life during the time the Prince Regent lived his riotous life in Carlton House, with his morganatic wife, Mrs Fitzherbert snugly ensconced at No. 111 Pall Mall from 1789 to 1796. Respectability, in the form of the Victorian clubs, such as the Athenaeum, the Naval and Military Clubs, the Travellers and the University Clubs changed the face of the south side, leaving a few shops and offices on the north side. It is no longer a busy bustling residential and shopping street but a most prestigious thoroughfare through which every year the hundreds of thousands of visitors to the royal palaces still pass.

6 St James's Street

St James's Street's development started a few years later than Pall Mall's. In 1585 the fields were described as a quagmire. Much of it was then in 'Mr Pewlteneys estate', granted to an ancestor by Henry VIII. In 1599 Mrs Anne Poulteney had a house 'ten houses up on the west side from Cleveland Row'; Sir William Poulteney was still living there in 1660. In 1603 Mrs Poulteney had a neighbour, Mrs Baldwin, who was paying 21 shillings in rates.

On the eastern corner with Pall Mall, before 1694, was an old inn, the Horse-Shoe Ale House, but soon afterwards it was renamed the Poet's Head, probably in honour of John Dryden who had died in 1700. This house is usually regarded as No. 1 St James's Street.

An early neighbour was Edmund Waller, the poet and composer of the song 'Go, Lovely Rose', who lived in the same house from 1658 until his death in 1687. Another was Sir John Fenwick, one of the 'thirty Knights, Gentlemen and Captains . . . known as *The Conspirators*' who were involved in 1696 in the Jacobite attempt to murder William III. Fenwick lived there from 1682 until 1692; he was executed in January 1697. Nearby, in 1686, were the Earl of Castlehaven and Sir Thomas Poulteney, as well as the well-known portrait painter John Gaspar Baptiste, friend of Charles II, who lived there from 1686 to 1688.

Significantly there were Lady Scroope and a Miss Isabella Pise, both of whom were already renting out to 'tenants' – the euphemism for loose ladies. Far more respectable was the Widow Bourne, who lived at No. 3 on the east side, whose grocery shop was popular with the gentry. In 1704 it passed to the first of the Pickering family until about mid-century it became Berry Brothers & Rudd.

Although by 1662, by command of Charles II, the street had been 'new pav'd . . . the better to keepe the streate cleane', there were by 1671 only nineteen houses on the west side 'looking into St

Sharing the Spoils
In contrast to the poor whores who shared out whatever they could steal or cozen from their cullies, these St James's ladies – purporting to be Lady Buckinghamshire, Mrs Concanen and Mrs Sturt are sharing the spoils from fleecing at their Faro Tables. Their crimes merited perhaps the pillory and a fine: the others could be hanged or transported

James's Park' and only nine on the east side. By about 1690, helped by the up-grading of St James's Palace and the influx of great numbers of courtiers and their servants and suppliers, as well as the spread of the new coffee- and chocolate-houses, the street began to burgeon.

It was still badly lit. Edward Hemming's monopoly, which required that every tenth house had to have an oil lamp, had not yet reached Westminster, and not until 1709 was Michael Cole's 'new-fangled lighting' installed. There were only lamps burning whale oil on cotton wicks suspended outside the entrances of the richer houses and an occasional lamp on a pole. Linkmen's torches helped to avoid pot holes and turds. John Gay in his *Trivia* (1716) warned:

> Tho' thou art tempted by the Linkman's call
> Yet trust him not along the lonely Wall;
> In the mid-way he'll quench the flaming Brand
> And share the Booty with the pilfering Hand!

The inhabitants had to accept the fact that they lived in an age of robbery and violence against their persons and their property. Only a handful of illiterate constables – many drawn from the criminal classes themselves – and only the 'Charlies', the old, unarmed and often corrupt night-watchmen, were available against malefactors. In serious cases the military had to be called in.

> Give to the Man half-a-Crown for a Lanthorn & a Plaister
> And Somewhat for Drinking & then, Good Night, Maister.
> Thus one Cull is acquited, Confederate Whore
> Is dispatch'd with a Charge to Decoy-in some more.

Less than half a mile away, at Knightsbridge, highwaymen were to be found. Indeed, one famous highwayman was living at No. 8 St James's Street, hobnobbing with the very gentry whom he was robbing. This was James MacLeane, 'the Gentleman Highwayman', who lodged there with his companion, Plunkett. Said Walpole: 'Their faces are as well known about St James as any Gentleman who lives in that quarter.' When MacLeane was hanged at Tyburn in August 1750, Lady Caroline ('Polly') Petersham and Elizabeth ('Lucy') Ashe, after visiting him in gaol, 'mourned his hanging' – and they were but two of many of 'the Quality'.

In 1720 Strype described St James's Street as 'a spacious street with many good Houses well-inhabited by the Gentry . . . the upper End is the best . . . on the west side'. He also noted that Cleveland Row now contained several houses and that there was a yard for stabling – the present Stable Yard in the palace grounds, and a pillory in front of the palace 'for malefactors'.

About this time there was a resurgence of rakes' clubs, the principal one being the Duke of Wharton's Hell-fire Club, the residuary legatees of the earlier hooligans known as Nickers, Mohocks, Scourers and Sparks. Each generation indulged in the excessive vices of its time, drinking, gambling, wenching, rioting, blaspheming and duelling. All were young men of 'the Quality', the direct descendants of the insolent, empty-headed ruffians of Jacobean and Stuart times, a little more sophisticated in that they tempered their brutality with an outward show of wit and elegance. As Lord David Cecil put it, 'If they were sporting, they raced and hunted; if artistic they collected marbles and medals; if intellectual they read history and philosophy; if literary composed verse and platitudinous orations – but their spare time was taken up by Balls, Clubs, private Theatricals, cultivated friendships and every variety of platonic and less platonic love.'

In a period when the country was governed by an oligarchy of

Newgates Lamentation or the Ladys Last farewell of Macleane

> *Farewell my Friends Let now your Hearts be Fill'd*
> *my Time is Near & I'll with Calmness Yeild*
> *Fair Ladies Now your Grief I pray forbear*
> *Nor wound me with Each tender Hearted tear*
> *Mourn Not my fate Your friendships Hase been kind*
> *which I in tears Shall Own till Breaths Resign'd*
> *Oh may the Indulgence of such Friendly Love*
> *That's Been Bestow'd On me, Be doubled from Above*

*The 'Fair Ladies' included Lady Harrington, Elizabeth Ashe and many
others of 'The Quality'*

wealth and political talent, by the middle of the century manners were more important than morals. There was little consideration for the ordinary man in the street and even less for the ordinary women: most petty crimes warranted transportation or death – even children suffered such penalties, while the oligarchs wasted their time and money in senseless orgies, gambling and duels. Their public rioting began to give way to gatherings in clubs, wherein physical violence could be sublimated to violent argument, even debate at times, and occasionally illegal duels, even into the middle of the nineteenth century; but mass violence, such

St James's Street in 1800 showing White's Club on the left and Crockford's on the right

as rolling defenceless old women in barrels down the steep slope of St James's Street for the fun of it, was dying out.

Although there were splendid shops along both sides, the great reputation of St James's Street was bound up with its clubs, which over a period changed from coteries in coffee-houses to exclusive gatherings in private premises, from simple backgrounds to the most luxurious settings. The most famous gambling clubs, such as White's, Brooks's, Boodles and Crockford's, brought St James's Street constantly into public notice, but there were many others famous in their day.

The Thatched House Tavern

Even before 1676, when the besotted King Charles II bought the Earl of Berkshire's estate to give to his mistress Barbara, Duchess of Cleveland, there had been an ancient ale-house known as the Thatched House in existence. In 1689 the Duchess leased part of the property to the speculative builder Joseph Rossington to develop, and when he had finished, though the Thatched House still

The Thatched House Tavern, c. 1733

stood, its frontage had been pushed back a few yards from the highway, with a narrow alley, Thatched House Court, running alongside and angled so as to make an entry into the newly created residential enclave known as Park Place.

The earliest known host was Thomas Williams, in 1707, and under his management the Thatched House quickly became a favourite resort of many writers, poets and wits, such as Joseph Addison and Richard Steele. Jonathan Swift, in his *Journal to Stella* on 20 December 1711, wrote: 'I dined, you know, with our Society, and that odious Secretary would make me President next week; so I must entertain them this day Sennight at the *Thatched House Tavern*. . . .' A week later he noted that '. . . at Dinner Brother Bathurst sent out for the wine, the house affording none', indicating that it was still but an ale-house; he moaned that this dinner had cost him 7 guineas.

The Thatched House was the headquarters of the Society of Dilettanti, founded in 1734 as a fraternity for those who had been in Italy and admired the Italian arts – although Horace Walpole said that the real qualification was that of being drunk during the tour: '. . . the two Presidents, Lord Middlesex and Sir Francis Dashwood . . . were seldom sober the whole time they were in Italy . . .'. Nevertheless, the club's splendid publications made known the beauties of Italian art and culture and influenced the design of many fine public and private buildings in London and elsewhere.

One of the rules was that each member must have his portrait painted and present it to the club to be hung on the walls of the ornate room in which their meetings were held. The Resident Painter was George Knapton, but other portraitists were Sir Thomas Lawrence, Sir Joshua Reynolds and Benjamin West. The ceiling was painted to represent the sky and was crossed by interlacing gilt cords from the knots in which three magnificent chandeliers were suspended. Two finely carved marble mantelpieces served as a focal point for the splendid furniture.

From about 1746 the tavern's proprietor was Thomas Wilson, and he was host also to several other clubs, such as the Linnaean Club, the Catch Club and the Literary Society. In 1755 the tavern was taken over by William Almack, who ran it till on 7 September 1759 he secured a licence for 'a Common Ale-house or Victualling House' at No. 49 Pall Mall, from which he made his great leap to fame.

Almack left the running of the Thatched House first to Francis Lawson, then from 1766 to 1768 to Benjamin Frere, both of whom

A dinner of the Thatched House Club

were also responsible for paying the rates, and then James Willis, who was later to marry Almack's niece, became manager. The tavern flourished mightily, and the tally of noble and gentle clients was impressive – although there were occasional grumbles, such as in 1780 when William Hickey thought that the food was 'only tolerable'.

No tavern, however elitist and masculine, could be isolated from female *divertissement*, and the adjacent court provided much of what was required. In Jack Harris's *List of Covent Garden Cyprians* for 1764 there was Miss South in Thatched House Court, St James's, who was 'Young, genteelly educated, a fine Woman full of Fashion and as sound as a Roach, with black piercing Eyes, much Tenderness in Looks, dark Hair and delicate Features, snowy Bosom and elegant Shoulders and sprightly Behaviour – but she will have her Price.' In her case this was a minimum of 5 guineas, although some negotiation was possible with other young ladies elsewhere in the court, and in Park Place.

In 1785 the premises burnt down and James Willis moved over to Almack's famous rooms in King Street, taking the portraits with him. Thenceforward they were to be known as Willis's Rooms.

Willis retained an interest in the Thatched House at least until 1793. In 1791 the Architects' Club was initiated there, the original members including George Dance, James Gandon, Henry Holland and James Wyatt, and the Literary Society, which had moved for a spell over to Parsloe's, returned to the Thatched House in 1799.

About 1795 the opposite corner of the court was to harbour a personage whose product was to become famous and a necessity in every nineteenth-century household. Monsieur Rowland, a French émigré much attached to the Bourbons, had fled to Britain after the outbreak of the French Revolution and had opened his highly fashionable hairdressing salon, charging 5 shillings for a simple haircut! The *haut ton* flocked to him, especially for his famed 'Macassar Oil'. In turn, because his preparation stained the backs of high chairs and sofas, a new industry was created in the manufacture of lace 'anti-macassars': they are in use to this day. Rowland departed from Thatched House Court in 1814 but his fame still marches on.

In June 1815 the Yacht Club – later the Royal Yacht Squadron – was founded within the tavern, which now enjoyed the highest reputation for respectability. In 1843 a part of the premises was demolished and the clubs removed to No. 86 St James's. In the next year a more pretentious edifice was erected – Thatched House Chambers.

St James Coffee-House at No. 88

Just before 1690 a coffee-man named John Gaunt opened a small place on the north side of Pall Mall, about seven doors up from the market, and ten years later he decided to improve his prospects by moving westwards to the corner where St James's Street met Cleveland Row. It was a most strategic position right opposite the palace gates. There were in fact two premises, one with an entrance on Cleveland Row and the other on (what is now) No. 88 St James's Street, linked to each other by a narrow alley at the back. Thus it had two names – the St James Coffee-House and/or John Gaunt's, causing much confusion to subsequent chroniclers.

By 1707 Gaunt was gone and Edward Burnaby became the occupier. He continued as Gaunt's until about 1760, but Gaunt's came into prominence only in 1733, when Francis White's chocolate-house burned down and for three years occupied the premises until his old home had been rebuilt. Then Burnaby took over again and was succeeded by several undistinguished persons until in

Gaunt's Coffee-house in St James's Street

1768 James Fitzpatrick became the lessee and St James Coffee-House once more became a popular rendezvous. In 1784 the vintner Stephen Phillimore turned it into a tavern, and ten years later it had become the St James Hotel and Coffee-House, the hotel entrance being in Cleveland Row and the coffee-shop entrance from No. 88 St James's Street. (Lowndes' Directory for 1799 says that, 'The name St James Coffee-house applied at different times to three different premises which had no connection with each other save proximity.')

Things began to be livelier in 1801, when Phillimore was succeeded by Samuel Miller, who owned Miller's Hotel in Jermyn Street, a house of ill-repute which in 1793 had been Grenier's Hotel. *The Times* for 20 March reported: 'Simonet the Dancer and Grenier, who keeps the Hotel in Jermyn Street were last week ordered to depart the Kingdom. . . .'

Under Miller's direction the St James's establishment flourished: 'It was favoured by Gentlemen of the Army and Navy . . . excellent Dinners dressed and good Beds made up. . . .' Samuel Miller sold out in 1809 to Messrs A. & T. Lewis under whose management the St James obviously deteriorated, for in 1812 Captain Rees Gronow – nicknamed 'No Grow' for his general pessimism – stated that the Guards had become dissatisfied with the accommodations and the company and had founded a club of their own at Watier's.

On 25 January 1813 '. . . an alarming fire broke out about nine o'clock . . . which in a short time utterly consumed the St James' Coffee House as well as the house next door of Mr Percival the Music-seller . . .'. When the hotel was rebuilt in 1815, it incorporated a music-shop, the hotel now being let to the vintner Edward Barr Dudding.

Soon afterwards it was to be known as the St James' Royal Hotel, being 'a well regulated House elegantly appointed in all things fitting for the vicinity of a Royal Palace . . .'.

White's Coffee-House

The most famous, and certainly almost the oldest, of the clubs in St James's was first a coffee-house in St James's Street, opened in 1693 – a year before the establishment of the Bank of England – by an Italian refugee named Francesco Bianco. A Veronese by birth, he had worked in the busy international seaport of Genoa and must have decided that a better future lay in Dutch William's England where Protestants were not discriminated against. Soon after his arrival he changed his name to Francis White and married an Englishwoman.

Coffee-houses were flourishing as far west as the Strand and Charing Cross, but a move to the Piccadilly end of St James's Street, as early as 1693, was something of a gamble. As an Italian, White was familiar with Turkish coffee and knew how to treat its drinkers. Four years later he moved to larger premises on the western side of the street, soon afterwards taking the house next door, to cope with the business. In addition to serving his gentlemen with 'that bitter black drincke for quickening their wits', as well as with beer and spirits, there was another diversion – gambling, which was to prove the most profitable activity of all.

Although in the early days anyone could come in, put down his penny, call for a cup of coffee (or even tea!) for which he would pay an extra twopence, sit down at a table and talk to his neighbour whether he knew him or not, at White's coteries of Whigs began to form and outsiders were frozen out. 'The Men of Fashion and Courtiers' gathered to discuss rules to regulate their social intercourse, forming a club which recruited its members from leaders of fashionable Society. Soon there were so many of them that the proprietor found it necessary to devote the whole house to them and exclude the general public.

Not everybody was impressed. One critical view was: 'At these

Beau Brummel at White's

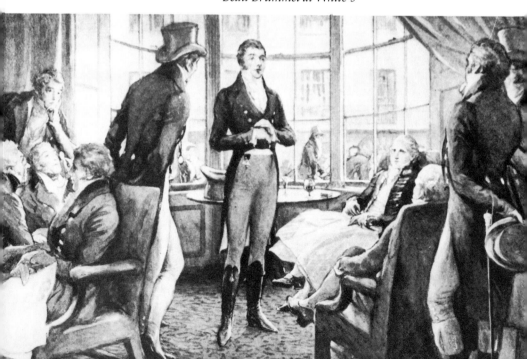

Coffee-houses neare the Court called *White's* and *Williams'* the Conversation turns chiefly upon the Eqipages, Essences, Horse-matches, Toupees, Modes and Mortgages. . . . At all Coffee-houses there is Lying, Cheating, Tricking Widows and Orphans and committing Spoil and Rapine upon the Publick . . . a Surgeon and a Sollicitor are kept in Waiting, the one to dress the wounds of Disputants prone to Duelling or Mayhem . . . the other, in Case of Death to get the Survivor off with a Verdict of Manslaughter. . . .'

The less respectable houses allowed tobacco, and these were said to be 'loathsome, full of Smoake like a Guard-room and as much crowded . . .'.

To cope with the growing business White employed John Arthur, first as a servant and later as manager.

White's was often in the news. One of the earliest reports is in an advertisement in June 1701 a few days after Theophilus Hastings, seventh Earl of Huntingdon, had died in nearby Charles Street: 'LOST . . . one of the late Lord Huntingdon's FUNERAL RINGS. WHOSOEVER brings it to Mr White at his Chocolate House in St James' Street shall have TWO GUINEAS Reward.'

Between April 1709 and December 1710 there are about sixty references to the coffee-house in *The Tatler*, including advertisements for tickets for various entertainments and functions. It was already known as a high-class gambling house with a rather murky reputation. Robert Harley, later Earl of Oxford, '. . . never passed by White's Chocolate House, the common Rendezvous of infamous Sharpers and noble Cullies, without bestowing a Curse upon that famous Academy as the Bane of half the English nobility . . .'.

Francis White died in February 1711 (his Will had been made two years previously, describing him as 'Gent . . . weak and infirm'), and he was buried in St James's Church in Piccadilly. He left a considerable fortune. His four children, Bartholomew, Elizabeth, Francis and Frances each received £600 and were to get an extra £200 each 'if their mother remarried'. He also left £600 to his sister Angela-Maria Casanova, £15 to her husband and £150 to his aunt Nicoletta Tomasi, all of Verona. The rest of the estate was left to his widow Elizabeth, who carried on with the help of John Arthur. Sometime around 1722 Elizabeth White did remarry, her choice being Major George Skreene 'of Chelsea', and when he died, intestate, in 1724, it was reported that, '. . . the Widow White, that keeps White's Chocolate House . . .' was granted Letters of Administration.

A description in *The London Journal* (1727) is revealing: 'At *White's*

*Old White's Club and the King's Head Tavern on the corner of Little Jermyn
Street's chains*

we see nothing but what wears the Mask of Gaiety and Pleasure. Powder and Embroidery are the Ornaments of the Place, not to forget that intolerable Stink of Perfumes which almost poysons the miserable Chair-men that beseige the Door. Conversation is not known here. The enquiries after the News turn cheifly upon what happen'd last Night at the Groom-Porter's. The Business of the Place . . . above all is to solicit a Share in the direction of the Money'd Interests which is establish'd here under the name of a FARO-BANK. . . .' (There was a rank of sedan-chairs outside White's, and the chair-men would crowd the entrance to take elderly gamblers home or to a whorehouse.)

Alexander Pope in one of his *Miscellaneous Poems* (1727) observes:

> Then Lords and Lordlings, 'Squires and Knights
> Wits, Witlings, Priggs and Peers,
> *Garth* at St James and at *White's*
> Beat up for Volunteers.

Another humbler versifier says of a frequenter of White's,

> Cibber! write all thy Verses upon Glasses,
> The only way to save them from our Arses.

The Widow White's connection with the club ended with her death in 1729, but her sons Francis and Bartholomew White successfully petitioned for renewal of the leases, mentioning *inter alia* that the house '. . . is an olde decay'd Messuage . . . erected many yeares since and by reason thereof is growne soe weake and

(Overleaf) *Promis'd Horrors of the French Invasion, 1796*
In October 1796, King George III warned Parliament that the French revolutionaries would invade England and terrible things would happen. Gillray shows William Pitt tied to a pole in St James's Street being flogged by Charles James Fox while hanging from the lamp-post are George Canning and Charles Jenkinson, Lord Hawkesbury (later Earl of Liverpool). Lord Lansdowne is working the guillotine and the severed heads of Thomas Townshend, Lord Sydney, William Windham and Richard Pepper Arden are displayed on a dish on the balcony. Richard Brinsley Sheridan is sneaking into Brooks's Club clutching the swag of the Treasury while French soldiers are storming White's. St James's Palace, in flames, is seen in the background. The revolution had created great unrest amongst the working class and 'Fashionable St James's' had reason to fear that the unrest, already creating riots might lead to an uprising

The picture shows St James's Coffee-House at No. 87 and Gaunt's at No. 88

oute of Repair that without rebuilding it will scarce stande oute the Terme in beinge . . .'. The premises were restored in 1730, and the names of Francis White and later his widow Sarah are listed as ratepayers until 1786, although the White family played no part in the running of the club. From 1731 to 1733 John Arthur was the proprietor, while his son Robert occupied the premises next door.

In April 1733 the houses were destroyed by fire. It was reported that, '. . . the young Mrs Arthur leaped out of a window two flights of stairs upon a feather-bed without much hurt . . . Mr Arthur had the value of £300 in Plate and Cash buried in the Ruins but a fine Collection of Paintings belonging to Sir Andrew Fountain valued at £3000 at the least were entirely destroyed. His Majesty [George II] and the Prince of Wales [Poor Fred] were present above an hour and encouraged the Firemen and others who worked the Engines. His Majesty ordered Twenty Guineas for the Firemen and Five Guineas to the Guard and the Prince ordered the Firemen Ten Guineas. . . .' The royal presence clearly demonstrates the esteem in which the club was held. Unfortunately the premises were insured for only £400. The records and betting books had perished.

On 3 May 1733 Robert Arthur advertised that he was moving to Gaunt's Coffee-house. He was to stay there for three years and when the premises had been rebuilt in 1735 he went back to occupy the middle house, because '. . . the houses on either side were no longer occupied by members of the Arthur or the White families . . .'. However, by the next year all three premises had been telescoped into what was afterwards called 'The Great House'.

Still in 1735 the Reverend Dr Trusler described it as 'a House against which for its continued Iniquity Heaven seems now to direct its severest Vengeance' – a remark attributed to a stroke of lightning which struck during a storm in 1738. Turner wrote:

Some rob at Hounslow
Others rob at *White's*

thus equating the exactions of the highwaymen on Hounslow Heath with the behaviour of the gentry at White's: William White-head, in his satire upon *Manners* (1739), called it 'a Den of Thieves'.

In 1743, in order to regulate entry to his exclusive establishment, Robert Arthur founded 'The Young Club at Arthur's', a sort of probationary stage. No 'foreigner' was admitted, and this covered such as Irishmen, Scotsmen and Jews. The 'Old Club' was even more exclusive, even rejecting 'Old Q' (the Marquess of Queensberry), as 'a foreigner', and his friend George Augustus Selwyn, a rich and famous dilettante, had to wait eight years!

In addition to gambling at cards or dice and 'E & O' and heavy betting on horses there was no hare-brained idea on which the gentlemen would not gamble. On occasion a slight leaning towards culture might be discerned: a good game of chess could be played. In April 1750 Handel conducted his *Messiah* in aid of the Hospital for the Maintenance & Education of Expos'd and Deserted Children in Lambs Conduit Fields (the Foundling Hospital). Tickets were sold at White's for half a guinea each.

Still, Sir Charles Hanbury Williams could contrast it with Moll King's Covent Garden shack where they kept as late hours and as much company as at White's: '. . . but as there is more Politeness and Politicks at the latter so is there more Wit and Humour at the former'.

In 1755 Robert Arthur transferred the management to Robert ('Bob') Mackreth, previously his billiards-marker and latterly the waiter, retiring to his house in St James's Place where he died in June 1761. His estate passed to his daughter Mary, who shortly afterwards married Mackreth. Backed by Mary's money, Mackreth determined on a career in politics, being supported by Selwyn, who had great influence in political circles. In April 1763 Mackreth circularized the membership '. . . that he had quitted Business entirely . . . and let his house . . . to his near relation the *Cherubim*'. (This person's identity has never been uncovered; the term is likely to have been a euphemism for a group of whores.)

In 1770 John Martindale is described as 'Master of the House'; it was under his management that '. . . the club entered upon a period of unrest . . . because he concentrated upon entertaining and refreshing the Nobility and Gentry . . .'. There was other trouble: William Pitt, just after he had been made Prime Minister and returning from a banquet at the Grocers' Company, was savagely attacked '. . . just outside *White's*, his servants much mauled, his carriage destroyed and with great difficulty . . . [he] managed to get into *White's* away from the mob'.

> See the sad Sequel of the Grocers' Treat;
> Behold him darting up St James' Street;
> Pelted and scared, by Brooks' hellish Sprites
> And vainly fluttering round the Door of *White's*.

Martindale complained that the removal of the high players to Brooks' had caused his membership to fall, but a committee set up in 1795 to look into 'certain unlawful happenings' decided to have him watched. He was then deeply in debt. One of his unlawful activities was the conducting of a Faro table. In March 1795 Henry

Martindale (presumably his son) was fined £200 at Marlborough Street; also involved was Lady Elizabeth Luttrell ('who play'd high and cheated much'), the daughter of 'the King of Hell', Lord Carhampon. Another was one of 'Pharaoh's Daughters', Lady Albinia Hobart, Viscountess Buckinghamshire, whose income was derived mainly from 'fleecing young Ensigns at Faro-tables' in aristocratic houses at the parties she held there, and Lady Mary Anne Sturt, wife of the rich brewer Charles Sturt.

Martindale went bankrupt in 1799. In the following year his assignee conveyed the house to Benjamin Martindale (probably his son), although there was a note saying that Mackreth, now MP for Castle Rising and soon to be knighted, '. . . was in possession of the Club's premises'.

That the club's members had interests other than gambling is evidenced by the portrait of Kitty Fisher which hung in the hall of Arthur's Club. She had of course been involved with many of the gentlemen before she died in 1767 and obviously her memory was treasured. The portrait was eventually removed to Pratt's Club, when the membership divided between that rendezvous and the newly formed Carlton Club.

White's still queens it over St James's Street as the most exclusive political and gambling club, quietly ensconced in its elegant Regency mansion and certain types of 'foreigner' – ladies – are still not admitted to membership.

Williams' Coffee-House and the Smyrna

Williams' coffee-house, in 1702 described as 'being near the Courts', stood near the lower corner of St James's Street on the western side, very near the palace gates. The proprietor was Roger Williams, a coffee-man. It was quite a popular resort of the literati of the day. In April 1715 John Gay, writing to the young Thomas Carlyle about Pope and Addison, says that '. . . in the meantime amidst clouds of tobacco at Williams' I write this letter.'

The premises, which were already old and decrepit, forced Williams to make a covenant with the Crown lessee Henry Nelthorpe to rebuild the house at a cost of some £800, and in 1736 Williams managed to get a new lease directly from the Crown. In the intervening years it was frequently mentioned in the Press, for example with the advertisement in *The Daily Journal* of 4 September 1734: 'CHIMNIES infallibly prevented from Smoking by J. DAWSON. . . . If any Chimney that I have undertaken has not proved effectually CURED, upon Notice left at Williams Coffee House in St James' Street . . . I will alter it at my own Expence.'

From 1745 to 1747 the occupier was Francis Williams, probably the original proprietor's son, but in 1749 it was taken over by a well-known local character named James Rowles, coffee-man and vintner, who also occupied the next door premises, No. 87. Nothing noteworthy disturbed the even tenor of his stewardship but things were to change radically in 1770, when Talbot Condon, proprietor of the famous Whig rendezvous the Smyrna in Pall Mall, took over. For Condon it was an upward step because St James's Street was now becoming the centre of fashion and politics, as well as of clubs. Now known as 'The Smyrna in St James Street', it carried on its implacable Whig tradition.

Condon was not long to enjoy his new address for he died at the end of 1772. His place was taken briefly by one of the waiters, James Goosetree, until in 1774 Richard John Atwood, the tenant of the next-door house, No. 85, took over and ran both premises as a coffee-shop and a club. Both houses were destroyed in a fire in 1785 and were rebuilt in the following year – the new premises being known as No. 86, in which, as the Smyrna, it flourished for many years. In 1801 it was advertised as the place '. . . where Gentlemen meet on purpose to play at Billiards'. It had by then become a public house, which between 1809 and 1811 was run by Mrs Elizabeth Law. After 1817 it became the home of the Union Club, until 1820, when the pub closed down and the premises were taken over by G. & J. Carey, the famous map-makers. It was demolished in 1862.

The St James Coffee-House at No. 87

The coffee-house was established at No. 87 in about 1705 by Arthur Goffe, who gave way in the same year to John Elliott, who was the proprietor when in September 1707 Richard Steele wrote therefrom one of his love letters to his second wife, Mary Scurlock, his 'Dear Prue'. It was mentioned in *The Daily Courant* of 6 January 1708, and between then and 1710 there are more than fifty mentions in *The Tatler*.

Very interesting is the announcement in July 1708 by a young Irishman, Michael Cole, of his newly invented and patented *Globular Lamps*: 'There is a new sort of Light call'd a GLOBE LIGHT at St James Coffee-house neare St James Palace which is observ'd to enlighten the Street and all Parts neare it with a True and Steady Light in no way offensive to the Eye. . . .' He could be interviewed to answer all queries relating to it. Unfortunately no details are extant about this wonderful invention, or about Michael Cole, but it was clearly done with reflecting mirrors; it was about 150 years before regular gas lighting was installed.

Jonathan Swift's letters were put 'in the Glass Frame at the Bar' which was the receptacle for all other items in this *poste restante*. The first issue of *The Spectator* stated: 'I appear on Sunday nights at St James Coffee House and sometimes join the Little Committee on Politicks in the Inner-room', but the issue of 28 March 1711 had a warning: 'TO PREVENT all Mistakes that may happen among

Sequel to the Battle of Temple Bar, 1769
In March 1769 a delegation of 130 City merchants marched to hand over a
Loyal Petition *to George III. They were harassed by an anti-Government mob and there was a* fracas *at the Temple Bar, where they were insulted, pelted and maltreated. The dozen or so who eventually arrived 'were so daub'd with Dirt' that they were in peril of their lives, the mob shouting anti-monarchist slogans, preventing them from handing-in their Petition, which was made known to the King 'privately by water from Whitehall' later that evening. Five of the rioters were sent for trial and all were discharged by a Grand Jury, which infuriated the King, since the mob had chanted 'Wilkes and No King!' and 'Wilkes and Liberty!'*

Gentlemen of the other End of the Town who come but once a Week to St James Coffee-house, either by miscalling the Servants or requiring suche Things from them as are not properly within their respective Provinces . . . Kidney, Keeper of the Book-debts of outlying Customers and observer of those who go off without paying, having resigned that Employment is succeeded by John Sowten . . . Samuel Burdock comes as Shoe-cleaner. . . .'

In 1716 Lady Mary Wortley Montague mentions that her *Town Eclogues* had first been 'read over' at this place.

John Elliott died in 1722, much missed by the clients, and his widow Thomasina carried on until 1746 when the licensed victualler James Rowles, 'Coffee Man and Vintner', succeeded her. In 1749 he took over the house next door, No. 86, which he turned into a tavern, carrying on both businesses with great success for many years, very respectably.

In an advertisement in *The Daily Advertiser* in 1761 a lady advertised that she would like to meet a gentleman, with a view to matrimony. She was answered by a gentleman 'who had long despair'd of meeting a temptation to enter the Holy State of Matrimony' but finding her sentiments so close to his own went on to describe his situation: 'I am a Gentleman of exceptionally Good Family, but Losses and Crosses had reduc'd my Fortune to my Wardrobe, a Diamond Ring, a Gold Watch and an Amber-headed Cane . . . my Person is far from disagreeable, my Skin smooth and shining, my Forehead high and polish'd, my Eyes are sharp tho' small, my Nose long and aquiline, my Mouth wide and what Teeth I have, perfectly sound . . . a flaxen full-bottom'd Wig . . . suitable to age between forty and fifty, with good Heart and sweet Disposition. . . .' The lady was to direct her reply to 'S.U at the St James's Coffee-house'. Unfortunately history does not give the outcome, if any.

The lease was renewed by the Crown in 1765, together with the house adjoining to the south and two small timber outhouses. The increase in the rateable value suggests that Rowles had rebuilt the coffee-house. He vacated it in 1767 and handed over to Thomas Staplyton but stayed at No. 86 until 1786.

From 1773 onwards there are many references to notable characters who met and dined there, including David Garrick, Sir Joshua Reynolds, Oliver Goldsmith and Edmund Burke, as well as such lesser lights as William Hickey. The critic Joseph Warton could often be seen '. . . at Breakfast surrounded by Officers of the Guards who listened with the utmost pleasure to his remarks'. Less pleasant was the incident in 1776 when, for no apparent reason, the Baron de Lansing '. . . ran a French officer through the body . . . for laughing at the St James's Coffee-house . . .'. Prime Minister Disraeli's father, Isaac, used to come up from Enfield to read the newspapers there.

The house was still in use as a coffee-house in 1785, the lessee then being James Carr (who was to establish Carr's Coffee-house in King Street in 1787). In 1802 under William Graham it was described as 'in turn, a Public House, an Hotel and Graham's Club' and also as 'the Headquarters of Whist' where Lord Henry Bentinck invented the call for trumps known as 'petering' or 'Blue Peter'. The St James's Coffee-House at No. 87 was closed down in 1806, '. . . its Whig Friends having deserted its doors it passed quietly away, superseded by Brooks's Club . . .'.

Peyrault's Bagnio

Amongst its earliest amenities, St James's Street had a bagnio – a hot bath establishment. In the last quarter of the seventeenth century some members of the aristocracy had popularized this new idea of the ancient Turkish hummums not only as an aid to cleanliness but also as a new type of social amenity. Hot baths were not a new idea: the bishops of Winchester had run eighteen 'stewes' on the Bankside in Southwark from the time of the Norman Conquest until the middle of the sixteenth century, when Henry VIII closed them down because they had long since become licensed brothels. At first confined to men only, with a women's day once a week, bagnios became bi-sexual, favourite places of assignation, and later – when furnished with retiring rooms – turned into brothels.

By 1679 the first one appears at No. 19 (on the east side) St James's Street, when it was described by the Surveyor as 'verie meen and not answerable to ye other howses nowe building in ye same streete'. Very shortly afterwards the owner moved across the road to No. 63, more commodious premises. The proprietor was a Frenchman named Peyrault, whose tariff in 1699 was: 'Five shillings going in, but if to lie all night Ten shillings each person. Here also is to be found a Cold bath, Two shillings and Six Pence per person.'

Originally it was a single house with a frontage of fifty-one feet, and eighteen feet in depth, but very shortly afterwards the premises were extended on both sides by the property-developer Joseph Rossington and designed as a bagnio.

In 1700 the business was being run by one Bartram Aumaillé

(whose name was transformed by the Rate Collector as Peter O'Malley and even Peter de Omela, though there is also a mention of a Widow Potter between 1702 and 1714, who was presumably the woman who attended to the female section.

During his visit in 1710, the young Baron Zacharias von Uffenbach reported that 'he had been received civilly by an old Frenchman' – most probably Aumaillé. Uffenbach described the premises as being smaller than the Royal Bagnio in Newgate Street but much cleaner, and added: 'Some of the rooms are hung with Tapestry . . . the Hot Room and Baths were made of porcelain, with Dutch tiles on the floor: the seats were of Marble . . . the Hot Baths were under the long cold bath, which was graduated in depth and had water constantly flowing in and out . . . in the middle was a hanging Rope by which one can pull oneself and roll in any direction. . . .'

By 1720 the bagnio was being run by Peter Delescot, and after his death in 1734 his widow Benique extended the business by taking the house next door. William Stevens took over in 1745 and gave way to Edward Wilson in 1757. None of these people was of exemplary character. Jack Harris's *List of Cyprians* in 1764 mentions a Miss Corbett, 'a fine delicate creature lately come onto the Market'. She was a tall, genteel young lady, with flashing black eyes with snowy skin and bosom, and was often to be seen in riding-habit because she mixed with the *haut ton*, but '. . . she made no secret of her prostitution', which, she said, '. . . was due to the eternal perfidy of the Keepers of the *bagnio* in St James Street . . .'. (By this time Peyrault's bagnio – or Pierault's or even Pero's, was commonly called 'The Bagnio'.)

On 13 February 1766 James Boswell remarked that it was much patronized by a fashionable clientele. Then a discreet silence falls over the activities of the next years, until about 1780, when Edward Wilson's tenure ceased. In 1800 Francis Fenton opened the house up as an hotel and bagnio, advertising it as 'Fenton's Hotel, late *Pero's*', altering the description in 1803 to 'Medicinal Baths'. He went bankrupt in 1835, leaving the running of the premises to one F. H. Fenton (a wife or son) but managed to compound with his creditors (at which time the hotel was refurbished and extended rearwards) and leased the hotel again in 1838. Nevertheless, in 1850 a disgruntled guest reported: '. . . the room was dark and small and furnished less well than a common boarding house . . . I had to write my letters on my knee or on the window sill, for there was no table. The dirt and the darkness . . . was most repulsive. . . .'

In 1865 F. H. Fenton gave way to Ann Fenton, who carried on till 1881, and a few years later the building was demolished.

Boodle's Club

Edward Boodle first appears on the scene in 1761 when he was managing Almack's Virtue Club at No. 50 Pall Mall. He was then about forty, a 'genial man who liked to have young people around him' and who, according to William Hickey, had already squandered a handsome fortune, being 'reduced to managing a fashionable gameing house'. At this time he was ostensibly a partner of Almack, who was also running the Savoire Faire club from the same address. When Almack established his new assembly rooms in King Street in 1764, he maintained his interest in this club until 1768, when the partnership ended, with Boodle keeping on No. 50, where he did very well.

In 1770 he moved to more commodious premises at No. 28 St James's Street, advertising that, 'A NEW ASSEMBLY . . . is set up at Boodles' called *Lloyds* Coffee-room, Miss Lloyd being the Sole Inventor. . . .' There were twenty-six subscribers, with the promise that 'others will be chosen by ballot' to ensure exclusiveness.

The members met every morning to play cards, chat 'or do whatever they please'. The membership included such political luminaries as Charles James Fox, William Wilberforce and the rich country squire Sir Frank Standish, immortalized by Gillray in *A Standing Dish at Boodles*. The Duchess of Bedford and 'Old Q' had been blackballed. Regarded as a country gentleman's club, its most famous member was Edward Gibbon, who used it as his 'writing room', and gives a valuable *vignette* of a function at the Pantheon in Oxford Street, at which clubs were wont to hold balls and masquerades on special occasions: 'Last night was the Triumph of Boodles: our Masquerade cost two thousand guineas – a sum which might have fertilised a Province vanished in a few hours, but not without leaving behind the Fame of the most splendid and elegant *fete* that perhaps ever was given in a Seat of the Arts and Opulence. . . . I left . . . about five this morning. . . . Two Gentlemen coming from the Masquerade and still dressed in their costumes . . . used a woman very indecently . . . and were so mauled by some spectators that they had difficulty in escaping with their lives. . . .'

Edward Boodle was not long to enjoy his fame: he died in Pall Mall on 8 February 1772 and was buried in the village of Chipping Ongar.

Brooks' Club

In the latter part of the eighteenth century Brooks' was the most famous political club in Britain. It had originally been established by Almack at No. 50 Pall Mall about 1763 and speedily became one of the most recklessly extravagant gambling houses ever known, all the features of White's being found there, the main distinction being that White's was the stronghold of the Tories, Brooks' that of the Whigs. In 1770, says Walpole, young men could lose between £5,000 and £15,000 in an evening's play – the two sons of Lord Holland lost £32,000 in two nights. From 1774 Brooks' name appears.

Edward Gibbon, who was fond of clubs, wrote in June 1776: 'This is the only place which still invites the flower of English youth. The style of living is exceedingly pleasant although somewhat expensive: and notwithstanding the rage of play I have found more entertainment and even rational society here than in any other club to which I belong.'

The *rouleaux* for the minimum stakes were £50, and at any time there might be £10,000 in gold on the table. The number of members was always limited, and one blackball was enough to exclude any unwanted interloper. Charles James Fox was naturally a member, but others were Sir Philip Francis, George Selwyn, John Wilkes, Brinsley Sheridan, the Duke of Queensberry, Topham Beauclerk (grandson of Charles II) and Sir Joshua Reynolds, later the Prince of Wales before he became Prince Regent. Charles James Fox, when Lord of the Admiralty in Lord North's administration, spent so much time gambling there that his clerks had to bring official documents and '. . . with pen in hand and his cards in the other he signed Warrants and Orders'.

In 1778 the club passed into the hands of William Brooks, a wine merchant and moneylender, who moved over to No. 60 St James's Street into a house specially built for his purposes. It opened for play on 1 October 1778. By May 1779 the gambling was so fast and furious that Selwyn complained that, '. . . we are all Beggars at Brooks' . . .', threatening to leave the place because it 'yielded him no profit' and penning the lines:

> Liberal Brooks, whose speculative skill
> Is hasty Credit and a distant Bill;
> Who, nursed in Clubs disdains a vulgar Trade
> Exults in Trust, and blushes to be paid.

147

This indicates that part of Brooks' success lay in lending money to his punters and delaying demands for payment, but considering that he was also a moneylender, this could only add to his profits – although the risks of non-payment were always high, as was the rate of interest.

The gentlemen would bet on anything no matter how bizarre or in bad taste. When in 1778 George III was afflicted by one of his bouts of insanity, there was great jubilation. Some gamblers, when playing a king, would say, 'I play the Lunatick!'

One of the club's greatest benefactors (for he was a consistently heavy loser) was Charles James Fox, who lived just round the corner in a flat at No. 2 Park Place. He borrowed large sums from the Jewish moneylenders who were so often in attendance in the club's ante-room that it was called 'the Jerusalem Chamber'. In 1781 Horace Walpole remarked that when Fox had a run of luck at Faro '. . . it aroused his Creditors . . . but it would not have yielded much of a Sop to each . . .'. He once saw '. . . a Cart and Porters outside Charles' door carrying off his furniture . . .' for unpaid debts, but Fox was quite philosophic about it, knowing that there was always someone who would bail him out. He even borrowed money from the club's waiters and '. . . upon occasion the very Chairmen in St James Street would importune him to pay their trifling charges'.

A less welcome member was the 'rumbustious Irish ruffian, *Fighting Fitzgerald*', Captain George Robert Fitzgerald, who was constantly fighting duels provoked by his murderous temper, although '. . . a great favourite with the well-born Ladies . . .'. (It transpired that he owed his success and survival to a metal cuirass under his shirt!)

On 28 February 1784 William Pitt, then Prime Minister, was attacked by ruffians in St James's Street, 'was pelted and scar'd by Brooks' hellish sprites' and managed to escape into White's. Pitt rarely attended the club since he was not a 'Man about the Town', and he eschewed the company of light ladies – one of his nicknames was 'the Virgin Minister' – but he paid his subscription until he died in 1806.

By this time William Brooks was dead. He died in poverty in 1782. By this time too the Prince of Wales had gone, upset by the blackballing of two of his friends. In revenge he helped Louis Weltje open a club, then called 'The Dover House and later known as Weltje's, which '. . . began to alarm the devotees of Brooks's for it lived well, increased in numbers and was very chary in its choice of members'.

Among the members was the Duke of Cumberland, '. . . who holds a *Pharaoh Bank* and deals standing the whole night', and the Duke of Devonshire, who was told when he sat down to play that there were two rules, 'not to punt more than ten guineas' and 'No Tick!' Otherwise the club was described by Lord Dudley as the 'dullest place in the World, full of Bores . . . an Asylum of Doting Tories and drivelling Quidnuncs'. Lord Byron thought it 'the most tiresome of the London Clubs'.

In 1857 the premises were enlarged by taking in No. 2 Park Place, Fox's old home, where it still stands to this day as one of London's premier political clubs.

The York Coffee-House

The York Coffee House was a comparatively late comer to the St James's scene. It stood at the Piccadilly end of the eastern side of St James's Street at one corner of what was then known as Villiers Court, about three houses down from Piccadilly. The occupier between 1756 and 1780 was Matthew Towne, who had moved there from the lower end of the street nearer the palace, where he had been from 1744.

The earliest mention of the York Coffee House is in *The Morning Post* of 15 February 1776, where a seemingly lesbian advertisement appeared: 'FEMALE COMPANION: A LADY OF Independent FORTUNE and Liberal Sentiments would be glad if in procuring to herself an Agreeable Companion she could at the same time perhaps prevent from Utter-Ruin . . . some unfortunate Fair One. . . .' The person wanted must be affable, know something of music, be genteel with an agreeable voice, not under twenty and not over twenty-five, but not a Kept Mistress or Lady of Pleasure.

Apparently the coffee-house was known as a place for such assignations, for in 1777 similar types of advertisement appear in *The Morning Post* and *The Public Advertiser*. In 1778 a Member of Parliament, '. . . upwards of thirty years of age . . . with an estate of £1600 a year, a single man was desirous of marrying a Lady of Good Temper and some Fortune as near as may be sufficient to pay off the Encumbrance on his Property'. He claimed to have a comfortably furnished country house and a park well stocked with deer.

On 17 December 1779 *The Morning Post* presented a Mr J.R.C., who knew a method which almost certainly guaranteed a substantial sum by 'insuring the numbers in the Lottery'. All replies were to be sent to 'The York'. In 1793 it was said to be used 'by the most respectable Merchants and Inhabitants at the West End of the Town'. It was still appearing in various directories as late as 1833, when it had become 'The York Hotel and Coffee-House' and by no means as respectable as of yore.

Curiously enough, not many of the noble and rich lived in St James's Street itself – they could be found packed together in such side streets as Arlington Street, Park Place and St James's Place or within the shadow of the palace, Cleveland Row and the Stable Yard. Apart from being famed for clubs, by the middle of the century the street was known for its *de luxe* shops, many shopkeepers having been driven out of Pall Mall because of the erection of the great houses. A great deal of rebuilding was also going on in St James's Street, so that the new shop premises were larger and more sophisticated than before, and the range of goods was much wider.

The first real information about the shops and the shopkeepers comes in 1749, when for the first time the businesses were mentioned in the electoral register. Besides the victuallers – the owners of the clubs and taverns – there were three peruquiers, two apothecaries, three grocers and three tailors, two booksellers and coffee-men, a silversmith and a toy-man, three watch-and-clockmakers, several chandlers, a china-man and assorted craftsmen, and eight gents and esquires. For the ladies there was a linen-draper, a milliner, and a pastry-cook's.

The three clockmakers have since become famous, particularly Benjamin Gray, who was on the west side from before 1744 and became King's Clockmaker; his son-in-law Vulliamy became even more famous after they had moved in 1751 to Pall Mall. John Jolyffe the bookseller started about 1740, and Jane Jolyffe was still there in 1793, next door to Robert Arthur, then described as a coffee-man. On the corner with St James's Place was, from 1762, Peter Wirgman, Jeweller and Silversmith to the King, who was still there in 1822. In 1778, when Dr Johnson wanted a pair of silver buckles, he found initial difficulty in finding the shop, and he grumbled, '. . . to direct one only to a corner shop is toying with one'. It would seem that Wirgman also stocked toys – although to Johnson jewellery was just baubles or 'toys'. Johnson wanted a small pair, not the fashionable large ones, and there was some haggling over the price, since in the end he remarked, '. . . and I will give you no more than a Guinea for the pair!' Wirgman became an eccentric, giving his money to various peculiar organizations before he died.

The best-known inhabitant on the west side was undoubtedly

Elizabeth Neale. Betty's Fruit Shop was a household name, and as 'the Queen of Apple-Women' her activities masked the real nature of her establishment.

She was born in St James's Street in 1730, her father being one Edward Neale. She boasted that she had slept away only twice (when she went on holiday to the country and again when she was at Windsor Castle for an Installation of the Knights of the Garter). By about 1758 she was installed at No. 62, '. . . dispensing her Opinions on Persons and Politicks as she served her Pears and her Pine-apples . . .'. She could also discourse on fashion and was a mine of information about the family histories of her aristocratic customers. She had a pleasing manner and a spontaneous *bonhomie* with a fund of good stories and much gossip, which enabled her to become very friendly with many of the *haut ton*. She was also a very good businesswoman. Her shop became the rendezvous '. . . of Wits and Politicians, of the Nobility and the Gentry and of Ladies of the Quality . . .'.

There was a more sinister side to her career. In 1760 she leased the house next door 'for tenants' and a little later another in Park Place for the same purpose; between 1776 and 1793 she leased numbers 29 and 30 St James's Street, also 'for tenants'. This occasioned Edward Thompson's reference in *The Court of Cupid* that, 'Mrs Neale's is a *Stewes*.' The chapbook entitled *The Fruit Shop* (1766) says that, in addition, her real fruit shop was for assignations to the nearby brothels, explaining that a 'fruit shop' was a collo-quialism for a whorehouse – women being described in terms of fruit. It also alleged that it catered for homosexuals.

> GO WHERE we will, at ev'ry Time and Place
> *SODOM* confronts and stares us in the Face.
> They ply in Publick at our very Doors
> And take the Bread from much more honest Whores.
>
> Those who are mean, High Paramours secure
> And the rich Guilty screems the guilty Poor . . .
> For Pleasure we must have a *Ganymede*,
> A fine, fresh *Hylas* – a delicious Boy
> To serve our Purpose of a beastly Joy. . . .

Thompson echoes this in *The Meretriciad* (1770):

> You may daily deal
> For Fruit or Ladies with good Mrs Neale;
> The sweetest *Belle* here meets her stinking *Spark*
> After a Morning's stroll about the Park. . . .

Betty gave up the fruit shop about 1783, retiring to her house in Park Place where she died, a very rich woman, on 30 August 1797. Her memorial is the present Neale House at No. 62 St James's Street.

At the corner of Blue Bell Yard in 1768 James Kelsey opened a pastrycook's and coffee-shop – a café in today's terms, but by 1793 he had moved over to No. 7 St James's Street, where his son Frank catered mainly for the officers of the Guards (stationed across the road at the palace), who would pop in for a quick snack when on duty, leaving one of their number at the door to give warning of the approach of any superior.

Miss Fawkland's Temples of Love

Undoubtedly the most *recherché* establishment in St James's devoted to the sexual peccadilloes of the high and mighty in the latter half of the eighteenth century was the elegant brothel run by Jane Frankland.

She came from a well-known family, established since about 1727 in nearby St James's Place. Jane was one of the numerous progeny of Lady Elizabeth Frankland who had resided since about 1762 in St James's Street as a neighbour of Betty Neale, but was back in St James's Place soon afterwards, dying in her house there in 1791.

Quite why Jane operated under the name of Fawkland is unclear, but she was at one time mistress to Lucius Frederick Carey, eighth Viscount Falkland (a gallant soldier who was killed in action at Tobago in 1780), who 'paid off his mistress when he married' in 1760, giving her 'a very considerable sum'. As 'Miss Fawkland' she founded her Academy of Love and by about 1766 was occupying three houses on the west side.

The house on the left was the Temple of Aurora, because it was to be the dawn of a new life for a dozen children between twelve and sixteen. In the middle house was the Temple of Flora to which they graduated later, and the right-hand house was the Temple of Mysteries for, so to speak, post-graduates.

For the Aurora the little virgins were '. . . handpicked from those brought to the establishment by their Parents . . . many from homes of a superior quality'. While many a hard-pressed middle-class family might sell a daughter in the hope of her becoming a high-class courtesan, earning much money and mixing with the *haut ton*, there can be little doubt that most of these children were taken from orphanages or sold by destitute parents or even from 'wholesale dealers' around St Giles.

There were two 'governesses' who taught them to read and write, to be clean in body, neat and tidy in habits – in short to behave like little ladies. They were well fed, well clothed and given regular medical checks by a resident doctor. They were also enjoined to visit the library to look at books which were 'designed to arouse their sexual consciousness'. They were taken every day for walks in St James's Park to get fresh air and exercise, the two duennas ensuring that they behaved correctly and were not molested or importuned.

At this stage in their careers, Miss Fawkland averred, '. . . no clients were allowed to have any contact with these little virgins' – although this may be taken with a pinch of salt considering that virgins were what this exacting clientele usually demanded, but it was good publicity.

When they reached sixteen they were transferred to the Temple of Flora where they began their new careers in earnest. If they showed real flair and skill, they would be transferred after a while to the Temple of Mysteries. It would seem that some manoeuvring was possible, for '. . . there were never more than a dozen *nymphs* in that house' of whom 'six came up from *Aurora*'. By this time, however, none of them would still have been virgins, however elastically that term was then construed.

The subscription fee for the limited number of personages was prohibitively high. Clients numbered two royal dukes and a group of earls headed by James Hamilton, eighth Earl Aberdeen, and the goat-like lecher John Campbell, fourth Earl of Loudoun, joined later by Henry Thomas Carey who had become Viscount Falkland in 1785. He was a lieutenant in the 43rd Regiment of Foot and a real chip off the old block. He claimed to be a Whig but this earned from another Whig nobleman the caustic comment that '. . . to be a *Bully* in a brothel, a *Hector* of a tavern, or a *Keeper* of a Faro-table is the highest point to which . . . this Noble Peer soars; Noise and Ribaldry . . . supply the place of Wit, obscene songs are the only Tribute he can offer to the Whig Party.' Fortunately for all concerned, he died, dead drunk, in the White Lion Inn in Bath in May 1796, at the age of thirty-one.

There was no lack of 'fresh goods': the onset of the Industrial Revolution brought thousands of young women into London. There was not yet enough industry to employ them, so that they were thrust into abject poverty. Indigent parents were forced to abandon their children or sell them to procuresses. Little boys were

bought to be catamites for rich homosexuals. In 1739 Captain
Coram had founded his Foundling Hospital in Bloomsbury '. . . to
rescue those Infants misbegot of Respectable Girls . . .' and within
a few weeks it had been overwhelmed. In the next four years, of
more than 15,000 admitted, no fewer than 10,000 died from tuberculosis, whooping-cough and diarrhoea, although the 'nurses' got
a bonus of 10 shillings for every child who survived.

In 1754 the Government ordered that female foundlings should
be taught to read but not to write: they were destined to go into
domestic service or be sent out as 'apprentices' when they were
nine. This was a godsend to procuresses who operated as 'milliners' and 'mantua-makers'. It was not unusual for the ill-paid
'nurses' – themselves untrained and really only child-minders – to
sell the children to bawds.

In fact Miss Fawkland protested that her girls were 'no worse
off than domestic servants and could always earn much more'.
Prostitution was the only profession, then as now, in which an
untrained young virgin could bring maximum payment. The contemporary scandalsheets contain many instances of 'auctions' of
children and young women described as virgins. Noblemen such
as Lord Bathurst and Lord Baltimore actually bought them to be
installed in their harems – both were subscribers to Miss Fawkland's Academies.

In 1779 she received great publicity in *Nocturnal Revels* and was
stated to be flourishing mightily, but in 1780 the premises are
found occupied by one Joseph Parsloe. This does not necessarily
imply that she had departed – there were after all three houses, and
she may have still been in business for she is still mentioned in 1786
as being active.

Parsloe's Subscription Room

At the bottom of the street was a well-known chocolate-house
owned, from 1758, by a licensed victualler, Richard Saunders, who
in 1772 was succeeded by Richard John Atwood, who established
yet another club, called Atwood's, one of whose members was the
historian Edward Gibbon, who wrote that 'he had been chose'. In
1774 he took over No. 86, next door, but dying shortly afterwards
his son Bartholomew carried on until 1779, when Joseph Parsloe,
also a licensed vintner, took over. Parsloe established a 'subscription club' to ensure only visitors of a superior nature. Both buildings were then known as 'the Subscription House'.

In 1785 both buildings caught fire and were '. . . entirely consumed before any water could be got to extinguish the flames'; The Thatched House Tavern immediately on the north side was also seriously damaged. Parsloe covenanted to build 'a house of the first rate' and the new building was thereafter known as No. 85. He gave up the lease of No. 86 but remained proprietor of the subscription club, now licensed as Saunders' Coffee-House.

From 1792 the highly respected Literary Club and the Dilettanti Society both held their meetings at Parsloe's, his house being 'fam'd for its excellent dinners and its Chess Club. NB, the only one in England'. (Actually a chess club had existed as early as 1747, meeting at Old Slaughter's Coffee-House in the Strand.) The star attraction was the great chess-player François André Danican de Philidor who, had first been in London in 1747 playing against Lords Elibank, Godolphin and Sunderland. He stayed in Britain until 1751, going back to his native France in 1754.

In 1771 and 1773 Philidor played again in London, and in 1774 British chess enthusiasts founded Parsloe's Chess Club with a distinguished membership limited to one hundred, raising a fund to enable the Master to visit the club for the next twenty years, from February to May each year, to give lessons at a crown a time and, in 1783, his first blindfold display to the London public. In 1795 Parsloe advertised: 'By particular desire Monsieur Philidor, positively for the last time will play on Saturday the 20th of June . . . three games at once against three good players: two of them without seeing either of the boards and the third looking over the Table. . . . Ladies and Gentlemen not being members of the Club may be provided with Tickets . . . at Five shillings each.'

Philidor's opponents were Count Hans Moritz von Brühl, the Saxon Envoy, who lived in St James's, and Thomas Bowdler, whose censorings brought the word 'bowdlerize' into the English language. These two were then reputed to be the best chess-players in London, but Philidor beat them both.

In 1766 Philidor received a pension from Louis XV of France, but this proved a misfortune, for after the Revolution he was considered an *émigré* and could not return to France, although one of his chess-friends was Robespierre! Depressed, hard up and ill of gout, he died in his lodgings in Ryder Street in September 1795 and was buried in St James's Church.

In 1811 the premises changed hands, the new occupier being John Giles, who renamed it the Albion Club at Saunders' Coffee-House, but for several years afterwards it was still known as Parsloe's, 'fam'd for its Chess Club', the last mention being in 1814.

On the other side of the street John Pickering is listed in 1749 as a grocer. He and his brother William were Yorkshiremen who had come in the 1730s and who occupied numbers 2 and 3. By 1744 William also had No. 4. Between numbers 3 and 4 there was a narrow alley known in 1734 as Pickering Court which the brothers developed into an exclusive enclave today known as Pickering Place. (Until a few years ago the Consulate for the State of Texas could be found there.) William died in 1755, and the business passed to the ancestors of the present occupiers, the well-known wine merchants Berry Bros & Rudd.

At No. 6 there was a famous hatter, James Lock. The business was founded by Charles Davis, who had a small shop on the other side of the road in front of the Thatched House Tavern. His daughter Mary married Lock, who opened at No. 6 in December 1764, retiring in 1797. He will always be best known for the invention of the bowler hat – although he also made Lord Nelson's hat for the Battle of Trafalgar and the Duke of Wellington's for the Battle of Waterloo.

At No. 7 was Kelsey's coffee-shop, much patronized by Guardsmen, and No. 8 at one time harboured the notorious highwayman James MacLean – Lord Byron lived there for a while in 1811. At No. 9 might be found the famous shoemakers J. Lobb, established in 1850. No. 10 was the scene of Crockford's one failure – the St James's Bazaar.

At No. 29 is the chemist's shop opened by James Harris in 1790 next door to Boodles. 'Old Q' (the Duke of Queensberry), and doubtless many of his friends, used to patronize the establishment when he needed a sexual stimulant: he always asked for a 'cock-stand'.

By 1765 most of the buildings had been reconstructed, and the street began to assume the character of a fashionable and elegant parade ground, although there were still problems, and some amenities lacking.

The Westminster authorities were still foot-dragging about lighting. (A new ordinance came about only in 1792.) They insisted that only the sewers were their concern, and all the rest, such as clearing the cesspits 'was up to the property-owners'. Street-cleaning was still primitive although the enterprising 'flyters' were still carrying on their useful services to distressed citizens.

From about 1770, thanks to the efforts of men like Fox and Wilkes, who were genuinely concerned with social problems, some measure of care and compassion was creeping into the body politic – although democracy was still fragile, trade unionism still a

Hero's recruiting at Kelsey's or Guard-day at St James's, 1797
James Kelsey opened a fruit and confectionery shop in 1760 on the corner of
St James's Street and Blue Bird Yard. In 1793 his son, Francis, moved over
the road to No. 7 almost facing the palace gate, dispensing cold drinks, jellies
and confectionery to the officers of the Guards and Dragoons. Captain
Thomas Birch of the 16th Light Dragoons is here partaking of a jelly, while a
very young officer sits on the next stool eating sugar plums. Another officer
watches the street scene as a royal carriage passes

Very Slippy Weather
The scene outside Miss Humphrey's shop in St James's Street, over which
Gillray lived. There was a tremendous demand for caricatures of all kinds. It
was from this house that Gillray committed suicide by jumping from a
second-storey window

crime, and although dreadful poverty and crime could be found cheek-by-jowl with the heedless 'Fops' and 'Beaus' now parading up and down. These were now superseded by the 'Macaronis' trying to catch the public eye by fanciful attire. By 1790 these had given way to the 'Dandies', whose presence was marked by meticulous attention to their dress. They were also of a different breed – many were brave and distinguished soldiers, but nevertheless all were described as 'Well-groomed but pompous, parading daily between *Crockford's* and *White's*, up one side and down the other . . .'. One purpose of these parades was to establish one's status as a gentleman and thereby impress tradesmen to grant credit. In those days the appellation 'Gent.' signified someone with a regular income who did not need to work. It frequently hid a confidence-trickster and certainly did not connote a gentleman in today's sense, nor gentlemanly behaviour.

The 'High Impures' could not parade so easily. The street was too muddy or dusty, and too steep for elegant perambulation. The park was better suited to them, but in any case there were convenient lodgements. In 1820 there were whorehouses at numbers 1, 2 and 50 St James's Street!

Crockford's

Crockford's is a real story of rags to riches. It shows that it was the sharp and quick-witted sons of working- and middle-class people who created the gambling palaces of the rich and powerful, making themselves rich in the process.

William Crockford was the son of a small fishmonger in the Strand. He was a fish-salesman and then a stall-holder near Temple Bar, but he studied the habits of betting men, determined to turn their weaknesses to his own benefit. In dingy gambling-hells around Billingsgate he graduated to betting at Newmarket, amassed a considerable sum and set up about 1817 a 'Hazard-bank' in Bolton Row, Piccadilly, with a partner named Taylor.

Crockford's manner towards those who gambled against him '. . . was deferential to the point of servility, his speech that of the East End', but he was shrewd enough to buy the loyalty of his staff by sharing a part of his profits with them: in 1824 he divided £1,000 among the waiters, and the head waiter got £500. He had a faculty of calculating odds while giving the appearance of being stupid.

Crockford's ambition was to cream off the richest takings in town, so in 1827 he commissioned the architect Benjamin Wyatt –

himself a noted gambler – to build a luxury house at No. 50 St James's Street, immediately opposite White's. This occasioned the verse:

> CROCKFORD, voting Bolton Row
> On a sudden, vastly low,
> And that Gentlemen should meet
> Only in St James Street,
> Broke his Quarters up, and here
> Entered on a fresh career.

He secured the services of the great French chef Louis Eustace Ude, a brilliant, hot-tempered genius whom few gourmets would care to argue with. His salary ranged between an unheard-of £1,200 to £2,000 a year, but he proved to be worth every penny – some members enjoyed provoking him into storming into the dining-room to argue with them, thus enhancing his publicity value.

In November the subscription list was opened and two of the first members were the Earls of Chesterfield and Lichfield; later the

Crockford's Clubhouse, 1828

Duke of Wellington was to become a member, only for the food and excellent amenities. The entrance fee was 30 guineas, the highest in London. From the official opening in January 1828, it was a tremendous success. Crockford's gross income in the first two seasons was estimated at about a quarter of a million pounds. His expenses too were enormous. He spent £2,000 a year on dice, providing three new pairs made from the finest ivory at a guinea a pair, at the opening of the play at Hazard each evening. If any nobleman, sitting at the gaming table, took a fancy to, say, grapes or peaches out of season, his whim would be gratified even if it meant that a servant had to search all London to get them. Every foreign dignitary and ambassador belonged to the club as a matter of course, whether they gambled or not.

The 'Old Fishmonger' watched the tables like a hawk, giving credit to large losers only against approved signatures – it would be difficult to say how many families were ruined to make Crockford the millionaire he was when he retired in 1840 to his house in Carlton House Terrace, where he died in 1844 at the age of sixty-nine.

Crockford's was still in St James's Street until a couple of years ago, when it moved to its present address in Curzon Street.

7 St James's Place
and Cleveland Row

When Barbara, Lady Castlemaine, later Duchess of Cleveland, decided to improve her new properties, she called in the master builder Joseph Rossington to develop Cleveland House and its extensive grounds. One of the streets was the present St James's Place, which by 1685 contained eight small tenements, all occupied by 'Persons of the Quality', including the Earls of Inchiquin and Nottingham. It was home to many celebrities in the years to come.

One of the earliest was the Reverend Thomas Parnell, the poet, later Archdeacon of Clogher. In 1755 Robert Henley, early lover of Charlotte Hayes and later to be Lord Northington, lived at No. 22. From 1748 until she died in 1768 the famous actress Molly Lepell lived here. She married Lord Hervey and was constantly praised not only for her beauty but for her excellent behaviour, which was rewarded by her being appointed a maid of honour to Queen Caroline. Charles James Fox lived at No. 2 when he was not gambling next door at Brooks's. His mistress (later to be his wife), Elizabeth Armistead, had been living there since 1773.

The famous fencing-master Domenico Angelo lived at No. 3 from 1758 to 1762. The historian Edward Gibbon had an 'indifferent lodging' at 2 guineas a week at No. 2 in 1766. Mrs Mary Delany, prolific gossip and friend of George III, is first found there in 1749 and again from 1771 to 1788 at No. 33. 'Perdita' Robinson and her mother lived at No. 21 from 1784; Mrs Robinson died in this house but 'Perdita' stayed on at Colonel Tarleton's charge long after she had been rejected by the Prince Regent.

More dubious characters were Colonel James Chauvel of the Middlesex Militia, who had two houses Nos. 26 and 27, 'for tenants' from 1767 to 1786, and Miss Frankland (of Miss Fawlk-land's Academy) who retired there in 1785 and died there in 1788. In the 1749 Electors' List every resident was described as either a 'Gent' or an 'Esquire'.

By far the most famous inhabitant was the ravishing beauty Fanny Murray, the greatest courtesan of her time: daughter of a poor musician in Bath, a flower-girl at eleven, seduced by Jack Spencer at fourteen, a street whore in London, boosted in the Harris List in 1747 and from then until 1758 'the unchallenged Toast of all London'. Even the dour old Dr Johnson paid her compliments. The list of her 'conquests', before she married the actor David Ross, included half the nobility, but after her marriage 'there was no breath of scandal'. From 1750 until her marriage in 1758 she lived in 'an elegant lodging' at No. 22 St James's Place.

In the nineteenth century the street harboured such eminent people as Chopin, who stayed at No. 4 when in 1848 he gave his last concert at the Guildhall, the famous caricaturist Cruikshank, at No. 11 from 1820 to 1826, and the great banker Sir Francis Burdett who restored Molly Lepell's house in 1816 and lived there until 1844. Today it is a quiet elegant by-way dominated by the Stafford Hotel and the Royal Ocean Racing Club.

In front of the palace was Cleveland Row, where Rossington erected seven houses, one of which was occupied by Hugh Chol-mondeley, whose descendants were to be created Marquesses of Cholmondeley. His house at No. 3 was taken over in 1695 by John Poulteney, and members of his family were to live there until 1763, when it was occupied by 'Golden Ball' Hughes, the immensely rich playboy.

'Mad Jack' Ogle lived in Cleveland Row from about 1668, when he came of age. He had £200 a year and gained notoriety by 'his duels, his licentious pranks and low humour'. Through the influence of his sister, Anne Ogle, maid of honour to the Duchess of York (and mistress to the Duke), he became an officer in the Royal Horse Guards, although he had not enough means to secure the necessary equipment so that his shifts and subterfuges became the subject of many anecdotes. 'Captain' Ogle '. . . lost more in cock-fighting than he gained at the gaming-table'. His excesses killed him in 1685, and his name was long a byword for his eccentric profligacy.

Ogle's activities, however, were as nothing compared with those of 'Lord Fumble', William Stanhope, Earl of Harrington and Baron Petersham, who was 'a man of the most exceptionall immorality

George James, 4th Earl Cholmondeley, '. . . a womaniser . . . a man who has lost all sense of moral rectitude and has no bounds for his sexual indulgences . . . a byword for insane Vices, dirty Songs . . . boasting of all the women he had seduced . . .' Here seen in 1801 promenading along St James's Street on the prowl

. . . who sacrificed all appearance of Decency . . . for the lowest amusements at the lowest Brothels . . . as lecherous as a Monkey.' The *Town and Country Magazine* chronicled his amours for several years, starting with the opera singer Signora Caterini Ruini Galli, who 'could not be ranked as a Beauty because she was too corpulent'. She was dropped in favour of Kitty Brown, who was compared with the Venus de Milo, with 'a fair complexion, brilliant blue eyes a commanding but modest presence and with small pouting Bubbies'. His entanglement with that 'Imperios Thaïs' Kitty Fisher did not last long, and his next 'Dulcinea' was the actress Mrs Houghton, who was snatched away by General Keppel. When the Duke of Dorset died, Harrington acquired his mistress, Jane Courteville, but she succumbed to 'the corpulent charms' of the 'Lena', Mrs Rushton of King Street. About 1775 Stanhope maintained a harem in his mansion '. . . which comprised a Negress in a feather'd Turban, a young girl in pseudo-classical Dress, another as a Countrey-wench, as well as a Mandolin-player . . .'. However it was his affaire with Miss Lisle (widow of Captain Parker who was killed at the siege of Savannah) who had become a professional whore, that aroused the magazine's venom: 'His Lordship is an impotent Debauchee and his Lady a professional *Messalina*, who has little cause to be jealous – she would rather be inclined to laughter at this *liaison*. . . .'

Lady Harrington was not far behind her husband in the immorality stakes. She was also inclined to lesbianism as was demonstrated in her liaison with 'the Pollard Ash', Walpole's nickname for the spritely Elizabeth Ashe. When Elizabeth became mistress to the popular diplomat Count von Haszlang, Lady H. complained that she was '. . . quite devastated . . . her character had been demolished by this desertion'. Lady Harrington in addition to her own Messalina-like adventures attended Mrs Cornelys' routs and concerts, making assignations for her friends as well as for herself.

There were two other residents distinguished for their expertise, the best known being Mrs Mitchell 'of Cleveland Row' and the other, much later, Mrs Welch.

Elizabeth Mitchell had started in 1765 in Berkeley Street in a luxurious seraglio with a motto emblazoned over her door, 'In Media Tutissimus'. She kept only one or two selected beauties as boarders. One was the 'proud and haughty' Emily Colhurst, born in 1757, daughter of a highly respectable haberdasher in Piccadilly. While serving in the shop she had been cozened and seduced by the equally haughty Earl of Loudon, '. . . who set her up in an elegant house in St James with a fine Equipage and £500 a year' but

Charity Covereth a Multitude of Sins, 1781
A young officer knocks at Mrs Mitchell's bordel door in Cleveland Row,
immediately opposite the gate of the palace. Two of her young nuns welcome
him in, while he gives a tip to a crippled beggar. A poster advertising Dr
Leake's Pills is pasted on the wall. Two itinerant hurdy-gurdy players
serenade the gallant

dropped her after six months. She then became the 'Temporary Companion' of a large number of Beaux, being then only seventeen. She would '. . . often refuse a £20 Note . . . if she did not fancy the presenter . . . she would have no commerce with the Sons of Circumcision . . .'.

The other *mignonne* was the entrancing Lucy Palmer, daughter of Alderman Palmer, 'a gracious, well-bred and well-spoken' girl who, like many a wealthy citizen's offspring, was seeking an aristocratic, impecunious husband.

Meanwhile Mrs Mitchell had moved into Charlotte Hayes' old house in King's Place, extending her clientele to include the champion of liberty, John Wilkes, and lesser luminaries such as the Earls of Fife and Carlisle. Her special ploy now was finding 'Studs of the Quality' for ladies of that ilk, thus ensuring impeccable social and sexual intercourse. Another successful ploy was recruiting the young wives of elderly City merchants who needed sexual gratification, as well as young ladies of good breeding who needed a partner or extra money to buy fine clothes and jewellery.

In 1772 Mrs Mitchell moved into Cleveland Row, where she had as neighbours two of her clients, Admiral Lord Rodney and George Augustus Selwyn. The Prince of Wales dropped in quite often. As the Temple of Prostitution (1777) observed:

> Each Degree from Lords to Cits
> From Authors, down to puny Wits

were to be found there. Emily Colhurst, still riding high, came there 'to rest' between exertions. She caused quite a flutter in 1778 when her head-dress caught fire while she was in the Haymarket Theatre but happily it was '. . . extinguished by Esquire Glynn, although with some difficulty before more serious injury was caused'. Mrs Mitchell was indicating that she now had facilities for flagellation for those so minded. The ultimate accolade came when Rowlandson caricatured her in 1781. She was still in business in 1784.

The activities of 'Mother' Welch were chronicled in *The Rambler Magazine* and similar publications but not with the same degree of flamboyance as with the earlier 'abbesses'.

The Stable Yard bordels have long gone, giving way to the eminently respectable official palaces of Lancaster House and Clarence House, the residence of the Queen Mother. The yard could hardly go further up-market!

8 Park Place and Mother Needham

Only the south side of Park Place, which marked the boundary of the old Poulteney estate, belongs to St James's parish, but all of it has always been regarded as being within St James's.

John Poulteney lived in one of the houses from 1680 to 1696, and all his neighbours were of the nobility – Lord Brounker (Pepys' patron), the Countess of Tankerville, John Vaughan, Earl of Carbery, and Thomas, Lord Clifford. In 1691 the third Duke of Schomberg lived there while his mansion in Pall Mall was being completed.

By 1698 Lady Tankerville's neighbours were George Hamilton, Earl of Orkney, and the Duchess of Cleveland, as well as the Marchioness of Halifax. There was only one commoner, John Philip Hoffman, whose family were still in occupation till 1780. On the death of the Marchioness in 1726 the Halifax family gave way to the Earl of Essex – so there was no loss of status, but from 1766 to 1780 the house on the corner with St James's Street became a lodging house run by John Ludiman for 'tenants'.

Undoubtedly the most famous resident was 'Mother' Elizabeth Needham, the veritable Princess of Procuresses, who kept her 'House of Civility' at No. 12 from about 1709. She was born about 1675 'of obscure parentage' and was said to have been an orange-girl who became a prostitute when she was fourteen, '. . . but having a good skin and fine features made many a conquest and quickly amassed a large sum of money from rich admirers' became a bawd. One of those admirers was certainly powerful enough to get her a house in Park Place. By then she was a handsome woman 'of imperious mien', Hogarth, in 1725, describing her as 'the handsome old Procuress . . . middle-aged, well dressed in silk and simpering beneath the [fashionable] patches on her face . . .'.

'Mother' Elizabeth Needham, the most famous inhabitant of Park Place, procuring a young country lass for Colonel Francis Charteris in 1731. This was the incident which led to her downfall and death

She was a first-class organizer who maintained a very strict regime in her establishment, recruiting many of her minions from the countryside. Richard Steele, in *The Spectator* of January 1712, mentioning a visit to the coaching station at the Bell Inn in Cheapside, wrote: 'But who should I see there but the most artful Procuress in the Town examining a most beautifull Countrey girl who had just come up in the same Waggon as my Things. . . .' John Brown of Shifnal confirmed these activities as '. . . plying close at Inns upon the coming-in of Waggons and Gee-Ho coaches & there you may hire fresh plump Country Wenches sound and Juicy . . . for her Busines . . .'. They were impressed by this smart London Dame in her fine clothes promising regular, pleasant employment as a release from the dull drudgery of the village. They were not to know of her hot temper and command of foul language – *vide The Dunciad*:

169

Try not with Jests obscene to force a Smile
Nor lard your Words with Mother Needham's style!

She hired out the girls' clothes 'like a Tally-woman' and pocketed all their earnings. Any girl who failed to pay the exorbitant sum she charged for clothes-hire, laundering and the purchase of trinkets was mercilessly harried to redouble her efforts. The girls were compelled to drink with and fondle every drunken and diseased noble lout who would reel into the house at any time. Those who could not pay were hurried to a debtors' prison and left to rot or to gain release on Mother Needham's own savage terms. Those – mostly teenagers – who were sent on the streets faced the hazards of arrest by venal constables or watchmen if they could not bribe them, to be hauled up before the magistrate and sent to Bridewell. Those who grew too old or were unlucky enough to catch a disease were just thrown out into the street.

The women who served in the brothel were treated like cattle. In addition to 'satisfying' the clients, they had to carry out the many ordinary domestic tasks, scrubbing floors, acting as chambermaids and laundresses. To give her her due, Mrs Needham never claimed she was doing any Christian duty of rescue.

She was lucky with her neighbours. One was George Hamilton, Earl of Orkney. Another, briefly, was the Duchess of Cleveland. And there was Lady Camilla Tankerville, well known for her promiscuity, and George Montague, Marquis of Halifax. With such neighbours and with the protection of Philip, Duke of Wharton, and his ineffable cousin, Colonel Francis Charteris, she prospered mightily. The young Prince of Wales was among her clients. The first recorded brush with the law came in November 1721, when she was committed to Newgate, 'being accessory to a felony', but we know her business was not affected because in 1722 the poetess Mrs Blount burbled, '. . . for want of you, to Needham's we must hie . . .'. Her protection was now wearing thin, for on 23 July 1724 it was reported: 'On Monday last the noted *Mother* Needham and *Mother* Bird were committed to Newgate, their Houses having been searched the night before. . . .' The peace officers had found two women in bed 'with two Gentlemen of Distinction'. The gentlemen were bound over but the women were sent to hard labour in the Tothill Bridewell. Worse was to follow. The *London Journal* on 10 April 1725 reported: '. . . the famous *Mother* Needham, *alias* Bird *alias* Howard alias Blewitt [the different names were used when hiring rooms of premises when procuring girls at the register offices] was again apprehended on Sunday last April 4th for

All Sorts in St James's Park, 1770
From the luscious Tid-bit
To the bouncing Jack Whore;
From the Bunter in Rags
To the gay Pompadore!

keeping a Disorderly House. 'Tis likewise said she has made ample discoveries relating to several of her own Profession . . .'. She was sentenced to a derisory fine of one shilling and an hour in the Westminster pillory, but there is no record of the pillorying. The sentence was minimal because she had 'split' on the other bawds, whom she alleged had tipped off the constables, although it may have been a disgruntled employee.

Her downfall was certainly due to Charteris, whose scandalous behaviour had earned him the sobriquet 'Rapemaster-General of Britain'. He was saved from trouble only because he was a scion of the Wharton family and had served in the Army (although cashiered for embezzlement). He made money by cheating at cards – he won £3,000 from the Duchess of Queensberry by using a small mirror, and was barred from several clubs for this. In 1717 he had been before the magistrates for drawing his sword against a constable in St James's Park – he got only a wigging for this, but then he raped a young virgin in the Scotch Ale-house in Pall Mall and had to pay maintenance for her bastard child. In his Scottish home he kept a seraglio, often being indicted for assault. He was once described there as 'a huge raw Beast . . . I ken him weel by his nastie Legg for he has wrapt it round my Arse mony a guid time!' His weakness was a terrible satyriasis coupled with inordinate arrogance.

In court it was testified that Mrs Needham had supplied him with '. . . strong lusty countrey girls . . . their Buttocks hard as Cheshire cheese that would make a dint in a wooden chair and work like a (parish) Fire Engine at a Conflagration'. For such a virgin he would pay 20 guineas but on one occasion Mrs Needham angrily protested that 'he was using her ill' because he had used and rejected a girl and '. . . she would be compelled to sell her to some Player or even a Barrister . . .'.

Alexander Pope in the first of his *Horatian Odes* warned:

> Not thus at Needham's your judicious Eye
> May measure there the Breast the Hip the Thigh –
> And you will run to Perils – *Sword* and *Law*. . . .

The end came when Mother Needham sent a young maid-servant, Anne Bond, who wanted a 'respectable Situation' to Charteris's townhouse. She fought off his attempt at rape, called the constables, and charged him with assault and rape. At the Old Bailey on 17 February 1730 he was sentenced to death. On the intervention of Lord Wharton he was pardoned by the King after a short spell in Newgate, to great public anger at this travesty of justice.

Mrs Needham was charged before her arch-enemy, 'The Whorehunter', Sir John Gonson, on 24 March 1731 and convicted of keeping a 'Disorderly House' in Park Place. She was committed to the Gatehouse and brought back to court on 29 April and sentenced to stand in the pillory 'over against Park Place next day' and once in the New Palace Yard, besides finding sureties for future good behaviour. She was allowed, exceptionally, 'to lie down upon her face on the pillory', though, as the *Daily Advertiser* reported, '. . . notwithstanding which evasion of the Law and the diligence of the Beadles and a number of Persons who had been paid to protect her she was so severly pelted by the Mobb that her life was despaired of . . . [and] a Boy was kill'd by falling upon iron-spikes from a Lamp-post which he had climb'd to see Mrs Needham on the pillory . . .'.

The *Grub Street Journal* said Mrs Needham died on 6 May but in a trial of keepers of houses of ill-fame held on 14 July 'Elizabeth Needham *alias* Bird *alias* Trent' was committed to Newgate. She probably died in August, for in September a broadsheet was published entitled *Mother Needham's Elegy & Epitaph*:

> YE LADIES OF DRURY, now weep
> Your Voices in howling now raise
> For *Old Mother* Needham's laid deep
> And bitter will be all your Days.

After all this excitement Park Place sank back into respectability, although sinfulness was not entirely eradicated, for from 1765 to 1792 Mrs Margaret Pocock kept a discreet establishment at No. 12, Mrs Needham's old residence.

Among the later residents were William Pitt, from 1785 to 1802, Sir William Musgrave, compiler of the famous *Obituaries*, from 1780 to 1792, and Admiral Hugh Pigott, from 1780 to 1792. From that date the only nobleman living there was Lord Vernon.

9 Arlington Street

When Henry Bennet, newly created Earl of Arlington, sold a small piece of land at the top end of St James's Street to a Mr Pym about 1678, he said that he wanted the new street to be 'an *enclave de luxe* for the Nobility'. By 1680 it was completed and in 1689 Mr Pym constructed Bennet Street to link it with St James's Street. By this time his lordship was dead. And thereby hangs a tale.

In the post-Restoration period the Court and Society had been

Arlington Street looking north towards Piccadilly. On the left is Pomfret House, popularly known as Pomfret Castle, the wall of which stands to this day. On the right is Bennet Street on the corner of which stands The Blue Posts Tavern, still going strong

much diverted by the activity of Lady Bennet, one of the most famous procuresses of the time, entertaining such royal intimates as Lords Buckhurst and Rochester, the Earl of Dorset and Sir Charles Sedley. These aristocratic hooligans were members of 'The Ballers' who were not above mayhem and even murder. It was reported: 'Lady Jane Leeke, famous by the name of Lady Bennet . . . was ruining her child [Katherine] by her evil Precepts and Examples . . . and laying waste [her late husband's] lands by her Profligacy. . . .' Hence when King Charles, wishing to show goodwill to Sir Henry Bennet, then Secretary of State, offered him the title of Earl Bennet, he informed His Majesty that he could not have his own name in any title because '. . . he had to avoid any opprobrium in his future Lady's name, Lady Bennet being of too infamous a Reputation in the World'. He therefore became Lord Arlington in 1664 and honour was preserved.

Among the earliest residents were Barbara, Duchess of Cleveland, in 1685, soon after the death of Charles II, Lady Dorchester, Sir Charles Sedley's ennobled daughter Catherine, Sir Robert Walpole (Horace Walpole was born in No. 6) and the Duke of Kingston, whose daughter, the famous Lady Mary Wortley-Montague, was born at No. 17. Edward Walpole asserted, 'Nothing can be more dignified than this position.' In the mid-eighteenth century there were politicians such as Charles James Fox (No. 9) and William Pitt. No. 18 was originally called Pomfret Castle, built in 1760 by Lady Henrietta, Countess Pomfret, one of 'the Two Bitches' who were said to be the bane of George II's life. The original front lodges may be seen to this day.

A most dramatic incident occurred in 1801, when Lord and Lady Nelson were lodging there: '. . . a cheerful Conversation until My Lord Nelson remarked on some thing that "My Dear Lady Hamilton" had said or done, whereupon Lady Nelson rose from her chair and exclaimed with much vehemence "I am sick of hearing of My Dear Lady Hamilton and I am resolved that you shall give up either her or me!" Lord Nelson said quietly "Take care, Fanny, of what you say, but I cannot forget my Obligations to Lady Hamilton." Whereupon Lady Nelson left the house without any further word and went away in her Carriage.'

At No. 22 lived Sir Sampson Gideon, Bart., son of the great Jewish banker of the same name, who had coveted a title but could not be granted one because, although he had all his children baptized and was estranged from the congregation at the Bevis Marks Synagogue, he never apostasized and was buried as a Jew. As a compensation, a grateful Government created Sampson Jr, a baronet during his father's lifetime and after his father's death Earl of Eardley.

At No. 5, from 1755, lived Charles Sackville, second Duke of Dorset, and his charming mistress Jane Courteville. When he died in 1769, she was briefly 'protected' by Lord Harrington but when he lost interest she found herself heavily in debt and in the King's Bench prison. In 1773 she had sufficiently recovered her esteem that she was reported as 'well known along Piccadilly'.

One famous denizen was not an aristocrat at all, although greatly in demand by them. This was Charlotte Kelly of Arlington Row, the small alley leading into Park Place. She had started life as an apple-seller but by 1765 was keeping a 'House of Civility' in Duke Street. Hickey described her in 1768 as 'the useful Mrs Kelly with her bevy of Beauties'. He and his brother used to dine there, sometimes taking their own doxies. He introduced many friends and acquaintances, although sometimes he was let down.

One was the 'Surly Nabob', Captain Henry Mordaunt of the Bengal Lancers, illegitimate son of the fifth Earl of Peterborough by the actress Anastasia Robinson. He was 'an envious jealous man' because he could not succeed to the title – he called himself Lord Mordaunt – and carried his rancour everywhere. He was then the 'protector' of Charlotte Berry who later became Hickey's beloved common-law wife.

The Hickey brothers ran foul of Mrs Kelly's temper when some years later they introduced another Bengal Lancer, Captain Mackintosh. When they came back a couple of days later, she assailed them with a volley of abuse for having introduced '. . . such a dirty Dog and arrant Pickpocket Blackguard . . . he had had every girl in the house without giving any of them a single coin, always paying them with lavish Compliments . . . he had run up a Bill for more than a hundred Pounds for suppers and wines . . . he had now decamped to Copenhagen . . . without paying his Lodgings or his Servants and owing thousands of Pounds to Tradespeople and Others'. Hickey did not offer to recompense her.

Amongst Mrs Kelly's bevy of beauties were the popular 'Toasts' Betsy Coxe and Sally Hudson and, somewhat later, the 'Kelly Girl', the ravishingly beautiful Emma Lyon who was to become Lady Hamilton. Mrs Kelly owed her success mainly to the fact that she procured very young girls, *The Rambler Magazine* (October 1784) noting, 'TO BE SOLD by Inch of Candle at Mrs Kelly's Rooms several Orphan Girls under sixteen imported from the Countrey & never shewn before. Gentlemen of sixty-five and over are invited.'

Hickey reported that, while at Margate, 'Mrs Kelly of Arlington

Street arrived with a child of twelve and two *nymphs'*. He described her then as 'an old woman'.

Mrs Kelly ran an establishment in Duke Street, but from 1791 to 1800 had moved to No. 18 Berkeley Square and disappears from St James's history.

By this time too the aristocracy were moving westward to Mayfair, and Arlington Street thereafter assumed respectability and quietness.

10 Piccadilly

Only a part of the southern side of Piccadilly is in the parish of St James – that is, the portion between the Haymarket and St James's Street. The highway itself was anciently the route to the west and as late as 1585 was called 'the waie to Colbroke' (Colnbrook) and also 'the waye to Readinge'.

The earliest record of the name seems to be 'the Old Pickadilla Hall' shown on a plan in 1585, when it was marked as 'the Gameinge House'. In 1623 this was in the possession of Robert Baker who sold 'Pickadilla Cakes'. Ten years later Gerarde's *Herbal* recorded that, 'Wilde buglosse was growing aboute the drye ditche-bankes on either side of Pickadilla.'

All the land on the south side between the Haymarket and St James's Street formed part of the estate of Henrietta Maria, Charles I's Queen. In 1658 there were only a few buildings at the

The Piccadilly Turnpike. The turnpike barring the road from London to Reading and the west was originally situated at a point near today's Clarges Street, Piccadilly. In 1761 it was removed to a point opposite St George's Hospital at Hyde Park Corner where it stood until its removal in 1825

Haymarket end. In 1661 the Queen's trustees granted thirty-year leases to her son's friend, Henry Jermyn. (The freeholds of most of the area still belong to the Crown.) These thirty-year leases were later extended to 1740. In 1674, however, Charles II granted to Colonel Edward Villiers the freehold of the site at the eastern corner of St James's Street – a little alley, Villiers Court, existed there for many years.

In 1674 Sir Christopher Wren was appointed architect to the new church which was to serve the newly carved-out parish, and the foundation stone was laid in 1676. Wren was very pleased with his design, which became the prototype for many of the eighteenth-century churches.

The site was known much earlier: John Stow mentions that when, in 1245, work was being started on the famous water conduit-house in Cheapside in the City, its pipes ran from the source in Paddington '. . . to James' Head on the hill to the Mewsgate, from the Mewsgate to the Crosse in Cheape . . .' (a distance of about two miles). The Mews Gate was on the site of the royal mews where now stands the National Gallery. This was the conduit which in 1273 flowed all day with wine to celebrate Edward I's coronation.

Although the exterior was modest, the interior was very elegant, the limewood reredos was carved by Grinling Gibbons, as was the Harris organ case – the organ was made for the Chapel Royal but was donated to the church by Queen Mary II in 1691. John Evelyn noted that there was no altar in England 'more handsomely adorned'. The church can hold about 2,000 people who can clearly hear the preacher.

Among the famous people buried there are Robert Dodsley, the great publisher, James Gillray, the caricaturist, Tom D'Urfey, writer and collector of bawdy ballads, James Christie, the auctioneer, and Francis White, the founder of White's Club, as well as quite a few of the light ladies who inhabited King's Place.

From 1661 Piccadilly was known as Portugal Street, in honour of Queen Catherine's birthplace, but the name never caught on and by 1685 there is a reference in an Act to 'Pickedilly street *alias* Portugal Street'. John Strype in 1720 shows it as Piccadilly but Roques' map of 1746 extends Piccadilly to Half Moon Street. The Piccadilly turnpike stood at that point but had been moved in 1761 to Hyde Park Corner, where it stood until 1825.

By 1681 the stretch from the Haymarket was covered with undistinguished buildings, many of them inns and taverns. In 1720, from St James's Street eastwards, there were the White Horse

Inn, the Elephant Inn and the King's Arms Inn (where Fortnum & Mason's now stands), all three 'of an indifferent trade'. Where now stands the Criterion Theatre was before 1685 the White Bear Inn, a huge property reaching back to 'Germin Streete', with Fleece Yard running through it; at the Piccadilly end were a covered archway and two small shops. In 1717, when Mary Fitzgerald was the leaseholder, it was also known as the Fleece Inn, but in 1740 it was known as the White Bear & Fleece, and in 1743, when a licensed victualler, William Miller, took over, it was again the White Bear and 'in a ruinous condition and must soon be rebuilt'. In 1770 it was reported to be 'in good condition' and was then a very important coaching-station. 'Diligences' left every morning at five o'clock for Dover, Ramsgate, Rochester and Canterbury. There was a night-coach to Dover every evening. It was a pick-up point for all coaches going westward, and it survived well into the railway era.

In the early 1800s the White Bear Public House was the resort of 'sporting Characters, thieves and prostitutes' from the Haymarket. It was demolished in 1870 to make way for the famous Criterion Restaurant.

From what is today Lower Regent Street going westward there were a great many small shops with living accommodation up-stairs; from very early times these upper parts were let off as lodgings for visitors and more often to prostitutes – the earliest one recorded being Anne Hill, 'who dwelt nigh unto the White Beare' and was found dead there on 8 June 1685.

Of unusual interest was the large number of booksellers in this stretch between the church and St James's Street. Many had gravitated from the City and the Strand in the early 1700s. In 1749 there was Robert Dawes, one of the electors on the Parliamentary Register, and Robert Davis, who was associated with John Debrett.

The first to make his name was John Almon, a Liverpool apprentice who had come to London to be a printer but became a bookseller and publisher in 1765 at No. 178 (now 176) when he was only twenty-eight. He was already known as a supporter of John Wilkes by 1761 – indeed, this association cost him a term of imprisonment for libel in 1770 for his polemics. The back of his shop was patronized by all the prominent Whigs, becoming a sort of political club. Almon's bitter satirical tongue landed him in more difficulties, and in 1781 he had to sell out to John Debrett, although he remained active. In 1784 he founded and edited *The General Advertiser*, but after yet another libel action he had to '. . . retire to France because of financial difficulties' and fear of the debtors' prison. He died in London in 1805.

St James's Church in 1684

John Field Debrett was twenty-seven years old when he took over. The *St James' Gazette* for 11 July 1780 printed the advertisement: 'JOHN DEBRETT begs leave most respectfully to acquaint the Nobility and Gentry and his Readers in general that he is removed from the late Mr William Davis' to Mr Almon's Bookseller and Stationer opposite Burlington House in Piccadilly where he hopes he will be honoured with their commands.'

In 1769, when he was with 'R. Davis of Piccadilly', he had published his *New Peerage, or The Present State of the Nobility of England*, although his name does not appear on the title page. The 1784 edition, however, does mention his name. In 1802 he published his famous *Peerage of England, Scotland and Ireland* which is to this day an essential directory of the nobility. In 1808 he produced the companion volume, *Debrett's Baronetage*. Both represent what was popularly known as *The Snobs' Bible* by the irreverent. He moved from Almon's original premises in 1788, and in 1814 retired from the bookshop which he had occupied at No. 180 (now No. 178) but continued to edit the *Peerage* from his home until he died in November 1822.

Debrett's easy-going temperament and thriftlessness, compounded by gambling, kept him poor and he died in poverty, in his lodgings near Regent's Park. A Notice was published: '. . . all Communications are requested to be sent to Rivington's, Waterloo Place'.

Debrett's shop was taken over by Richard Jackson, a direct descendant of that John Jackson, chandler and oil-man, who started in Piccadilly about 1680. Richard Jackson, who was then described as a tallow-chandler and oil-man, expanded his business to include groceries. His nephew William was to carry on until 1765, and it was one of his kin who took over Debrett's premises and started the great expansion, while still living over the shop. He moved to Nos. 171–2 in 1840. From Victorian times Jackson's, with its many Royal Warrants flourished mightily, only to close down in 1980 after 300 years in Piccadilly.

In 1781 John Stockdale, who had started life as a porter in Almon's, opened his own shop on the corner of Duke Street (then No. 181) but in 1810 he moved into the premises formerly occupied by Debrett. Another very strong-minded character, he was often at loggerheads with authority. He was prominent in the anti-Warren Hastings camp – Hastings sued him for libel but Stockdale was acquitted. His most impressive publication was Dr Johnson's *Works*. When he died, in 1814, his son John Joseph Stockdale continued the business. The firm also dealt in 'rare Books'. James

Ridgeway, Stockdale's brother-in-law, was to open his own shop a few doors away in 1806 at No. 170 (now 169), and the firm was to carry on there until 1894.

In 1797 John Wright, author turned bookseller, took over the shop at No. 169 (now 166–73) which had formerly belonged to John Owen, publisher of *The Anti-Jacobin*. Two years later he took over the shop next door. He was a close friend of William Cobbett, author of the famous *Rural Rides*, although they quarrelled in the end. He was also a friend of George Canning, who was frequently to be found, with other politicians and *literati*, in Wright's rear room – it was the rendezvous of Pitt's Ministers, which earned Wright's the sobriquet 'the Political House'. All the same, this galaxy of famous customers did not save his business from failing in 1802, landing him in the Fleet debtors' prison the following year, and Piccadilly knew him no more. He died in 1844.

Far and away the most famous – and the longest lasting, for it still exists – is the bookshop established in June 1797 'in the shop lately occupied by Mr White at 173 Piccadilly by the young Evangelical Tory' John Hatchard (then twenty-nine years old and already married seven years). The son of respectable and devout parents, he had started work at fourteen at a Strand bookshop but left after a month to be apprenticed to another bookseller. Seven years later, on 10 October 1789, he celebrated his freedom at his father's expense after a farewell party 'with a good Supper, a flowing bowl of Punch, some good Songs, Toasts and Sentiments'. It had cost Hatchard *père* £5. He then entered the employ of a well-known City bookseller, Thomas Payne, as a shop-assistant.

There Hatchard met many of the *literati* and *cognoscenti* who were later to support him – the Shakespearean scholars Edward Malone, Dr Johnson's first biographer, Sir John Hawkins, and the spiteful but brilliant George Alexander Steevens, great classical scholars like Richard Porson, Charles Burney and William Beloe, and such rich collectors as Lords Stormont and Charles Spencer. He also made a useful acquaintanceship with George Canning, later Prime Minister. It was now time for him to set up on his own.

Accordingly: 'I quitted the service of Mr Thomas Payne 30.June 1797 and commenced business for my self . . . On July 1st I took the shop lately occupied by Mr. White, 173 Piccadilly, subject to £31.10s for Goodwill and £40 per annum. When I commenced business I had of my own Property less than Five Pounds.'

Amongst Hatchard's earliest publications were *Reform or Ruin* by John Bowdler (father of the notorious expurgationist) and Bishop Wilberforce's *Reports of the Society for the Betterment of the Condition of*

The south side of Piccadilly in 1800, showing Hatchards with its bow-fronted window two doors away from the museum

the Poor. Macaulay and Hannah More took a long-abiding interest in this serious and very honourable young man. Their 'Clapham Set' met often in his rear room for debates and decisions on their various objectives and charities, and the first meetings of the Anti-Slavery campaign started at Hatchard's. Empowered to receive large sums of money on their behalf, his ledgers show *en passant* that Wilberforce once borrowed half a guinea and Robert Heber (brother of the bishop) bought books and 'paid 2/- for Gloves'.

The Hatchard family lived 'on the upper front floors' because 'the back and lower rooms, narrow staircases, dark corners, low ceilings and even the attic were stuffed with books . . . in a sombre and religious atmosphere'. Business was very good: '. . . in four years he had converted his Five Pounds into Five Hundred'. In the summer of 1801 Hatchard moved to larger premises at No. 190 (now No. 187), buying a twenty-four-year lease for 1,000 guineas, 'half-down and the other half within two years'. He was able to pay the balance within a year.

His customers included the Duke of Wellington, who used at first to come on horseback; later he sent his coach for whatever he needed. Gladstone, Peel, Palmerston and Lord Derby were served, as also was Isaac d'Israeli when he came up to town. Peers and prelates came in droves, but he thought that the 'Grandes Dames' did not come to buy books but just to be seen and be amused. Their 'powdered and breeched Flunkeys', however, had a special bench outside on which to rest themselves.

Hatchard was entrusted to form collections and stock libraries. Cecil Rhodes, when creating his library at Groote Schuur near Cape Town, stipulated that no book should be expurgated or abridged and all workers should be well paid – an arrangement made only with John Hatchard and a close secret between them.

Longman's *Focus on Literature* (1816) said: '. . . Hatchard's, Bookseller to the Queen . . . shops which are frequented as Lounging Shops . . . Ridgeways, Stockdale's and Hatchards, all in Piccadilly . . .'. And Beloe, in his *Sexagenarian*, had booksellers divided into 'the Dry', 'the Finical', 'the Opulent', 'the Honest', 'the Queer', 'the Cunning' and 'the B . . . s', but Hatchard was 'the Goodly': 'a worthy and conscientious man'.

He died in June 1849, aged eighty-one, leaving an estate of about £100,000, disappointed that his eldest son preferred the Church to business (he became a bishop eventually) but satisfied that his second son Thomas would carry on. Thomas, however, died in 1858 and was succeeded by the founder's great-grandson, Henry Hudson. In 1881 A. I. Humphreys took over and launched the business that became the hallmark of book-selling and internationally famous.

One other bookseller deserves mention, William Pickering, who founded the Aldine Press. He moved into No. 177 Piccadilly in 1842 but, dying in 1854, the business was carried on by James Toovey. Describing the house as 'unquestionably the ugliest house in Piccadilly', Toovey rebuilt it in 1866. He was famous in the world of rare books.

In 1749 the other shops along this stretch harboured several cheesemongers, three peruke-makers, no fewer than ten victuallers and two apothecaries but only one tobacconist, a large number of craftsmen such as smiths, carpenters, saddlers, tallow-chandlers, grocers, plumbers and breeches-makers and John Broadbelt 'engine-maker'.

In 1761 Charles Fortnum entered the service of Queen Caroline as a footman. He was then twenty-three years old. His wage was only about £45 a year but the perks were considerable. He had the advantage that his grandfather, William, had been a royal footman in Queen Anne's time and knew all the ropes. All sorts of perks were a source of profit, particularly the immense quantity of candle-ends, which could be melted down by a neighbouring tallow-chandler and supplied to the mass of ladies, gentlemen, Grooms of the Pantry, the Buttery and the Cellar, and maids of honour.

Great quantities of foodstuffs and drink as well as table and other linen, were being supplied to the Court, and Charles was able to secure a useful share through his contacts. In 1770 he decided to cash in on the situation and took the shop on the eastern corner with Duke Street. In 1720 this had housed the 'indifferent hostelry' known as the King's Arms Inn. (One William Fortnum, very likely his father, was already living in Duke Street in 1768.) Charles, however, still remained in the royal service to be able to direct business of an ever more diverse nature into his shop. In 1778 he begged leave of Her Majesty to retire owing to ill-health but continued to attend the palace part-time since the Queen had a liking for him.

The shop was then known as Fortnum's – Mason was to appear a little later. At the beginning of the century one Hugh Mason had a small shop in St James's Market, and grandfather William Fortnum lodged with him. About 1707 he became a footman in the Royal Household, in his spare time trading as a grocer and chandler. In the 1730s a licensed victualler, Henry Mason, lived on the west side of Duke Street – Mason's Yard is probably his memorial, it was used as a stables as well as supplying saddlery and all other items needed for the hundreds of horses thereabouts.

In 1817 John Mason's name appears, and thenceforth the business was to be known as Fortnum & Mason's, over the centuries to achieve an eminence unrivalled in its sphere. Charles Fortnum died in 1814, leaving all his property to his three children. The eldest, Charles, was then a page to the Queen, and the younger brother, Richard, ran the business, acquiring the adjoining premises to cope with the ever-increasing demands, in their 'Celebrated Italian Warehouse'.

John Mason died in 1837, leaving '. . . £2,000 to my worthy friend Charles Fortnum . . . and to Richard . . . all the houses in Piccadilly, Duke Street and the Yard, the Stock-in-Trade and Book Debts . . .'. Charles Fortnum was still in the royal service when he died.

Immediately opposite, on the western corner of Duke Street,

was the White Horse, a coaching house in existence long before its first mention in 1680.

In 1718 George I granted a new lease to his Sergeant-Painter, Thomas Highmore, with '. . . a frontage on Piccadilly of 167 feet . . . including nine small shops and houses . . .'. The entrance was through an archway on Piccadilly which led to two small houses fronting Jermyn Street. In 1742, when Highmore conveyed the lease to Samuel Rush, it included '. . . some olde timber houses in verie bad condition needing rebuildings . . .'. By 1762 the inn, 'with an indifferent reputation', was taken over by an upholsterer (or undertaker), John Mackay. The Jermyn Street entry had meanwhile been blocked off. In 1784 the inn had gone and the site was a stable yard, remaining so until 1805 when another John Mackay, an oil-man (possibly a son) became the lessee. Next year the whole frontage was demolished, and in 1812 Mackay surrendered the lease to the proprietors of the Egyptian Hall.

This famous building was part museum, part exhibition gallery

The Egyptian Hall, Piccadilly in 1812

and part auction-rooms. Till 1819 it was known as 'the Museum of Natural History', but its exhibits also included Napoleon's carriage from Waterloo in 1816 – 800,000 people rushed to see it. Siamese twins appeared in 1829 and again forty years later. Tom Thumb was there in 1846. It was demolished in 1906.

While respectability was now invading this part of Piccadilly, much less respectable activities were also rife: large numbers of thieves, muggers, pickpockets, confidence-tricksters and incredibly large numbers of prostitutes abounded. Even the famed Harris *List of Covent Garden Cyprians* in 1764 described some of the sorority operating in Piccadilly: Miss Sophy, tall and genteel and with a passionate eye, with 'all the arts of thumbing the Guineas', and Miss Nancy Portland, short and plump and a fine body for lust to guarantee satisfaction '. . . altho' at times her breath is not most savoury'.

In 1585 to the north of Piccadilly there were only green fields stretching as far as the Tyburn Road. By 1600 there were more houses and many lanes and alleys. One of them, Air Street, was soon to be full of small whorehouses; it linked Piccadilly with Golden Square, which was the northernmost point in the bailiwick, and Great Marlborough Street, built in 1704 and named after John Churchill, the famous Duke of Marlborough.

Great Marlborough Street soon became famed because of Jane Goadby's magnificent French-style bordello which was copied by other ladies, such as Charlotte Hayes and became the prototype for all the luxurious 'nunneries' in King's Place, in the southern part of the parish.

From the time of Queen Victoria's accession, the south side of Piccadilly became one of the most fashionable shopping streets in the kingdom. Between 1905 and 1910 Piccadilly was widened and modernized so that today only the church, Hatchard's bookshop and Fortnum & Mason remain to give the passer-by an idea of its former aspect.

11 Jermyn Street

Jermyn Street, which is Lord St Albans lasting memorial, was completed by 1680 as a thoroughfare between the Haymarket and the newly built St James's Street, although the western entrance was very narrow. At first the western end was more fashionable, and from 1675 onwards it housed John Churchill, first Duke of Marlborough, Charles Mordaunt, first Earl of Monmouth, Sir Charles O'Hara, first Baron Tyrawley and Charles Beauclerk, first Duke of St Albans – Nell Gwyn's boy.

By 1702 there were at least three coffee-houses, Betty's, Carter's and the Widow Chapman's, and on the corner with St James's Street the Nag's Head Tavern.

By the middle of the eighteenth century the street was known mainly for its lodging houses. Amongst the most famous lodgers were Sir Isaac Newton, the great astronomer John Flamstead, the poet Thomas Gray and 'La Belle Stewart', Duchess of Richmond. Mary Delaney – when she was still Mrs Pendarves – lived there for a while in 1741. William Pitt lodged there in 1763.

The only tradesman still in existence is the perfumier's Floris. Juan Famenio Floris came from Minorca and opened his shop in 1730 – the shop is still run by his descendants. There were, however, a number of gambling establishments, known as 'Sunday Houses'. About 1790 at No. 77 Jermyn Street was George Smith, George Pope & Company: 'The scenes which nightly occur at this House beggar all description. It is a Hazard-table where the chances in favour of the uninitiated player are little. The first Proprietor is as low in stature as he is in breeding – a corpulent, self-sufficient, strutting, coxcombical, irreligious Prig. Mr Pope is a respectable decent modest personage in his way; he is humble and forced to succumb to his monied partner.' The same source says that, '. . . large sums are paid to the police officers. . . . Hush

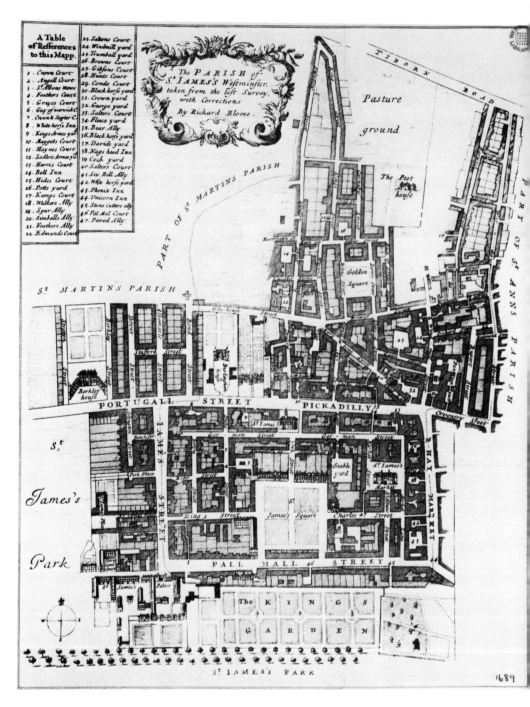

The PARISH of
St IAMES's Westminster,
taken from the last Survey,
with Corrections
By Richard Blome.

Richard Blome's map of 1689 showing how the parish had extended. Colman
Hedge Lane has now become Wardour Street, but the un-named street going
to the Pest House was later to become Great Marlborough Street. Carnaby
Street was a sleazy alley

money varies according to the magnitude of the concern, from £250 to £1,000 per annum. . . .'

Jermyn Street had a host of small whorehouses masquerading as boarding-houses or small hotels. In the nineteenth century there were Blake's, Miller's (Sam Miller was later to move into St James's Street), Topham's and the Waterloo.

By the latter part of the century Jermyn Street had become famous for its fashionable men's shops, mainly hatters and shirt-makers, some of which are still trading in their original premises.

Duke Street was the first street to have a paved way for pedestrians. As early as 1726 there is a mention of Madam Gould's – which might conceivably be connected with Elizabeth Gould of the Covent Garden bagnio in the 1750s. In 1749 it was a busy little street with two chandlers, a stockingmaker, a peruke-maker, an upholder (a funeral director), a number of craftsmen such as carpenters, plasterers and a baker, and six persons who described themselves as 'Gents'. In Mason's Yard the forerunner of the partner of Mr Fortnum was to be found. The most distinguished inhabitant was the well-known surgeon Dr Robert Young.

In 1764 Jack Harris' *List of Cyprians* had a puff for: 'Lucy Seales, in York Buildings, Duke Street, very genteel and well-made Lass, with black eyes and light brown hair . . . she has not seen much service yet . . . [because] . . . she shows little passion in her amours. . . .'

In 1765 comes the first mention of Mrs Charlotte Kelly at No. 30 Duke Street; she was to reach fame and fortune in Arlington Street. In Duke Street she had Miss Benson and Miss Hudson, as well as Sarah ('Betsy') Hastings, then 'kept by Archer the Musician'. (She and Sally Hudson were later to keep their own houses nearby.)

In 1771 the street leapt into notoriety when the *Town and Country Magazine* reported George, first Earl of Onslow, 'a noisy indiscreet little man' nicknamed 'Little Cocking George', as having a torrid affaire '. . . with Betsy Evans . . . a woman of low extraction, her father a knife-grinder near the Minories, who had passed thru' all the stages of prostitution. . . . He lavish'd a great part of his Fortune upon her altho' she was not faithful to him . . .'. In the event she was taken up by Admiral Augustus Keppel and had a son by him.

One of the brightest denizens of this street was that diminutive darling of the gods Elizabeth ('the Pollard') Ashe, intimate friend of Lady Harrington and of innumerable gentlemen. In 1751 she was living there with her (very brief) husband, Edward Wortley-Montague, before going on to greater fame.

191

A Saint James's Beauty, 1784
Portrait of a King's Place Nun gazing from her window opposite the gate of
St James's Palace. It is meant to imply that a royal client is expected

In 1788 Harris mentions that numbers 4 and 30 were brothels; doubtless there were several others.

Bury Street, built in 1670, is named after Henry Jermyn's estate at Bury St Edmunds. Dean Swift lived there at No. 26 in 1710. At the same time Richard Steele was at No. 22, 'third door right from Germin Streete'. 'Beau' Brummel's grandfather kept a lodging-house in the street, and there were two coffee-houses, Robinson's, from 1700 to 1714, and Cameron's, from c. 1700 to 1738, which was much frequented by freemasons. Walter Prendergast settled 'at the first house next Ryder Street' about 1750 and stayed till 1780, trading as a haberdasher. Sarah Prendergast lived there from 1773 to 1775, when she moved to King's Place and a prestigious future. When Ryder Street was widened in the eighteenth century, all the small whorehouses between numbers 11–13 and 24–30 and a host of little alleys and closes were cleared away, together with their histories.

12 King Street and King's Place

About 1670 Henry Jermyn projected a road to run between the Haymarket and St James's Street, to be known as King Charles II Street, being bisected by St James's Square. In the event, the eastern part became Charles II Street and the western section King Street.

In 1673 it was still 'in the fields' and not a very pretentious street: there were only a couple of prestigious houses, one the Earl of Ranelagh's. Leading off from the square, on the left-hand side, were a number of stables, the first, Cleveland Yard, being a narrow alley leading through to Pall Mall.

In 1676 there was a Rose & Crown tavern with its yard. The tavern is long gone but the name remains. The tavern was known to Pepys because '. . . *cundums* could be bought [there] in King Street almost outside the wall of St James Palace'. In both yards dwelt ladies 'of the poorer sort'.

By 1686 a few more nondescript houses had been built and at the end was the Pav'd Alley giving ingress into St James's Street for pedestrians. The houses on either side of the alley were occupied by poor prostitutes – it was designated as 'a whores' nest' until late into the 1830s.

Next on the left was a cul de sac called Binham's Yard (or Bingham's Yard) from the builder John Bingham who used it as stables from 1702 until 1756, when another builder John Baker took over and it was known as Baker's Yard. In 1763 a seven-foot opening was made into Pall Mall, and this alley became George Court, achieving great fame later as King's Place.

By 1720 important people were moving into King Street, now described by Strype as 'a fair street with many good houses', particularly that of the Earl of Ranelagh. In 1723 the famed bookseller Robert Dodsley was living at No. 22. In 1732, at the corner with Angel Court, a very prestigious hostelry, the Golden Lyon, was built. When it was rebuilt in 1763, the proprietor Richard Haines extended it along King Street to George Court. In Angel Court – most likely named after an ancient tavern – were half a dozen small dwellings leased to one Charles Kelly, perhaps connected with the lady of the same name whose whorehouse was across the way in Duke Street.

The last alley on this side was Crown Court, a busy little thoroughfare leading into Pall Mall, with another tiny alley leading into St James's Street. It was full of small shops and workrooms: in 1749 there were no fewer than twenty-two tradesmen including a well-known maker of gingerbreads, a peruquier and a perfumier. Crown Court today contains a number of such service tradesmen. By this time too even the Pav'd Alley had nine shops including two pastrycooks and a butcher; of the two chandlers one was William Pengras [sic], who as Prendergast was one of a family in a much more profitable occupation.

The houses between Angel and Crown Courts were originally part of Lord Ranelagh's estate. Between 1745 and 1767 they were occupied by a modest 'abbess', Mrs Ann Adams (1745–54), and a better-known one, Sarah Hastings (1759–67). The third house was the abode of the much esteemed 'High Impure' and reckless phaeton-driver Agnes Maria Townshend, first lauded in 1764 as 'a young courtezan of humble origin whose ambition is to . . . own her own *Vis-a-Vis*' (a light racing carriage, *the* symbol of the highest-class Impure). Through Lord Craven she reached the pinnacle as 'a furious Whip' in the Prince Regent's own circle. At the corner house with Angel Court, from 1759 to 1765, lived the even more desirable courtesan Elizabeth de la Roche, her next-door neighbour being the politician Bamber Gascoigne.

Cleveland Yard also had its share of lovelies. The corner house was occupied from 1774 to 1781 by Ann Chembre, of a distinguished Lakeland family (who tried to distance themselves from her avocation as a 'Lena') and a very intimate friend of the Macaroni 'Skiffy Skipton', otherwise Clotworthy Skeffington, second Viscount Massereene. The previous occupant had been the famous procuress Elizabeth Johnson, from 1745 to 1759, when she moved into Jermyn Street where she died in 1778, causing much anguish and anxiety to 'Old Lord Fumble' and 'Old Q'.

A few doors along King Street in 1775 the most famous of them all, Charlotte Hayes, maintained a house for the overflow of clients who could not be accommodated in King's Place.

In Cleveland Yard too, from 1763 to 1774, lived the famous opera singer Elizabeth Gambarini, much sought-after by diplomats such as the Russian Ambassador Count Sergei Musin-Pushkin and the Tripolitanian Ambassador the Aga Hamid, and by sundry noblemen – all of them eventually baulking at her excessive demands.

In 1776 the houses numbered 23 and 24 in King Street were taken over by John Nerot and transformed in an hotel and bagnio, which speedily became a most fashionable resort renowned also for its cooking, although William Hickey, eating there in 1778, complained that he had nearly died of the food, albeit praising the baths as 'famous'. Other visitors, such as John Wilkes and 'that hoary old lecher' Simon Luttrell, Viscount Irnham ('the King of Hell') found no fault with the cooking. In 1795 Edmund Burke stayed there, and also Admiral Nelson when on half-pay in London in 1782, again as Lord Nelson after his victory of the Nile and once more in 1800 after his bitter quarrel with his wife over Emma Hamilton. In 1810 Nerot's son William transferred the hotel to Clifford Street, and the premises were used as a warehouse until 1835, when the famous Jewish actor-manager John Braham bought it for £8,000 and built the St James's Theatre. The theatre flourished until 1958, when it was demolished to make way for the present office block, St James's House. And in 1830 the Pav'd Alley, still designated 'a disgraceful Rookery' was likewise demolished to widen King Street and at last make it a thoroughfare for traffic.

William Almack's venture prospered mightily, and when he died in 1781, a very rich man, he left the Assembly Rooms to his niece who had married James Willis. The Assembly Rooms now became known as 'Willis's Rooms', and were used for concerts and public functions. William Hickey visited the Rooms in 1796: '. . . to an elegant Ball and Supper . . . almost all the Indians in London being present . . . the like was never seen before . . .'. This was doubtless a function put on by the East India Company of which Hickey was a long-standing executive. In 1787 James Carr transferred his coffee-house there, staying till 1790.

The northern side of the street was lined with small shops and taverns. On the corner with Duke Street stood the King's Arms. There was also from 1702 to 1714 Burton's Coffee-House, but from 1803 this side was dominated by James Christie's auction rooms, which had started at numbers 8 and 9 then 'newly erected' and quickly spread along the street extending to Bury Street and Duke Street.

George Court, when renamed King's Place, kept the street in the limelight for nearly a hundred years for its brothels, whose fame and excellence was extolled reluctantly by Baron Johann Wilhelm von Archenholz during his visit to London in 1773 in his *Picture of England*. After describing the vast number of prostitutes accosting passers-by, he went on:

> . . . there are many noted Houses in . . . St James where a great number of them are kept for *People of Fashion*. A little street called King's Place is inhabited by *Nuns* of this *Order* who live under the direction of several rich *Abbesses*. You may see them superbly clothed at Publick Places . . . each of these *Convents* has a Carriage and Servants-at-livery for these Ladies never deign to walk anywhere but in St James Park . . . the price of Admission to these *Temples* is so exorbitant that the Mobb are entirely excluded . . . only a few rich people can aspire to the Favours of these Venal Divinities . . . the *bagnios* are magnificent buildings . . . the Furniture not unworthy of the Palace of a Prince. They can procure everything to enrapture the *Senses* . . . the Women are instantly brought in Sedan-chairs and only those celebrated for their Fashion, Elegance and Charms have the honour of being admitted . . . in these places more money is

Almack's Assembly Rooms in King Street, showing on the right, the archway leading into King's Place: next is The Golden Lyon Tavern with the opening into Angel Court

exhausted during one Night . . . that would maintain the Seven United Provinces [the Netherlands] for six months. . . .

He then remarked that the shopkeepers' best customers were these 'unfortunate women who will spend at one go their earnings of a week', but without them the theatres would be empty because they drew after them thousands of young men.

Because of the proximity of St James's Palace and the name of the alley, these 'nunneries' were known abroad as 'the King's brothels' – 'Les Bordels du Roy' – not altogether a misnomer, since all the royal sparks frequently made use of their facilities.

The alley still exists under the name of Pall Mall Place but instead of the exotic 'nunneries' there are the offices of the Department of Health and Social Security. *Sic transit gloria venerii!*

A Nun of the First Class, 1773
A King's Place courtesan, with a fashionable coiffure and the essential patch on her cheek

Mrs Sarah Pendergast

Among the most esteemed of the 'abbesses' was Sarah Pendergast (sometimes Prendergast) who came from a family well established in the sex business, there being Joseph Pindergas [*sic*] in Bury Street in the 1750s. His brother married Sarah Warren in 1731, and it was Sarah who seized the chance to take over 'Black Harriott's house in 1777, at No. 3 George Court (see pp. 201–4). The rent was a stiff £45 per annum.

Sarah kept only three young ladies on her permanent staff. One was the gay, sparkling Amelia Gosling, who did so well that in 1787 she was able to take over Lady Adams's premises. Another was Nancy Ambrose, daughter of a Portuguese-Jewish merchant named Abrahams. Her sister Eleanor was an actress, and a third sister was Sir Edward Walpole's *petite amie* – 'and like to marry him'. They were all well-brought-up, well-mannered and well-spoken girls, with several languages and well able to mix in fashionable society. Nancy was later also to become an actress and, with Eleanor, to become involved with the actor-manager Charles Macklin.

The third of Mrs Pendergast's employees was the youngster known as Charlotte Spencer, whose father was a substantial coal-dealer in Newcastle-upon-Tyne. She too had been well educated – taught music, dancing, French and Italian, being described as 'well-shaped, with flaxen hair, blue eyes, very good skin and long-limbs . . . and of immoderate Ambition'. She had eloped to London, made a 'Fleet Marriage' and been deserted. Her father had disowned her. She was 'discovered' by Jack Harris of the Shakespeare's Head, through whom she became mistress to Lord Spencer Hamilton in 1770, being thereafter always known as 'the Hon. Charlotte Spencer'. Among her intimate friends were the Duke of Devonshire (until he married), the Earl of Suffolk and 'the Cheshire Cornuto', Lord Richard Grosvenor. At Mrs Pendergast's she mixed with the *crème de la crème* of Society, to be numbered in the Prince of Wales's set. .

One of Mrs Pendergast's good friends was William, Earl of Harrington, known as 'Lord Fumble' and described in 1773 in *The Westminster Magazine* as 'a Person of the most exceptional immorality . . . a Goat of Quality'. He was very demanding and, when he turned down her three resident lovelies, she contacted Mrs Elizabeth Butler's 'warehouse' in the Sanctuary, Westminster, asking for a 'couple of fresh countery tits'. Mrs Butler at once sent over Elizabeth Cummings, 'Country Bet' and a youngster called

'Black-eyed Susan'. The aged Earl began 'his manual dalliance', announced he was highly satisfied and rewarded each girl with 3 guineas, though they had been led to expect something more generous.

The three girls' dissatisfaction boiled over when 'Mother' Butler demanded her 'poundage' of twenty-five per cent. Sue, the neophyte, agreed but Betty refused to pay, whereupon the beldam impounded her clothes. Betty went at once to the Rotation Office in Litchfield Street, Leicester Fields, and on Monday 10 November 1778 Mrs Butler was convicted of the theft of 'a Gown, a Handkerchief & other Garments and of keeping a house of ill-fame; and further, causing Elizabeth to go in company with another woman of the lowest order to meet the Earl of Harrington at the house of Mrs Prendergast who keeps a *seraglio* in King's Place'. It then transpired that Mrs Butler's husband was Sergeant Spencer Smith of the Royal Grenadier Guards, who was found guilty of '. . . aiding and abetting his wife by fetching Coaches . . . to furnish the *seraglios* in King's Place with girls whom she dressed as Country Maids . . . the Earl attended Mrs Prendergast's *seraglio* on Sundays, Mondays, Wednesdays and Fridays . . . having two Females at a time'.

The scandal Press picked up this story, and 'His Lordship flew into a great Passion, stuttering and Swearing and Shouting' that he would not be able to show his face in Court. Mrs Prendergast at once sent round to buy up every copy of the newspaper assuring him that neither girl would ever show her face in London again. (In fact, she gave Betty £5 to drop the prosecution.) She also advised all her noble clients that there would be no repetition.

However, something spectacular had to be done quickly to erase this misadventure, so Mrs Prendergast decided on a grand *bal d'amour* at which '. . . the finest Women in all Europe would appear *in puris naturalibis*'. She solicited subscriptions to cover the expense: 'Lord Fumble' started her off with 50 guineas and collected in all more than 700 guineas.

Among those present, apart from the professional ladies, were Lady Mary Adams, Isabella Wilkinson, 'The Bird of Paradise', Lady Henrietta Grosvenor ('of moderate beauty and excessive vanity') and Lady Margaret Lucan – the last two disguised 'as Mother Eve except that they covered their *Faces* with fig-leaves'. After the show everyone danced in the nude for a couple of hours – the orchestra faced the wall to avoid embarrassing the guests – and sat down to a marvellous cold collation. When the carriages were called, it was observed that the Ladies Grosvenor and Lucan and

'The Bird of Paradise' '. . . disclaimed their Attendance Fees and the cost of the hire of the Sedan-chairs, telling the Hostess to give the money to the servants'.

This wonderful affair netted Mrs Prendergast a profit of more than £1,000, and 'Old Lord Fumble' '. . . repaired to King's Place so long as he could crawl to Mrs Prendergast's four times a week to indulge his Whims with a Brace of new Faces'. He died a few weeks later, in 1779, 'to Mrs P's great affliction'. She had turned George Court into glittering King's Place as the finest place of bawdry in all England. Even so, the result of the ball was disappointing, and she left King's Place before the end of 1780.

The house remained empty for eighteen months, and then an old pro, Elizabeth Briscoe, became the new tenant. In October 1751 she had been sentenced '. . . to be whipt at the cart's Arse from the Turnpike neere unto Hyde Park Corner to the Lock Hospital . . .'. She was probably a surrogate for Mrs Prendergast, since the latter was still going strong in 1788, '. . . with two houses until she retired with a considerable Fortune after thirty years of trading unmolested by the Law or Reforming Busybodies'. In 1790 she was still running a seraglio in Bury Street. The class distinction is interesting: Mrs Butler ran a house of ill-fame; Mrs Prendergast ran a seraglio!

Black Harriott

The most curious and certainly the most exotic of the King's Place 'abbesses' was Black Harriott – the only black woman ever to have kept a 'house' in this 'royal' enclave.

She was a native of Guinea who had been captured as a child in a slave raid and shipped to Jamaica. There she was bought at auction by William Lewis, a captain in the merchant service who owned a plantation near Kingston.

She was a beautiful and intelligent girl, and Lewis, a widower, developed a great affection for her, making her his mistress and fathering two children on her. She was taught to read and write and to do accounts, and given lessons in manners and good deportment. To all intents and purposes she was Lewis's wife but in those contemporary colonial days he could never have married a black woman much less a slave.

About 1766 Lewis visited Britain, taking Harriott with him, spending much of his time in leisure and pleasure and introducing his 'jetty mistress' into the most fashionable circles. In those circles

Sandwich-Carrots! dainty Sandwich Carrots
John Montague, Earl of Sandwich, known as Jemmy Twitcher, *for his political manœuvres. He was 'as lecherous as a monkey' and not very particular in his amours. He is shown twitching the petticoats of a young carrotseller whom he is importuning*

there was not much sexual apartheid. Many ladies of 'the Quality' employed black men, ostensibly as servants or sedan-chair men, and several nabobs had black or brown mistresses. George Bubb-Dodington's lovely haughty Mrs Strawbridge was well known at Court, and Lord Sandwich's personal servant, the South Sea ex-slave Omai, was also his valued friend.

'The Captain' and Harriott kept house in Little Stanhope Street, off Piccadilly from about 1768, their next-door neighbour being Sarah Dubery, a high-class bawd. William Lewis, who had some pretensions as an actor, was on stage at Covent Garden from 1768 until 1772, when he died, leaving his mistress in dire financial straits, the *Meretriciad* sympathizing:

> But Harriott, like all Human things must fail
> In spight of Bricks and Mortar, Paint and Ball. . . .

For a while she was in the King's Bench debtors' prison but then was 'sprung' by Sir James Lowther, the much-disliked 'Jimmy Graball' described as a man of immense wealth but 'violent and arrogant almost to the point of madness'. (He was created Viscount Lonsdale in 1784.) Within a few months her clientele included a score of peers 'and fifty rich men none ever paying less than a soft Paper' (a £50 banknote).

One regular visitor was John Montague, Earl of Sandwich, famous as 'Jemmy Twitcher' and also as a lecher beyond description. He was a member of the notorious Hell-Fire Club and of the infamous Medmenham Friars set. Another was the East Indian nabob, Sir Thomas Rumbold, Bart., whose *petite amie* was one of Harriott's boarders.

Harriott quickly accumulated more than £1,000 in cash as well as an array of gold and silver trinkets, silver plate, furniture and jewellery. Although Little Stanhope Street was a good address, the richest pickings were to be found nearer the royal residence. In 1772 Elizabeth Allison, formerly of Jermyn Street, 'supplier to the nobility and gentry', who then occupied numbers 3 and 4 King's Place indicated that she was giving up No. 3 and in 1774 Harriott took the house over with all the furniture and fixtures.

The venture was at first highly successful and she was all set for great fame and riches when – so legend avers – she fell in love with one of her clients, an officer in the Guards. She was so besotted that she neglected her business and even refused the tempting personal offers which had helped in the past greatly to augment her income. Many clients deserted and some of her 'nuns' decamped without paying their debts. In June 1776 the Rates Collector's book noted that 'she had gone away' for two quarters: she was actually in a debtors' prison.

Harriott was back again in January 1777 but the crowning disaster came during the fashionable season in 1778 in 'Brighthelmstone' where the Prince of Wales and his entourage and cronies all went and to which bawds took their best 'pieces' to accommodate the gentlemen. During Harriott's absence her servants and 'nuns' stole many of her valuables, sold many of the best pieces of furniture and ran up huge bills on her account with the fashionable Bond Street shops. Harriott had to shoulder the debts and responsibilities and once again found herself in financial difficulties.

She was by now very ill, but her creditors were unrelenting, forcing her once more into the King's Bench prison – her establishment was taken over by Mrs Pendergast.

In 1778 it was reported that, 'Mrs Lewis a West Indian' was working from Charlotte Street but in 1779 she was at No. 2 King's Place.

Some of her *mignonnes* then were Miss Daniel, '. . . fresh coloured and good tempered who . . . had been missed from Piccadilly . . . but will never give any young fellow an unkind answer if his appearance bespeaks his ability both for Performance and for Cash . . .' and Betsy King, of whom it was said '. . . it is impossible to do justice to her beauty . . . her sweet pouting Lips her Neck her Breasts, all call for the pressure of a Loving Hand . . . she is not yet twenty . . . but she will not accept less than three or four Gold Pieces . . .'. There was also the very beautiful and infamous Miss Humphreys, 'a good-natur'd girl of twenty-three . . . with lovely firm round Breasts which have been greatly admir'd . . . by several liberal Admirers . . .'.

Black Harriott died shortly afterwards of tuberculosis to which denizens of tropical lands were prone, particularly if they had suffered a spell in a British prison.

Mrs Sarah Dubery

Sarah Dubery came from a long line of professional whoremongers, originating in Covent Garden with William Dewberry, who died in Charles Street in 1711, and his son Joseph, who was one of Lady Mordington's managers in her Faro table. Walter Dewberry operated a small but select brothel in Little Stanhope Street, Piccadilly, in 1766, his wife Sarah being the duenna. In 1770 she was described as '. . . the skilful Matron of the *Temple of Venus* in

Stanhope Street . . . where *Little Infamy* Betty Davis [mistress to John Manners, son of the Duke of Rutland] . . . was often to be found . . .'.

In January 1779 Sarah Dubery took over Charlotte Hayes' former premises at No. 2 George Court, at the exorbitant rental of £45 per annum. It was no handicap that her name resembled that of Madame du Barry – indeed she tried to emulate that lady in the luxury and refinement of her 'temple', being then eulogized as 'a Woman of the World . . . confining her activities to foreign diplomats and English Peers . . . her Accommodations are most worthy of the Diplomatick body . . . she speaks both French and Italian . . .'.

Her establishment was patronized by most of the 'Great Impures' as well as by well-known actresses enjoying a little harlotry on the side. She accommodated the Tripolitanian Ambassador, Sidi el-Hajji Abdurrachman, in his romance with the luscious opera singer Elizabeth Gambarini, whose terms were deemed exorbitant. There was also the famed stallion Count Alexei Semyonovitch Musin-Pushkin, the Muscovite Ambassador, who had retired from the pursuit of Signora Gambarini on the grounds of expense, and the Portuguese Minister, Count Louis Pinto de Balsamo, infatuated with the charming little Gertrude Mahon, 'The Bird of Paradise' and enjoying the sobriquet 'Mahon's Pintle'.

Another valued visitor was the famous Sadlers Wells ropedancer, Isabella Wilkinson, who was being 'protected' by the Swedish Ambassador, Count Gustav von Nollekens. When bored or needing extra money, Isabella would patronize one or other of the 'abbesses'. Mrs Dubery had promised His Excellency 'a new *nun*', and greatly to his astonishment and anger this was none other than his Isabella, '. . . whom he supposed was waiting for him at home as chaste as Penelope . . .'. Diplomatic and sexual relations were immediately severed, Mrs Dubery supplying the injured diplomat with a suitable replacement.

In January 1785 Catherine Matthews moved out of No. 5 King's Place, and six months later Mrs Dubery moved in, after redecorating the house.

In 1792 there was great excitement over the visit of a Special Envoy, Yussuf Adji Effendi, sent by the Sultan Selim III of Turkey to King George III, the more so when it was bruited about that this plenipotentiary '. . . had a Pintle so huge and powerful that it was past all Understanding and his Lust was insatiable'. It was reported that the King's Place abbesses '. . . were stretched to their utmost limits for the Great Plenipotentiary'.

Presentation of the Mahometan Credentials, 1792
The Special Envoy from Sultan Selim III of Turkey created not only a
sensation at the Court of George III but also much excitement in King's Place
circles for his sexual prowess. This was celebrated by Robert Burns in his
poem The Plenipotentiary

Mrs Dubery did very well out of this visit because her establishment was so commodious and luxurious and her 'nuns' experienced enough to cope with all comers. They earned large sums of
money with which they bought jewellery from Mr Lazarus of
Berwick Street, who would always buy back if a girl ran into
trouble. One essential to the successful 'Toast' was a gold watch,
which was the hallmark of the profession.

In 1789 Mrs Dubery's chief assistant was Becky Lefèvre, a
Frenchwoman raided from Mrs Chiappini's select bordel in Gerrard Street, Soho. In 1793 Becky was running her own 'house' in
Soho. The Duke of Queensberry's housekeeper, Maria Moreton, in
her *Memoirs* states that 'Old Q' '. . . employed that skilful Pro-

curess Mrs Dubery to procure his *Sultanas* . . . candidates were paraded for inspection . . . she seldom served him a Dish that he could not make one out of. If he approved, he rang a Bell and Mrs D . . . had to school the Novitiate in her duties . . .'. She used to entice young salesgirls from the Bond Street shops. One novice, however, spilt the beans, when she disclosed that '. . . he left me as good a maid as he found me . . . making a violent Fit of Coughing after an hour as an apology for his sudden retreat'.

Mrs Dubery continued to enjoy high esteem and support from the Quality, retiring in June 1814 'after a Reign of thirty-six years successful trading', leaving others to keep King's Place in the public eye.

Mrs Catherine Matthews

Catherine Matthews first comes into bawdry's history on Lady Day 1774, when she took over Charlotte Hayes' house at No. 5 King's Place. She was one of the seven panders employed by the ancient satyr 'Old Q', for whom she procured the youngster later to be regarded as 'the very *Thaïs* of London', Kitty Fredericks.

Kitty, who had been trained by Charlotte from 'a shaggy-tail'd uncomb'd unwash'd filly' of humble parents, had by the time she entered Mrs Matthews' sphere undergone a remarkable metamorphosis. She was now '. . . a delightful child, an only child and her mother's pet . . . well educated, well-spoken . . . a good little dancer . . . could speak French . . .'. Charlotte had first placed her 'at a good price' with the dissolute 'Baron Flagellum', Henry Paget, second Earl of Uxbridge, but he died in 1769 and she became the loving mistress of Captain Richard Fitzpatrick, till he was killed in action in America. Kitty then had to quit her comfortable home in Pall Mall, returning to her 'old home', now under Mrs Matthews' management. 'Old Q' settled £100 a year on Kitty straightaway 'for life' and gave her 'a genteel house', 10 guineas a week for its upkeep and, the ultimate mark of affection, a carriage. This love affair became so intense that Kitty became known as 'Duchess of Queensberry elect', and it was generally accepted that he would marry her. But in 1779 they quarrelled and the romance – and the settlement – ended. Kitty went on to become one of the most famous courtesans of the epoch, mixing with the highest in the land, even the royal circle and having money and jewels showered upon her.

Another of Mrs Matthews' successful 'placements' was a tall,

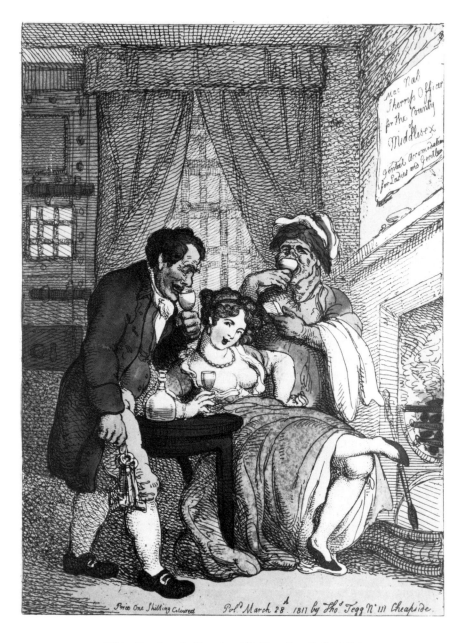

Kitty Careless in Quod or *Waiting Jew Bail, 1790*
A fashionable young prostitute held in a **Spunging-house** *while awaiting arrangements for bail by a Jewish Bail-bondsman. This was known popularly as Jew Bail, which involved collusion between the Head Jailers and Jewish entrepreneurs specializing in such arrangements. The prostitute, here seen drinking with her Bawd, would be allowed out to earn the extra money*

elegant beauty, the daughter of Sir Robert and Lady Harriet Hesketh. In 1771, when she was twenty-two, she was married to the Reverend Mr Bone, but this was not the sort of life she craved for and she ran into the arms of Colonel Francis Egerton, son of the Earl of Bridgewater. He set her up at No. 11 Suffolk Street, where she also received other gentlemen of rank. In 1774 her husband advertised, warning all tradesmen that he would not be responsible for her debts, and her father also washed his hands of her. She was then known as 'the celebrated Miss Hesketh' and numbered amongst her visitors Philip Stanhope, Earl of Chesterfield, and Francis, Duke of Bedford, known as 'the Bloomsbury Squirrel'. In Mrs Matthews' salon, where she was known as Mrs Bone, she was not popular with the other girls because she was always boasting of her noble descent.

Another of Mrs Matthews' much sought after 'nuns' was Margaret Cuyler, a well-born girl brought up at St James's Palace (her mother having been a lady in waiting to the Queen – Cuyler was not Margaret's maiden name, which has been carefully hidden from posterity). When she was fifteen she was taken up by the gallant young Colonel Cornelius Cuyler, who settled £300 a year on her and provided her with a house and servants. He was so often abroad that she became recklessly extravagant, holding frequent wild and often pornographic parties to match that charmed circle of High Impures which included 'The Bird of Paradise', 'Tall Dally' (Grace Dalrymple Elliott) and Lady Letitia Lade, all in the Prince of Wales' *entourage*. To find money for such extravagances, she patronized Mrs Matthews' establishment, and also appeared occasionally at Drury Lane. William Hickey had no great impression of her acting capabilities but described her as 'a great Jack-whore, without any pretension to manners or beauty'.

When the gallant Colonel arrived back in 1777 bearing bad tidings about Lord Howe's reverses in America, he paid Margaret's debts reluctantly, and appeared to condone her affaires, so long as they were confined to persons of 'the Quality'. By this time, she was also mistress to Captain Thomas Metcalfe of the Bengal Lancers – indeed, she pawned her jewels to provide him with his military outfit when he was subsequently posted to the West Indies. She eventually became mistress to Thomas Harris, manager-proprietor of Covent Garden theatre and bore him several children. This cost her Cuyler's support, as he objected to her 'being defiled by persons of a lower class'.

Mrs Matthews' house had facilities for flagellation, and she recruited 'the most skilled and beautiful high-class ladies who

A Meeting of Creditors
*The Prince Regent being dunned by Mrs Elizabeth Weston (of Berkeley
Square) and Mrs Windsor (of King's Place) with itemized bills for services
rendered, including 'first slice of a young tit only 12 years: £1,000' and for
'uncommon diversions' also £1,000. The coloured whore from Hedge Lane,
Black Moll is demanding payment for 'her Count' and on the far right is a
young girl asking for recompense for her lost maidenhead*

could wield the whip', but the roster of her clients has not been made public.

In the autumn of 1784 her house caught fire, but she was back in business in 1785. Then, in June 1786, the house was taken over by Mrs Dubery, and Mrs Matthews vanishes from King's Place. Although she is briefly mentioned about 1792, her whereabouts in the intervening years are not known.

Mrs Catherine Windsor

The longest lasting of all the King's Place 'abbesses' was Catherine Windsor, who opened her establishment at No. 4 King's Place in 1775 in the house originally occupied by Eleanor Leicester. Her name is noted with James Martin in 1773 but he was very likely the 'Cock-bawd' at that time.

She was already well known, for in 1775 *The Town and Country Magazine* reported that Sir Thomas Rumbold Bart., MP, '. . . a *Nabob* of the East India Company . . . frequented Mrs Windsor's . . . with the elegant enchanting Beauty, a daughter of a Shaftes-bury innkeeper . . . with whom he was besotted'. (Her name was Miss Keighley; he eventually established her as his mistress in a mansion in Manchester Square.)

A great deal of Mrs Windsor's fame and influence came from the patronage of the Prince of Wales and his brother William, Duke of Clarence. In 1779 *Nocturnal Revels* said that, '. . . there were some very fine Pieces', who included 'the sparkling youngster Betsy King, taken over from Black Harriott' and Mary Newsham.

Mary Newsham was 'a tradesman's daughter who had been seduced and deserted by a Person of Fashion . . . she is full of life, her eyes are full of expression and her temper mild and engaging . . . her complexion has rather too much vermilion yet on the whole few women can be called her superior at least in point of Beauty . . . she is not yet twenty but has several good friends . . . visiting all Public Places with her *Mama* [Mrs Windsor] . . . it must be owned they both cut a good appearance . . .'. *Nocturnal Revels* advised also that she was prepared to accept '. . . whoever came in her way whether it be a *Soubise* or little Isaac from St Mary Axe – the *Spankers* [golden guineas] will prevail, for she cannot discover any more Sin in yielding to a Blackamoor or a Jew than a Christian – even a Methodist'.

Another choice piece was a Welsh girl, Miss Meredith, who attracted such as Sir Watkin Watkins, Lord Barrymore and most of the Welsh noblemen and gentry because she was instructed in 'the tastes of the Ancient Britons . . . those females being modelled differently from English ladies . . . the Seat of Bliss is placed somewhat higher . . .'. Sadly, she was enticed away by an English baronet.

Mrs Windsor was one of the seven panders employed by the Duke of Queensberry and supplied him with the turbulent youngster Polly Talbot, 'whose attractions were sullied by her inordinate addiction to strong waters which made her noisy and rumbustious', which wearied the old lecher, who dismissed her summarily. She was not readmitted to Mrs Windsor's seraglio but was still active and popular elsewhere in 1790.

The *Rambler Magazine* (April 1783) had a caricature of Mrs Windsor and 'Old Q' in her Drawing Room, with Lucy (aged twenty), Polly (seventeen) and Priscilla (fifteen). His Lordship was haggling over the fee for Polly who 'only last night had passed for a Vestal to Father Solomons of St Mary Axe' but his lordship could have her for half-price since he was 'a special and regular customer'. Mrs Windsor wanted £200, however, for little Priscilla, and the argument grew acrimonious, especially when she indicated that 'old Mr Solomons' would pay even more. Mulishly the old 'Lord Dwindle' (by this time he was more a *voyeur* than a performer) said, 'They are very young. Will you warrant them?' To which the beldam riposted 'Warrant, my Lord! I am astonished at you! Neither of them was ever . . . served with a warrant. . . . They are chaste virtuous girls . . . one has almost got her maidenhead!' The old man ended the argument by saying, 'Very well! I'll take them all to Bath with me.'

She took her fillies every season to the fashionable watering places such as Bath and Tunbridge Wells, and later to Brighthelmstone (Brighton). These excursions are often described in *The Rambler* over the next few years.

Mrs Windsor and Mrs Johnson (of Pall Mall) used to parade their 'troops' in St James's Park, Mrs Windsor's to cope with the needs of the Grenadiers and Mrs Johnson's 'Heavies' to satisfy the demands of the officers of the Light Infantry. There were complaints that Mrs Windsor also '. . . engrossed almost entirely to herself and her *fillies* the whole of the right-hand corner of the Crown Gallery at the Opera House . . .'.

From 1782 onwards she was frequently mentioned in *The Rambler* and caricatured by James Gillray for her close connection with the Prince of Wales. Almost every one of the famous courtesans of the Regency were to be found at her house at one time or another.

King's Place: or A View of Mr Fox's Best Friends, 1784
Charles James Fox and the Prince of Wales were frequent visitors to the
King's Place Nunneries. Two courtesans praise the Prince, the one with the
feathered hat being Elizabeth Armistead, later Mrs Fox. One of the two

bawds is Mrs Windsor, the other most probably her neighbour Mrs Matthews. Of Fox it was said that 'His support, from Drabbs *&* Duchesses, Swindlers *& uncertified* Bankrupts *is exactly what could be expected'*

Most famous of all Mrs Windsor's girls was little Dorothea Phillips, grand-daughter of the Reverend Dr Phillips, a Welshman who had emigrated to Ireland. Her mother, Grace, ran away with a Captain Bland, and Dorothea was born in Waterford. The marriage having been annulled, the child was a bastard. When she was fifteen, working as a 'milliner' in Dublin, she had a chance to appear at the Dame Street theatre under Richard Daly, who seduced her and made her pregnant. By this time her mother had adopted the name Jordan, and the child was thereafter to be known by that name.

To escape Daly's brutalities, the family fled to Leeds, living in the most desperate poverty until one lucky day in July 1782 when the actor-manager Tate Wilkinson put her on-stage as a singer. Dorothy was then described as 'beautiful and warm-hearted but indolent, capricious, imprudent and refractory', and not sexually inhibited. The whole family moved to London in 1785, penniless, so Dorothy went occasionally to Mrs Windsor's to earn some money, at the same time appearing at Drury Lane theatre.

At Mrs Windsor's she met Richard – later Sir Richard – Ford, by whom she had four children. Then in 1790 she met William, Duke of Clarence. He fell in love with her, fathered ten children upon her, all of whom were named FitzClarence, recognized and supported by the Prince, who was a generous lover and an affectionate father. She was then known as Mrs Dorothy Jordan. Prince William allowed her £1,000 a year, but when his father, George III, had it conveyed to Dorothy that he thought £500 sufficient, in reply she sent him a playbill with her name as the Star Attraction, bearing the label 'NO MONEY RETURNED AFTER THE RISING OF THE CURTAIN'. The King took the hint and dropped his opposition. As Mrs Jordan, she appeared on stage at Drury Lane – despite the interruptions of regular pregnancies – until 1797.

There was a small *frisson* in December 1783 when Mrs Windsor turned one of her *mignonnes* naked out of the house, occasioning a newspaper headline 'The Naked Eve of St James'.

Charles James Fox was a regular visitor, one contemporary newspaper in the 1749 Election saying: 'The support of Mr Fox from *Drabbes* and Duchesses, Swindlers, uncertificated Bankrupts and Foreigners is exactly that which is to be expected.' The Prince Regent's ex-mistress 'Perdita' Robinson was often to be found at Mrs Windsor's when she needed money after the Prince had broken off the liaison.

In 1788 all the abbesses were complaining that, '. . . the late hours kept by the House of Commons prevented the Gentlemen from keeping their appointments and even when they came they were too tired to do their *devoirs'*.

The peregrinations of the 'Cyprian Corps' and their duennas were a constant source of interest to the readers of the many scandalsheets and magazines, and Mrs Windsor was singled out more frequently than most because of the royal association. The very large number of caricatures by such as Gillray and Rowlandson attest her great importance in the world of bawdry – indeed, the lack of interference by authority indicates the degree of protection which she enjoyed.

At Christmas 1809 Mrs Windsor moved into No. 1 King's Place and prospered there till she retired in 1821, having set a record of 'forty-six years of Honest Tradeing' and outlasting all her contemporaries. She died shortly afterwards.

Lady Adams

Last of the tally of prestigious abbesses was Mary Adams, who occupied No. 1 King's Place from about 1777 until 1785. She had formerly been operating from Little Ryder Street in 1771–2 and then in Duke Street until she moved across to 'fam'd King's Place'. About this period there were no fewer than six women of the same surname operating in the neighbourhood, including Catherine Adams in Pall Mall and Ann Adams in Little King Street.

Lady Adams was the widow of the Recorder of London, Richard Adams, who was knighted in 1753, but after his death in 1773 there was no more constraint and she could flaunt her title to best advantage.

Lady Adams' 'stable' was small '. . . but very select . . . her Best *Peices* being a delightful girl named Evelyn Roberts and a very pretty one named Miss Colebrook'. The great 'Toasts of the Town' were occasional boarders when their 'protectors' had tired of them or while they were awaiting the advent of a new lover. One such was the respectable lady known to Society as Mrs Elizabeth Mackay, née Sutton, who while serving in a shop in fashionable Bond Street had been seduced by Sir Henry Paget, Earl of Uxbridge. Elizabeth Sutton was then 'a skinny awkward' youngster full of girlish coquetry. His lordship thought it convenient to marry her off to John Mackay, a clerk in the East India Company, since an intrigue with a married woman was socially more acceptable. With the Earl's influence Mackay soon secured a senior position. Mrs Mackay, now filling out and becoming good-looking and *soignée*, was content, her husband complaisant. When she accompanied him to India, and gave birth to a dark-skinned child, this occasioned much ill comment, so the child was hastily baptized and the Mackays returned to Britain, where Mackay made a settlement of £1,500 a year on his wife, gave her a large credit with his bankers and promptly returned to India.

With such a splendid settlement Mrs Mackay attracted many a suitor but she was hard-headed and though she used Lady Adams's house for consummation of her amours, none was able to part her from her money. She remained friendly with Lord Uxbridge but lost her heart to the handsome heart-breaker John Palmer, then the idol of Drury Lane, although it was alleged that she gave him a £50 note 'for his first attendance upon her'. However, some kind friend apprised Mr Mackay in far-off India of his wife's life-style and he immediately cut her allowance to a paltry £500 a year and withdrew his bankers' credit, whereupon John Palmer's passion was much abated and he abandoned her. Not one to be trifled with, Mrs Mackay had him arrested for debt!

When Lord Uxbridge died in 1770, unmarried and intestate, there was a dispute over the succession to his barony, one of the claimants being Elizabeth's brother, Henry Sutton. Though the title and estate eventually devolved upon Henry Bayley, the magic of even an unsuccessful claim to aristocracy shed its aura on Mrs Mackay, making her activities *chez* Lady Adams even more lucrative.

In 1779 an acquaintance observed of Mrs Mackay: '. . . with Wonder and Astonishment we consider the sallow Skin, the withered Chaps, the wrinckled Forehead and flabby Neck of this antiquated Beldam which have not been insurmountable Obstacles to providing herself with Paramours . . .'. Of course a settlement of £500 a year, then a considerable sum, must have helped.

Lady Adams and her *mignonnes* were often to be seen in St James's Park and in the fashionable watering-places. Her title secured her admission to many otherwise exclusive places. She was invited to Mrs Pendergast's famous *bal d'amour* in December 1778, but an unkind spectator there observed that, '. . . having seen much Service she is somewhat weatherbeaten, having been in many a *Storm* and toss'd upon the *Rocks* and this Winter hath narrowly escap'd foundering . . . Lady Adams was to all intents and purposes a *Misnomer* . . . she should be call'd *Old Mother Eve*. . . .'

She carried on until 1785 when she was succeeded by Sarah Marquess.

Santa Carlotta's Saga

Far and away the most famous bawd of Georgian times was Charlotte Hayes, one of three pretty lively *gamines* who burst from a slum background of Covent Garden into the bright sunshine of popular prostitution to achieve fame and fortune and public acclaim.

All three were born about 1725 and were 'on the game' in their early teens. Lucy Cooper was to make her mark on Covent Garden, and poor Nancy Jones to die early of smallpox and syphilis in her twenties in the Lock Hospital at Kingsland. Charlotte Hayes had that mixture of charm and theatrical flair added to common sense and a business acumen which ensured success.

Very early in her career as a *demi-rep*, Charlotte had the good fortune to meet William 'Beau' Tracey, a barrister in chambers at the Temple – a gay if not exactly young spark. He was besotted with this 'lovely and charming and witty and lively girl who did not need to paint her Face, being as modest as a Saint and fair'. He was her 'protector', giving her money readily even though he knew she was drinking and whoring elsewhere, with Lucy and the up-and-coming 'Great Impure' Fanny Murray, at Sir Francis Dashwood's infamous Medmenham Priory, where as early as 1753 Charlotte was described as '. . . a Procuress and Courtezan bringing her *Nymphs* to participate in the outrageous Orgies . . .' organized there.

Then suddenly in 1756 Tracey died, leaving his financial affairs in some disorder, so that Charlotte's 'something' was not immediately forthcoming. Already in debt through her extravagance, she found herself in the Fleet debtors' prison – but this 'misfortune' was to lead her to fame and fortune, for there she met the young Irish con-man Dennis O'Kelly and fell in love with him. From this time their fates were inextricably and affectionately intertwined for the rest of their lives.

Kelly was the son of a poor squireen, Philip O'Kelly of Tullow in County Carlow. He came to England in 1748, when he was twenty, and after many vicissitudes rose, with Charlotte's support, to be a wealthy horse-racing Colonel of Militia, eventual owner of the Duke of Chandos's estate at Canons in Edgware and of the marvellous horse Eclipse which never lost a race – the basis of his friendship with the Prince of Wales and his brothers.

Many years later Charlotte claimed that: '. . . she fed and cloathed him and made him a Gentleman . . . in the Fleet when you fac'd famine and were in wretched Tatters scarcely covering your Nakedness. Remember the *Day Rules* I obtain'd for you and the Sums you won through that means . . .'. The prison's 'Day Rules' allowed inmates to go out to earn money, returning to spend the night in jail. Charlotte used these rules to run a brothel in the prison and to stand security for her feckless lover. *The Meretriciad* (1761) burst into verse:

> Blest in a Taste which few below enjoy
> Preferr'd a *Prison* to a World of Joy:
> With borrow'd Charms she culls th'unwary *Spark*
> And by th'*Insolvency Act* parades the Park. . . .

She was even then thinking of opening an elegant French-style brothel, like that of Jane Goadby, when by an unexpected piece of luck she and Dennis were released in the amnesty when George II died on 25 October 1760. In the following year she opened up her first 'Protestant Nunnery' in Great Marlborough Street, ten doors away from Mrs Goadby, and to her establishment came racing friends of Dennis's such as the Duke of Richmond and the (Catholic) Duke of Chandos, the Earls of Egremont and Grosvenor and a clutch of barons – all mighty gamblers and wenchers. Lord Foley, in payment for some undisclosed 'services', helped raise Dennis from a sergeant in the militia to a captaincy and eventually a colonelcy – but not all his powerful friends secured him membership of the Jockey Club!

By 1769, '. . . their gains in their different pursuits kept pace with each other . . . between them they have £40,000', which enabled Dennis to buy a half-share in Eclipse and to buy the other half in the following year.

Although this seraglio was highly successful, Charlotte realized that the way to greatest wealth and influence lay in running an even more luxurious establishment closer to the Court. In 1767 she opened another house at No. 2 King's Place, an event greeted by *The Meretriciad*:

> So great a *Saint* is heavenly Charlotte grown
> She's the First Lady Abbess of the Town!
> In a snug entry leading out Pell-Mell
> Which by the Urine a bad Nose can smell
> Between th'Hotel and the Tory *Almack's House*
> The *Nunnery* stands for each religious use.

The *Town and Country Magazine* allowed that this nunnery would '. . . administer Absolution in the most desperate cases without Confession', and called her 'a living Saint' because she could work miracles such as '. . . liquifying any amount of Golden Guineas

into Champaign Burgundy Clarett or Arrack-Punch instan-
taneously, cure the Evil of Love and broken-hearted Swains by the
Touch . . . make fair women Black and black women Fair . . . make
old Dotards believe themselves gay vigorous young fellows and
turn vigorous young men into old Dotards . . . she should be
canonised. . . .' Then it went on to say that she had her own box at
the Opera and that her girls were warned '. . . to eschew all Irish
Catholick *Beaux* because they have no money . . . it would be
convenient to confer with the Rabbis whose profundity of knowledge . . . may afford instruction and satisfaction . . .'.

Charlotte always considered Jews among her best friends and
clients and provided for the 'rich Levites' from Bevis Marks and St
Mary Axe in Bishopsgate, since most then lived in that quarter of
the City of London to be nearby the Synagogue.

The financier who backed her enterprise was the broker Isaac
Mendes, some of the members of whose family became regular
attendants at the various shrines to Venus. Charlotte was equally
scrupulous in fleecing both Jews and Christians but observed that,
'. . . rich Jews always fancy that their amorous abilities never fail'.
Thus she ensured that in her house 'they can forget all their worries
on the Stock Exchange . . . and even forget about the value of large
gold coins', referring to the generous way these 'Levites' always
treated her 'nuns'. They always spoke gently and civilly and
rewarded the girls with golden guineas.

She also had many good friends in the theatrical profession: not a
few of the successful actresses of the day owed much to Charlotte's
training in postures, airs and graces.

Towards her *nuns* she was businesslike. She sold them fine
dresses, beautiful French underwear, gold rings and jewellery as
well as the *sine qua non* of Georgian courtesans – a gold watch, the
ultimate sign of success. She supplied them with expensive knick-
knacks and adornments and charged them for food, board and
lodging, linen and washing. In this way she ensured that although
her girls earned large sums, they stayed often in her debt until
some 'Maecenas' bought them out – which was not infrequent.
Clients in this elite milieu were exigent and quirky, and there was
an insatiable demand for little virgins – in a brothel this is an elastic
term. Every bawd scoured the market for such prizes – from
indigent parents and orphanages and from 'wholesalers', but most
were girls whose deflowering had been rectified by artifice – some
of her best girls had been re-virginized many times. The remarkable Miss Shirley '. . . had gone through twenty-three editions of
virginity in one week, since, being a Bookseller's daughter she

Inspecting a Virgin, c. 1750
A doctor examines a young girl, to satisfy the seated procuress that her latest
recruit is a virgin. Such scenes were commonplace in King's Place and other
high-class St James's bordels

knew the value of repeated fresh Editions'. Charlotte opined that,
'A Maidenhead is as easily made as a Pudding.'

Every girl was medically vetted by Charlotte's resident physician, Dr Chidwick, to ensure they were free of all blemishes,
including bad breath, so as to be ready at a moment's notice. She
demanded that all her 'fillies' be sound in wind and limb (termin-
ology perhaps due to Dennis) and recalled Lord Rochester's sage
advice to use 'paper behind and sponge in front' to avoid unpleasant smells.

To avoid another type of mishap she supplied Mrs Phillips' 'fam'd new *Engines* – Implements for Safety for Gentlemen of Intrigue', although by that time 'cundums' of the best sort were imported from Marseilles. She also got John Gale to design his 'Elastick Beds' to give her more elderly customers better support and comfort. (When she eventually sold up there was a mad scramble for them among the other abbesses!)

Charlotte was often seen in the street with two or three of her juvenile beauties, 'exuding cheerfulness'. When the weather was inclement, they were taken around in the nunnery's own elegant equipage. The girls were allowed to wear any diamond crosses or necklaces and rings bestowed on them by grateful clients but not to fraternize with girls from the other King's Place houses.

Charlotte took into consideration that the actual numbers of the *haut ton* were at most a few hundreds and her prices were therefore necessarily high but that also ensured exclusivity. Even so, although the house was large and commodious, there were times when accommodation was overstrained – especially at week-ends, when she had to find room for anyone who demanded it, since a refusal would be resented and a noble client lost.

In her purported *Memoirs* there is a description of how such a quandary was dealt with on Sunday 9 January 1769. (There is a real substratum of truth – indeed, some clients can be identified.) Since the guest's wishes were known beforehand, outside 'experts' were brought in.

for Alderman Drybones	Nelly Blossom, 19, who has had no-one for four days and is *a Virgin*	20 guineas
for Baron Harry Flagellum	A girl younger than 19: Nell Hardy of Bow St or Bet Flourish of Berners St or Miss Birch of Chapel St	10 guineas
for Lord Sperm	A beautiful & lively girl. Black Moll of Hedge Lane who is very strong	5 guineas
for Colonel Tearall	Mrs Mitchell's servant – a gentle woman from the Countrey who has not been out in the world	10 guineas
for Dr. Pretext	(after Consultation hours) A sociable young Person with white skin & soft hands. Polly Nimblewrist or Jenny Speedyhand	2 guineas

for Lady Loveitt	(just come from Bath & disappointed in her love-affaire with Lord Alto) Now wants something better. Captain O'Thunder or *Sawney* Rawbone	50 guineas
for H. E. Count Alto	A fashionable woman for an hour only) Mrs O'Smirk from Dunkirk Square or Miss Gracefull from Paddington.	10 guineas
for Lord Pybald	To play a Hand at *Piquet* and for *titillatione mammarum* & no other object. Mrs Tredillo of Chelsea	5 guineas

Thus, two 'Posture Molls' will take care of Henry Paget, second Earl of Uxbridge, and cordially whack his noble backside: two hefty Samsons will satisfy Lady Sarah Lennox's nymphomania – she was then known as 'Messalina', and Count Alto can be recognized as her lover, Lord William Gordon. For the anonymous Colonel, a woman was borrowed from Mrs Mitchell's neighbouring seraglio, and for the worthy doctor a couple of supple-handed nymphs. The alderman was Robert Alsop, Lord Mayor in 1752.

The accommodation arrangements can only be explained be-cause the house was already crammed. The doctor was put 'on the landing of the three-pair of stairs', and Lady Lennox made comfort-able on a sofa in the drawing-room. The alderman had the 'small elegant chamber . . . used only for *Vestals*' and Lord Harry was appropriately whipped in the attic 'nursery'. Lord Sperm (prob-ably the Earl of Harrington) was given the 'High French Bedroom' (perhaps Charlotte's own) while Hugh, Viscount Falmouth, who was now able only to fondle a tit or two, was put into the card room, which was usually called 'Le Salon de Chastité' because while gambling no debauchee in his right mind would be diverted from that obsession for mere sexual acrobatics.

The year 1769, which had started off with such great promise, was to prove traumatic for both Charlotte and Dennis. He lost a great deal of money in gambling and she was loath to cover these debts from her own revenues because she was negotiating the purchase of a mansion at Clay Hill next to Epsom race-course. In April her old friend and lover Sam Derrick, whom she had been accustomed to feed and clothe whenever he was down and out, died in abject poverty.

Then in October the young Lucy Fields was cozened by the Hon. Mr Wimpole into making '. . . a rendezvous at Charlotte Hayes' diabolical dwelling . . . where she was made drunk and seduced . . .'. Having nowhere else to go, little Lucy became one of the residents until, shortly afterwards, his sick wife dying, Wimpole married her, whereupon she '. . . changed from a loving Mistress to a demanding Wife . . .'. During one of the ensuing quarrels she shot him dead.

At the beginning of the next year Charlotte was arrested for non-payment of some considerable sum 'while she supported her *Cyprian Temple* in King's Place' In the debtors' prison she comported herself in a most ladylike fashion, '. . . her conversation delicate and agreeable, her manner gentle modest and conciliatory . . .'. She was granted bail and her debts were paid by Dennis. It was said that she had neglected her King's Place temple because she had gone around with the militia wherever Dennis was inspecting and all this unaccustomed travel caused her to suffer from 'a lassitude and anxiety of mind and body'. Part of the anxiety was due to Dennis's irresponsible behaviour at York Races which resulted in a disagreeable scene which cost him £500 to save a scandal. Charlotte upbraided him, saying that, 'He had flung away in a drunken frolic more than she had cleared by honest industry in a month.' She complained that she was not well 'and had retired temporarily from George Court'.

In 1770 the couple went through a form of marriage but, because she was a Protestant and he a Roman Catholic, the ceremony was a 'Savoy marriage'. Henceforth – outside her business affairs she was known as Mrs O'Kelly.

In 1771 she took over No. 5 King's Place and turned it into what was to become London's most famous brothel. She also rented, under the name of Flammingham, a house just around the corner in King Street. Charlotte now began to divide her time between King's Place and her mansion at Clay Hill at Epsom, where she played hostess to such as the Prince of Wales, the Duke of Cumberland and the Duke of Orleans. The food, accoutrements and service were superb, but one rule was strictly observed: '. . . on no account whatsoever was any guest permitted to play or make bets of any kind at her Table or in her House'. Charlotte took little or no interest in the races.

For recruiting her staff she utilized the many new register offices which had sprung up to supply the ever-growing middle-class with domestic servants, nursemaids and the like. The girls were lined up in rows, the would-be employer walking up and down the

A Late Unfortunate Adventure at York
'Captain' Dennis O'Kelly discovered while trying to seduce a young lady in his hotel while attending York Races. He had to pay £500 to avoid publicity, earning a stinging rebuke from his wife, Charlotte Hayes for this costly indiscretion

lines examining and probing. Since each employer had to give an address to establish *bona fides*, Charlotte would rent a house under a false name for a short period. (At least twice she used the name Flammingham, which probably had some family connotation.) She made the rounds soberly dressed like any respectable matron seeking healthy young maidens 'to attend a lady', or she would leave an advertisement pinned-up inviting applicants to an interview. Any fears, apprehensions, scruples, or even anger would be overcome by the gift of a silver bracelet or the promise of a new gown. Since the girls were usually poor and friendless, it was useless to complain to a magistrate – in any case there would be nobody at the accommodation address. Most girls would be hooked; the most suitable would be groomed and trained for a new life. Quite a number eventually became well-known actresses or high-class 'Toasts of the Town'.

One was the little Betsy Green, 'born in profound obscurity' – probably a foundling, found by Captain John Fox ill and in direst poverty in a back room in a Windmill Street hovel. She had been forced onto the streets when her landlady badgered her for the rent – she was only fourteen. Captain Fox took her away and gave her into Charlotte's care, whereupon 'her wonderful beauty flowered' and when she was nineteen Captain John Coxe of the Guards took her into protection. As Betsy Coxe, she became one of the most famous 'Toasts of London'.

Even more successful was the 'shaggy-tail'd uncomb'd unwash'd filly of fourteen . . . bought from her industrious painstaking Mechanick of a Father for a Song . . .' whom Charlotte cleaned up, groomed and trained until she became the famous Kitty Fredericks, '. . . the veritable *Thaïs* amongst the *haut ton*, the veritable *Flora* of all London . . .'.

There was also the little Frances Barton, daughter of a poor Guardsman turned cobbler. After she had suffered some very unpleasant and degrading experiences, she found her way to Charlotte Hayes and went on to become Frances Abington, one of the most famous actresses of her time, renowned not only for 'so often exposing her lovely naked bosom to the gaze of lascivious leering gentlemen' but for the number and range of her love affairs. She died at the age of seventy-eight in her house in Belgravia, well respected and very rich.

The equally famous actress Clara Hayward was sent to Charlotte 'to be nursed and trained until she could meet a noble protector to ransom her out'. She met Evelyn Meadows, heir to the duchy of Kingston, and became his mistress, acquiring a marvellous reputation as actress and singer and maintaining for many years a leading place as one of London's prime Toasts. She often referred thankfully to Charlotte's training.

The young *roué* William Hickey often visited 'that experienced old Matron Charlotte Hayes in her *House of Celebrity* in King's Place'. One of the girls he admired was little Emily Warren, whom Charlotte 'had met in the street when she was leading her father, a blind beggar soliciting alms: she was then twelve years old, could not read nor write but was not awkward or deficient in conversation'. Hickey said he often saw 'the little sylph learning to walk under that ancient Dame's tuition' (in 1776 Charlotte was all of fifty), an art which Madame Hayes considered of great importance. Emily had 'a face of the most exquisite beauty . . . an air of grace – but she was still illiterate . . . and a divine woman'.

In 1776 she was mistress to Captain Robert Pott of the East India Service who set her up in Cork Street with a carriage and pair. This 'beautious Angel' later joined the Captain in India, only to die of fever in Madras in May 1782, buried in Calcutta before her thirtieth birthday. Her portrait as *Thaïs* by Reynolds hangs in Waddesden Manor.

Another inmate was Captain Richard Vernon's lovely sprite

Polly Jones, who helped him conduct wild parties entertaining the racing set. She was an aspiring actress appearing briefly in 1755 at Drury Lane and in 1762 at Covent Garden – although still resident with Charlotte. She was a very ignorant chit and rather simple. Encountering one evening the 'Wicked' Lord Lyttleton, he asked her if she knew Jesus Christ. She responded angrily that, '. . . she wondered at his Lordship's imperence . . . she never had no acquaintance with foreigners'. Polly lived with 'Old Fox Vernon' for many years and was still 'in residence' in 1792.

All these lovelies demonstrated Charlotte's great flair and business acumen, for many of them became friends and brought their friends and paramours.

Then in 1772 the Pantheon in Oxford Street opened with great *éclat* and became a serious competitor with its cotillions and routs. To counter its attractions, Charlotte came up with a brilliant idea. Captain Cook had just discovered Tahiti and had reported *inter alia* that there all handsome young men and nubile maidens copulated in public amid great encouragement from the onlookers. She at once circularized a couple of dozen special clients inviting them to attend a 'Tahitian Feast of Venus' at seven o'clock precisely, '. . . when twelve beautiful *Nymphs*, all spotless Virgins will carry out the Feast of Venus as it is celebrated in Oteite, under the instruction of Madam Hayes who will play the part of Queen Oberea, herself'. Some twenty-three gentlemen 'of the Highest Breeding', including five Members of Parliament, turned up on her doorstep.

The decor had been arranged to highlight the lewd 'Aretinian Postures' adopted by the participants. A dozen well-endowed athletic youths faced twelve 'nymphs' whose beauty could not be doubted although their virginity might be suspect. Each youth presented his nymph with a dildo-shaped object about a foot long, wreathed in flowers. The couple would then copulate with great passion and considerable dexterity since some of the Aretinian rites demanded a gymnastic suppleness which of a certainty could never be achieved by most of the onlookers. All this was accompanied by suitable music until the spectators had lashed themselves into such a state of lasciviousness that they invaded the floor, clutched the nymphs and tried to emulate the examples which had been shown.

This 'Cyprian Fete' went on for more than two hours, by which time most of the participants had exhausted themselves. All present then partook of a sumptuous banquet. It was reckoned a *succès fou* and none cavilled at the astronomical cost. Other hostesses copied this in after years, but not Charlotte, who was preparing for retirement.

By 1774 Dr Chidwick was treating her for exhaustion and neurasthenia and in 1775 she gave up No. 5 King's Place and concentrated on her house in Great Marlborough Street, although she still kept the small house in King Street. However, she must have kept her hand in, because in August 1776 she was charged with non-payment to a bankrupt lacemaker, James Spilsbury, in the sum of £50, 'for work and labour . . . in making fitting and adorning and trimming divers Cloathes, Garments & Masquerade Dresses . . . intending craftily & subtilly to defraud'. She admitted the debt but refused to pay and found herself in the Marshalsea. After a wrangle Dennis bailed her out, and she went to live at his town house in Half Moon Street, Piccadilly, and at Clay Hill or Canons Park.

Dennis died, aged sixty-seven, on 7 January 1788 and was buried 'in great style' in the nearby cemetery at Whitchurch. He left 'to his Wife (late Charlotte Hayes) living here with me' £400 a year for her lifetime, diamond jewellery, gold and silver cups – his trophies, silver plate, his 'Chariot' and coach and horses, and 'the She-Parrott called Polly'. This remarkable bird, which had cost him £50 according to *The Gentleman's Magazine*, '. . . talks and sings correctly a variety of items and corrects itself if it makes a mistake in a bar . . . reputed to be able to recite the 104th Psalm . . . unquestionably known to all who have seen it . . .'. (This would have been a tour de force considering the length of that psalm.) It died on 7 October 1802 of 'a bloody Flox', wrote Charlotte, who was very fond of it.

She was still prone to trouble by her extravagance. A deed of 30 June 1798 making over all her interests to Dennis's nephew states: 'late of Half Moon Street but now of the Fleet Prison'. In return he paid all her debts. The last heard of her is in 1811 when she was 'aged over 85 years' and still living at Canons. She died soon afterwards, forgotten by her generation, but her successors, Mrs Matthews and Mrs Dubery, carried on in the same house until well into the next century.

13 Haymarket

The Haymarket marks the eastern boundary of St James's, although at the southern end it bends a little to include Suffolk Street and what is now Whitcomb Street, which abuts on the National Gallery and was anciently the site of the huge royal stables known as Dunghill Mews. Whitcomb Street, formerly Colman Hedge Lane, is mentioned as early as 1509 by Wynkyn de Worde as a pleasant green spot suitable for the prostitutes evicted from Bankside by Henry VII.

In 1585 it is shown merely as 'the waye to Charynge Cross from Colbroke'. Faithorne's map (c. 1644) shows a few houses clustered at the Pall Mall end. The name Hay Market appears first in the Rate Book for 1657.

The freehold of all the land on the west side belonged to the estate of Queen Henrietta Maria, and in 1661 a thirty-year lease was granted to Henry Jermyn. A large plot of land on the east side stretching back to Colman Hedge was known as Scavengers' Close, appositely facing Dunghill Mews. By 1670 both sides of the Hay Market were lined with houses, shops and taverns. In that year the brewer William Whitcomb built some houses in Colman Hedge Lane, and the street is thenceforth known by his name.

The great number of horses required great quantities of hay, fodder, and straw, which were brought in by great lumbering hay-carts, parked along the way in haphazard fashion. In 1661 the Surveyor-General wanted the market removed but King Charles II merely appointed an inspector. The following year an Act of Parliament levied a toll on all hay and straw entering the capital, the money to be used to repair the pavements.

This measure being ineffectual, in 1663 the King granted the Earl the right to hold a twice-weekly market 'for the sale of cattle and sheep', the street being proclaimed 'a market for hay and straw' on Tuesdays, Thursdays and Saturdays. There were all sorts of stalls

The Fair Nun Unmask'd, 1769
A King's Place courtesan unmasking herself at a Ridotto, *before accom-*
panying her client to the rendezvous. She is wearing a magnificent diamond
cross, a gift from another client. She is most probably one of Charlotte Hayes'
girls, since Charlotte encouraged her nymphs *to wear their jewels. The*
poem by Alexander Pope sums up the situation:

> *'On her white Breast a sparkling Cross she wore*
> *Which Jews might kiss and Infidels adore.'*

as well as the usual food and drink sellers, the most fascinating being: 'TIDDY DOLL, the celebrated Vendor of Gingerbread, who with his stylish Clothes, ruffled Shirt, silk Stockings, lace Cuffs . . . a byword for Dandified Appearance. He was the King of the itinerant Vendors . . . [calling out] . . . "Here's your nice Gingerbread, your spiced Gingerbread, which will melt in your mouth like a hot Brickbat and rumble in your Belly like Punch-in-a-Wheelbarrow". He ended by singing "Tiddy Tiddy Dol, Lol, lol, lol . . .".'

Some early taverns were Rice's and Seager's and the Blue Posts, and the most notorious was Long's in which in January 1677

Tiddy Diddy Doll
Gingerbread, a plain cake made with treacle and spiced with ginger and formed into a doll-like shape has been known in England since Saxon times: it was a particular favourite at the Bartholomew Fairs founded by Rahere, Court Jester to Henry I in 1102. It was already known as a Tiddy Doll in Chaucer's day, at fairs and all public occasions such as executions. In the 18th century the most famous vendor was John Ford, a handsome man always dressed 'like a Person of Rank', whose stall in the Haymarket was a great attraction because he always finished his exhortations singing a ballad and ending with 'Tiddyty tiddyty tiddy-loll Tiddy-doll!' He had a long run, dying in 1752 when about seventy

232

'Borish Pembroke Brave' (Philip Herbert, seventh Earl of Pembroke), 'known for his deeds of drunkenness and manslaughter', killed a man in a duel, in which he 'played foul'. For this he spent a month in the Tower of London. In April 1678 in the same tavern he killed Nathaniel Coney 'with a blow of his Fist'. Agreeing to be tried by his peers, eighteen found him not guilty of murder against six who thought him guilty, but all forty present found him guilty of manslaughter. He claimed 'the benefit of the Statute' and was discharged. In January 1681 a Middlesex jury found him guilty of murdering a man in Turnham Green – on this occasion he secured a pardon from the King, perhaps due to the fact that he was married to Henrietta Mauriciette, sister of the King's mistress Louise de Quérouaille, Duchess of Portsmouth. Two years later he died of drink and syphilis at the age of thirty.

By 1685 the Haymarket had become so dangerous and filthy that James II granted Lord St Albans the right to move the cattle market to Mayfair, but not until 1690 was another Act passed regulating the hay and straw market. Complaints had been made about the disrepair of the pavements and the disruption in traffic caused by the ever-increasing number of wagons, despite a sort of one-way system whereby the wagons were unloaded on the east side but the contents stored on the west side.

The 'indifferent quality' of the buildings in 1774 was attributed to the market which in February was attended by more than 13,000 carts. The Piccadilly end was known as 'Hell Corner', having '. . . the greatest number of prostitutes, hatters, trimmers, laundresses, milliners, servants, shopgirls and fishwives. Brothels abounded . . . the women bare-headed in dirty white Muslin, disfigured Faces due to smallpox or syphilis, a large proportion being children used for stealing from shops . . .'. The Harris List for 1779 described one rough house where the waiters were often kicked downstairs, bottles and glasses flung after them.

Congestion grew worse with the years. In 1827 more than 26,000 loads were recorded, forcing the authorities in 1830 to shift the market east of Regent's Park – although crime and prostitution flourished unchecked.

At the top end of the Haymarket in 1619 Robert Baker, 'a taylor of Pickadilla Hall', bought four acres of land. One of the first houses was occupied by the Lord Chamberlain's barber, Simon Osbaldeston, who ran the Shavers' Hall, a popular eating-house later called the Gameinge House. In 1643 the estate came into the hands of Colonel Thomas Panton, a friend of Charles II, an 'absolute artiste at the card table . . . square or foul play'. By 1661 he had become a

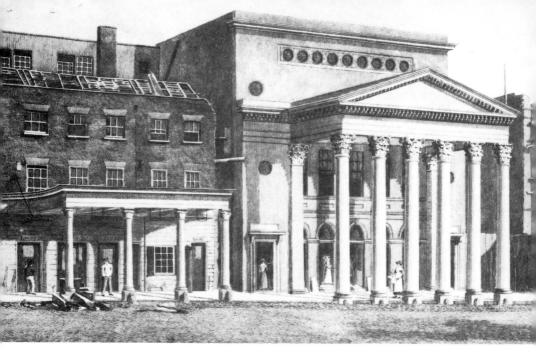

View of the new Theatre Royal, 1821

property speculator, and in 1673 he built Panton Square (where the new Trocadero now stands).

In 1762 the Moroccan Ambassador, who had a large house in the square, became displeased with one of his servants and sliced his head off. An angry crowd broke into the house, smashed all the furniture and threw it into the street, then 'threshed the Grand Moor' and his retinue down the Haymarket.

The 'little theatre' on the east side of the Haymarket, although just outside the parish boundary, cannot be omitted from this history. It was built in 1720 by a carpenter, John Potter, on the site of an old hostelry, the King's Head Inn, which had previously been leased 'for the performance of French Plays'. On 15 December 1721 it was announced: 'At the new theatre in the Hay Market between Little Suffolk Street and James Street, which is now completely finished will be performed a *French Comedy* as soon as the rest of the Actors arrive from Paris. . . .'

However, Potter had no licence. The actors arrived on 29 December, billed as 'The French Comoedians of His Grace the Duke of Montague', which enabled them to play, but subsequently the theatre could be used only by amateurs – it was not licensed until the 1736 Licensing Act was passed. Meanwhile, on 28 January 1723 there was a benefit performance for a well-known *danseuse*, Peggy Fryer aged seventy-one, who had played but once since the days of

King Charles but 'taught three queens to dance'. In 1726 the young Lavinia Beswick, famous in theatrical history as Lavinia Fenton, the original 'Polly Peachum' (later to become Duchess of Bolton), played in Gay's *What d'ye Call It?* A French company that came over in 1738 met with such a hostile reception that they gave only one performance.

Because of the Act, all sorts of fiddles had to be devised to get around it, such as musical concerts (paid for) followed by a play (*gratis*), and Sam Foote's wheeze: 'Inviting all friends to come and have a Drink on Chocolate with him . . . there will be a greatdeal of Comedy & some Joyous Spirits . . .'. Tickets were available at various taverns and coffee-houses locally, crowds attended, and Foote would 'instruct' some young performers while chocolate was being prepared – neither 'tay' nor chocolate was ever ready before the end of the (gratis) performance.

Foote was a great favourite with the royal family. After he broke a leg while a guest of the King's brother the Duke of York, to make amends the Duke secured a patent for the theatre to be opened during the summer months for Foote's lifetime. When it re-opened in May 1767, it was designated a Theatre Royal. Foote's scandalous satire landed him in dire trouble when he was branded a sodomite by one of the escorts of Elizabeth Chudleigh, Duchess of Kingston, and he was forced to kneel down on the stage and scream to his accusers that he was nothing of the sort.

In 1777 George Colman took over, and the theatre enjoyed a *succès d'estime*. Italian operas were played there in 1790, when the Opera House burnt down. There was a dreadful scene in February 1794 during a Royal Command performance when sixteen people were trampled to death trying to get out at the narrow pit entrance, and in August 1805 the Bow Street Runners had to be called in to quell a riot by journeymen tailors taking umbrage at Foote's satirical play *The Tailors*. In 1820 a new, larger, modern theatre was built next door by John Nash.

At the back of the theatre is Suffolk Street, built about 1664 on the Earl of Suffolk's stables. The best-known inhabitant was Moll Davis, King Charles II's mistress, who lived at No. 11 from 1667 to 1674, when he bought her the house in St James's Square. In this same house about 1760 'Mother' Elizabeth Courage kept her *maison de tolérance*, specializing in finding suitable stallions for bored and frustrated Ladies of the Quality and wives of City magnates, as well as lesbians. *The Meretriciad* (1770) called her 'a Female Banker', explaining:

'tis true she's old – but common, never known . . .
She slept with Men of ev'ry Rank and Age
Down from His Highnesse to his humble Page . . .
What could a Knight see in thy ugly Face
To be hum-bugg'd by Fifty Pounds of Lace?
But that's not rare, for thousands have before
Paid for a Maiden-head – and bought an Whore!

Sam Foote lived at No. 3 when he was managing the theatre, and about the same time Dean Swift visited his 'Vanessa'. No. 7 became notorious when the Marquess of Winchilsea accused the Duke of Wellington of 'treachery to the Protestant Cause' and was challenged to a duel. When the order to fire was given, Winchilsea kept his hand at his side and Wellington 'fired wide', whereupon Winchilsea 'fired into the air' and apologized, thus settling the quarrel.

On the west side of the Haymarket at the junction with Pall Mall was the Opera House built in 1704 by Sir John Vanbrugh on the site of the ancient White Horse Inn and parts of the equally ancient taverns the Phoenix and the Unicorne. In 1720, said Strype, the Hay Market '. . . harbour'd a greate number of people of foreign extraction . . . mainly Italians . . .'; by 1760 they were running 'many Perfume Shops'. It was a most elegant building, but after it was opened in April 1705 it was discovered that the acoustics were so bad that '. . . scarce one word in ten could be heard by the audience'. The theatre was then christened 'The Queen's Theatre' in honour of Queen Anne. William Congreve was co-manager with Vanbrugh, and such stars as Nance Oldfield and Thomas Betterton appeared there. The appearances of the famous *castrato* Grimaldi Niccolini in several of Handel's operas was always greeted with wild acclaim.

In 1711 John Jacob Heidegger took over. He was the son of a Zürich pastor and had arrived almost penniless in England but by his wit, humour and 'great charm' had ingratiated him with the nobility, particularly Philip, Duke of Wharton. He had another source of income, not trumpeted about – he was the paramour and partner of the well-known procuress 'Mother' Whyburn, purveyor to the *haut ton*, and mainstay of the famous courtesan Sally Salisbury. Heidegger's ridottos and masquerades were immensely popular but by 1713 had become so pornographic that he had to substitute concerts to avoid prosecution, though his aristocratic friends still stayed loyal – occasioning the panegyric starting,

Thou, Heidegger, th'English *Taste* hast found
And rul'st the Mobb of Quality with sound.

'Miss Chudley, Maid of Honour to the Princess of Wales in the caracter of Iphigenieia at the Holiday Masquerade in ye Daye time at Ranelagh Gardens in June 1749.' Elizabeth Chudleigh, even when she was Duchess of Kingston, would appear in the same fashion in many other Society functions

*King's Theatre, Haymarket. Under the colonnade on Pall Mall at No. 2,
Johnson and Justerini established themselves as wine-merchants*

> In Lent, if *Masquerades* displease the Town
> Call 'em *Ridottos* – and they'll still go down. . . .

When Queen Anne died, the theatre was re-named 'The King's Theatre' and the new King greatly enjoyed Heidegger's *risqué* entertainments – his son George II made him Master of the Revels, although in 1729 he was presented by a Grand Jury as 'the principal promotor of Vice and Immorality'. In 1732 'Poor Fred' gave a 'Grand Entertainment' to the nobility, and in 1749 his father, George II attended a 'magnificent Mascorade' at which Miss Chudleigh appeared as Iphigenia 'with so little clothing that she was more like Andromeda'. In 1799 the Knights of the Bath gave 'a magnificent Ball and hot Supper served at midnight on gold plate lent by His Majesty' provided by Louis Weltje.

On 17 June 1789 the theatre was destroyed by fire but was rebuilt quickly to the design of Michael Novosielski. It was one of the finest theatres in the world, its auditorium larger than La Scala, Milan. The lessee was Richard Brinsley Sheridan. The ballet *Bacchus and Ariadne*, on 9 December 1797, gave great offence, one critic saying, 'Have we advanced to the pointe of seeing people dance naked?' and actually hissing the dancers. Ten years later there was a riot because it was not nude!

In 1847 the marvellous Jenny Lind made her appearance, 'to the joy of an immense crowd', but in December 1867 Her Majesty's Theatre (Victoria was now Queen) was completely destroyed by fire. When it was rebuilt, a part was hived off for the Carlton Club, cutting it off from Pall Mall. Although almost everyone who owned or managed it lost money, the theatre survives to this day, once more as the Queen's Theatre – this time Elizabeth II.

238

Bibliography

Anon., *A Medal for John Boyes* (London, 1682)

Anon., *Almonds for Parrotts* (London, 1708)

Anon., *A Trip Through the Town* (London, 1735)

Anon., *A Trip from St James to the Exchange* (London, 1744)

Anon., *The Potent Ally* (London, 1741)

Anon., *The Nocturnal Revels* (M. Goadby, London, 1779)

Anon., *College Wit Sharpen'd* (For J. Wadham, 1739)

Anon., *History of the Human Heart, or The Adventures of a Young Gentleman* (London, 1749)

Anon., *The Fruit Shop or A Companion to St James' Street* (J. Harrison London, 1766)

Anon., *Characters of the Most Celebrated Courtezans* (M. James, London, 1780)

Anon., *London: A Satire* (London, 1782)

Anon., *The Genuine Memoirs of Denis O'Kelley* (London, 1788)

Archenholtz, Baron Johann von, *A Picture of England* (Byrne, Dublin, 1791)

Beaven, A., *Aldermen of the City of London* (London, 1913)

Beckett, Dr William, *An Attempt to Prove the Antiquity of Venereal Disease* (Royal Society's Philosophical Transactions, Vol. xxx) (London, 1717)

Bleackley, Horace, *The Life of John Wilkes* (Bodley, London, 1917)

Bloch, Ivan, *A History of English Sexual Morals* (F. Aldor, London, 1936)

Blyth, Henry, *Old Q of Piccadilly* [Lord Queensberry] (Weidenfeld, London, 1967)

Boswell, James, *Boswell in London* (Futura, London, 1983)

Bourke, Hon. A., *The History of White's* (London, 1892)

Bray, Alan, *Homosexuality in Renaissance England* (Gay Press, London, 1982)

Chancellor, H. B., *Annals of St James Street* (Constable, London, 1925)

Cokayne, G. E. (Ed.), *The Complete Peerage Harleian* (London, 1887–90)

Collins, Lydia, *George Seymour Crole: son of Geo. IV* (article in *The Genealogist*, No. 7) (London, 1984)

Cook, T. A., *Genuine Memoirs of Denis O'Kelly* (Private Ptg, London, 1788)

Dasent, Andrew, *History of St James Square* (Macmillan, London, 1920)

Evans, George, *An Old Snuff House* (Fribourge & Treyer, London, 1921)

Gay, John, *Trivia* (London, 1716)

Gentleman's Magazine, The, The Trial of Lord Baltimore for a Rape (London, April 1768)

George, Dorothy M., *Catalogue of Political and Satirical Prints in the British Museum* (London)

Graeme, Bruce, *The Story of St James Palace* (Hutchinson, London, 1929)

Hardy, Alan, *The King's Mistresses* (Evans, London, 1980)

Harris, Jack, *Lists of Covent Garden Cyprians* (H. Ranger, London, 1764–92)

Hickey, William, *Memoirs* (reprinted London, 1923)

Hickey, William, ed. A. Spencer (London, 1948)

Jones, Louis C., *The Clubs of Georgian Rakes* (Columbia U., USA, 1942)

Kronenberg, *The Life and Times of the Extraordinary Mr Wilkes*

Liber Albus, The, (Ed. T. H. Riley) (Griffin, London, 1861)

Lillywhite, Bryant, *London Coffee-Houses* (Allen & Unwin, London, 1963)

Lillywhite, Bryant, *London Signs* (Allen & Unwin, London, 1972)

Low, Donald A., *Thieves Kitchen* (Dent, London, 1982)

Macky, John, *A Journal Through England* (Rob. Gosling, Edinburgh, 1732)

Mandeville, Bernard de, *A Modern Defence of Public Stews* (Morel, Glasgow, 1730)

Margetson, Stella, *Leisure & Pleasure in the 18th Century* (Cassell, London, 1970)

Melville, R. L., *The Life of Sir John Fielding* (Williams, London, 1934)

Musgrave, Sir William, Bt., *Obituaries* (Harleian Society, London, 1899–1901)

North, Roger, *The Life of the Rt Hon. Francis North, Baron Guilford* (G. Bell, London, 1890)

Phillips, Hugh, *Mid-Georgian London* (Collins, London, 1964)

Pindar, Peter (John Wolcot), *The Royal Brood – A Poem* (London, 1792)

Rae, Dr James, *Deaths of the Kings of England* (Sherrad Hughes, Manchester 1913)

Rambler, Magazine, The (London, 1769)

Riley, T. H., (Ed.), *Liber Albus* (Griffin, London, 1861)

Rimbault, E. F., *Cock Lorells Bote* (Percy Soc. No. 30, 1843)

Rochester, Earl of (John Wilmot), *A Ramble in St James Park* (London, 1674)

Seymour, Robert, *Survey of London & Westminster* (London, 1734)

Shelley, Henry C., *Inns and Taverns of Old London* (Putnam, London, 1909)

Stone, Laurence, *Family, Sex and Marriage* (Princeton Univ., USA, 1977)

Stow, John, (Ed. H. B. Wheatley), *Survey of London* (Dent, London, 1956)

Stow, William, *Remarks on London* (St Aubyn, London, 1722)

Thompson, Edward, *The Meretriciad* (1765 and 1770 editions) (C. Moran, London, 1770)

Town and Country Magazine (1769 ff.)

Ukers, W. H., *All About Coffee* (Pitman, New York, 1922)

Walpole, Horace, *Letters* (Ed. W. S. Lewis) (Yale Univ., USA, 1973)

Wardroper, John, *Kings Lords and Wicked Libellers* (Murray, London, 1973)

Weinreb, Ben, *Encyclopaedia of London* (Macmillan, London, 1983)

Whitehead, Paul, *Honour – A Satyre* (London, 1747)

Wilkes, John, *An Essay on Women* (London, 1764)

Williams, E. N., *Life in Georgian England* (Batsford, London, 1962)

Wilson, J. Harold, *All the King's Ladies* (Harvard, 1968)

Yearsley, Dr McLeod, *Le Roi est Mort* (Unicorn, London, 1935)

Young, Sir George, *Poor Fred: The People's Prince* (OUP, 1937)

Ziegler, Philip, *King William IV* (Collins, London, 1971)

Index

Bath, Thomas Thynne, Marquess of (1734–96), 63
Baths and bathing, *see* Sanitation
Bathurst, Allan, Earl (1684–1775), 70, 127, *see also* Harems
Battersea Baron, The, 57, *see also* Bolingbroke
Beauclerk, Charles, Duke of St Albans (1670–1726), 86, 189
Beauclerk, Topham (1739–80), 58, 107
Bedford, Francis, Russell, 5th Duke (1745–1802), 117, 209
Bedford, Lady Georgiana, Duchess of (1781–1853), 118, 146
Bell Tavern, The, 73, 76, *see also* Old Bell Tavern
Bellasis, Lord John (1614–89), 76
Beloe DD, Rev. William (1756–1817), 183, 185
Bennet, Charles, 52
Bennet, Henry, 53, *see also* Arlington
Bennet, Lady Isabella, *see* Arlington
Bennet, Sir John, 52, *see also* Ossulston
Bennett, Lady Elizabeth (Lady Leeke), 175
Bentinck, Lord William (1649–1709), 20, 56, *see also* Sodomy
Berkeley, Charles, 2nd Earl (1649–1710), 125
Berkeley, Lady Elizabeth, 64, *see also* Germain
Berry Bros., and Rudd, 121, 156
Betty's Coffee-House, 189
Betty's Fruit Shop, 95, 151–2
Bevis Marks Synagogue, 58, 86, 175, 221, *see also* Jews
Bielefeld, Baron von, 29
Bill of Rights, The (1689), 17
Bingham's Yard, 117, 194, *see also* King's Place
'Bird of Paradise, The', 49,

200, 205, *see also* Mahon
Bitches, The Two, 175, *see also* Pomfret, Sundon
Black Death, The (1348–50), 2
Black Harriott, 199–201, 212, *see also* Lewis
Black Moll of Hedge Lane, 210
Bloomsbury Squirrel, The, 117, 209
Blount, Lady Elizabeth (1500–40), 10
Blue Bell Yard, 152
Blue Posts Tavern, The, 232
Boehm, Mr Edward, 65
Boleyn, Anne (1507–36), 10, 11
Bolingbroke, Visc. Henry St John (1678–1751), 20
Bolingbroke, Frederick St John, 2nd Visc. (1734–87), 57–8
Bolton, Lavinia, Duchess of, 235
Bone, Mrs Elizabeth (1749–), 209
Boodle, Edward (1722–72), 146
Boodle's Club, 125, 146–56
Bordels du Roy, Les, 198
Boscawen, Admiral Edward (1711–61), 52
Boscawen, Hugh, 3rd Visc. Falmouth (1706–82), 52
Boswell, James (1740–95), 46, 145
Bourne, The Widow, 121
Bow Street Runners, 235
Bowdler, Thomas (1754–1825), 155, 183
Bowman, Christine, 116
Bradford, Countess Mary (1661–1737), 20, 68
Braham, John (1774–1856), 196, *see also* Jews, St James's Theatre
Brett, Anne Margaret, 25, *see also* Macclesfield
Bridgeman, Sir Orlando, Bt., 68
Brighton (Brighthelmstone), 204, 213

Briscoe, Elizabeth, 201
Bristol, Earls of, 57
British Coffee-House, The, 84, 105–6
Broglie, Mme la Duchesse de, 29
Brooke, William and *Brooks's Club*, 58, 125, 139, 147–9
Brothers Club, The, 99
Brouncker, Henry, 3rd Visc. (–1688), 16
Brouncker, William, 2nd Visc. (1620–84), 168
Brummel, 'Beau' George Bryan (1778–1840), 132
Brydges, James, 59, *see also* Chandos
Bubb-Dodington, George (1691–1762), 89, 106–7, 203, *see also* Melcombe
Bubble and Squeak, 70, *see also* Sheridan, Wynne
Buccleuch, Anne, Duchess of (1651–1731), 58
Buckingham House, 38, 39, 113
Buckingham Palace, 37–9, 59
Buckingham, George Nugent-Temple-Grenville, Marquess of (1753–1813), 113
Buckinghamshire, Lady Albinia Hobart (1738–1816), 76, 140
Buckinghamshire, George Hobart, Earl (1731–1804), 76
Bull-baiting (1643–1714), 9
Burke, Edmund (1729–97), 143, 196
Burnaby, Edward, 129
Burnet, Bishop Gilbert (1643–1714), 57
Burney, Charles (1757–1817), 183
Burton's Coffee-House, 196
Bury Street, 193, 199, 201
Bute, John Stewart, Earl of (1713–92), 94, 104
Butler, Mrs Elizabeth (Mrs Smith), 199, 200–1
Byng, George, Earl of Strafford (1740–1812), 56

St Albans, Henry Jermyn,
Earl of (–1684), 50, 75
and *passim*
St Giles-in-the-Fields, 4
St James's Gazette, The, 182
St James's
Bailiwick, 1, 3, 4, 6
Fair, 2, 9, 12, 15
Fields, 2, 4
Market, 9
Palace, 3, 10–39
Park, 3, 40–9, 213 and
passim
Place, 139, 162–7
Square, 7, 16, 28, 50–77
Street, 6, 7 and *passim*
St James's Church, 7, 133,
179
*St James's Coffee-House,
The*, at No. 87, 141–4
St James's Coffee-House, The
at No. 88, 129
St James's Theatre, 196
St Margaret, Westminster,
1
St Martin-in-the-Fields, 4,
7
Salisbury, Sally
(1690–1724), 235
Sanctuary, 13
Sandwich, Lady Elizabeth
(1674–1757), 97
Sandwich, John
Montague, Earl of
(1718–92), 203
Sanitation, 29, 48, 51,
116–18
Cesspit, 156
Chamberpots, 9, 30, 117
Close-stools, 29, 117
Flyters, 117, 156
Lavatories, 117
Sewers, 15
Santa Carlotta Hayes, 220
Saunders' Coffee-House,
154–5
Saunders, Richard
(–1772), 154
Savage, Richard, Earl
Rivers (1654–1712), 89
Savage, Richard
(1696–1743), 52, 89,
see also Oldfield
Savile, George, 65, *see also*
Halifax
Savoy Marriage, 225
Scavengers' Close, 230

Schomberg House, 98,
108, 111
Schomberg, Marshal
Frederick van, Duke
of (1615–89), 18, 20,
108
Schomberg, Meinhard de,
Duke of (1641–1719),
56, 108
Schulenberg, Countess
Ehrengard Melusina
von (1667–1743), 24,
see also George I
Schulenberg, Melusina de,
Countess of
Chesterfield
(1720–78), 68, *see also*
Chesterfield
Scotch Ale House, The, 172
Scourers, 123, *see also*
Mohocks, Nickers
Scroop, Lady Mary
(*c.* 1600–85), 121
Seager's Tavern, 232
Sedan-chairs, 90, 98, 105,
135, *see also*
Duncombe
Sedley, Catherine
(1657–1717), 16, 25,
38, 62, 71, *see also*
Dorchester, Portmore
Sedley, Sir Charles
(1639–1701), 87
Seilern, Count Christian
Auguste von
(1717–1801), 59
Selwyn, George Augustus
(1719–91), 138, 147,
167
Seymour, Robert, 106
Seymour, Sir Thomas, 11
Shadwell, Thomas
(1642–92), 41
Shavers Hall, 233
Sheffield, Sir Charles Bt.,
38, 59
Sheffield, John, Duke of
Buckingham
(1648–1721), 38
Sheridan, Richard
Brinsley (1751–1816),
147, 238
Shirley, Miss, 221
Shoreditch Riots, 28
Shrewsbury, Charles
Talbot of (1660–1718),
53, 56

Sidi al-Hajji
-Abdurrachman,
Tripolitanian
Ambassador, 205
Sidney, Henry, Earl of
Romney (1641–1704),
64
Skeffington, Clotworthy,
Earl of Massereene
(1742–1805), 195
Skiffy Skipton, 195, *see also*
Skeffington
Skreene, Major George,
133
Smith, Letitia, *see* Lade
*Smyrna Coffee-house,
The*, 84, 97–9
Soane, Sir John
(1753–1837), 73
Society of Musicians, The,
102
Sodomy, 41–3, 46, 53, 56,
76, 151
Sophia Dorothea, Princess
of Hanover
(1666–1726), 21, 82,
see also George I
Southesk, Lady Anne
Carnegie, Countess of
(*c.* 1645–95), 16
South Sea Bubble, The, 21
Spankers (Gold coins), 212
Sparks, 123, *see also*
Mohocks
Spectator, The, 142, 169
Spencer, Lord Charles,
103
Spencer, 'Hon.' Charlotte,
199
Spencer, Lady Diana
(1734–1808), 58, *see
also* Beauclerk
Spencer, Hon. John
(1710–46), 163
Sprimont, Nicholas, 109
Squeak, 70
Stable Yard, 123, 150
Stable Yard Messalina, The,
48, *see also* Harrington
Standish, Sir Frank, 146
Stanhope, Sir William
(1719–79), *see*
Harrington 2nd Earl
Stanley, Edward, 59
Staplyton, Thomas, 143
*Star and Garter Tavern,
The*, 84, 94, 103–5

Index